Preaching as Testimony

Preaching as Testimony

Anna Carter Florence

Westminster John Knox Press
LOUISVILLE • LONDON

Scripture quotations from the New Revised Standard Version of the Bible are copyright © 1989 by the Division of Christian Education of the National Council of the Churches of Christ in the U.S.A. and are used by permission.

Book design by Drew Stevens
Cover design by Mark Abrams

First edition
Published by Westminster John Knox Press
Louisville, Kentucky

This book is printed on acid-free paper that meets the American National Standards Institute Z39.48 standard. ∞

PRINTED IN THE UNITED STATES OF AMERICA

07 08 09 10 11 12 13 14 15 16—10 9 8 7 6 5 4 3 2 1

Library of Congress Cataloging-in-Publication Data is on file at the Library of Congress, Washington, D.C.

ISBN-13: 978-0-664-22390-8
ISBN-10: 0-664-22390-7

For my father
David Martin Carter
1936–1993

Somebody's going to live through this.
Suppose it's you?
—Mark Doty, "Mercy on Broadway"

Contents

Acknowledgments

The book of Exodus, with its great liberation narrative, has always been one of my favorite sources for teaching. Not long ago I noticed a curious thing about its title. "Exodus," which is how English translations refer to the second book of the Bible, is actually a Greek phrase: it means, "a way out." But in Hebrew, the titles for books in Scripture are taken from the first words of the book itself. Exodus is known as "These Are the Names" because the story begins, "These are the names of the children of Israel coming into Egypt with Jacob, each with his own household: Reuben, Simeon, Levi, and Judah. . . ." *These are the names. A way out.*

I have thought about that a great deal. Our liberation, our crossing over into new life, is *a way out*. That is what we call it: not *the* way out, but *a* way out. And the story of our liberation begins with *These are the names*. These are the names of the ones who went with Jacob into slavery, and who found with him *a way out*. These are the names of the ones who crossed over with him into freedom, and a season of wilderness, and finally a land of promise that had been waiting for their return. *These are the names, and a way out.*

When a book has been as long in coming as this one has, acknowledgments take on a particular weight. How does one convey a depth of gratitude that goes beyond measure and beyond words? I draw on the wisdom of Exodus: These are the names. They have gone down with me into Egypt, and they have been for me a way out. If the book is to tell any story of liberation through the Word, it begins with the names.

I thank all the saints of Westminster Presbyterian Church in Minneapolis, who first called me to ministry and loved me into my vocation. When I left for graduate school in 1993, they gave me their blessing, and it is with me still, as they are. Always.

I thank my teachers, Thomas G. Long and Nora Tubbs Tisdale, for believing that a scholar would surface from this preacher. Without them, I would not have been able to imagine myself a part of this field, nor would I ever have found the way. With them, I have had the faith to keep reimagining.

I thank Columbia Theological Seminary, this amazing place where I am privileged to live and teach among students and faculty who are, quite literally, out of this world. President Laura Mendenhall and Dean D. Cameron Murchison never stopped believing. Walter Brueggemann was a generous conversation partner over multiple lunches. Students Chris Henry and Tricia Dillon Thomas provided editorial counsel and technical support at all hours and on a moment's notice; Chris did an outstanding job on the index. And Chuck Campbell, my colleague and partner in extreme homiletics, my big brother and my friend, continues to fill my teaching life with laughter, surprise, and awe. For his faith in the foolishness that might be, I am speechless, and thankful.

I thank Stephanie Egnotovich, my wonderful editor at Westminster John Knox, for seeing a book through the trees, and persevering with me right up to the end. She was always wise, and always right. I thank everyone who read and commented on drafts of the manuscript. These are the names: Emily Anderson, Anne Apple, David Bartlett, Brandon Brewer, Walter Brueggemann, Richard Buller, Chuck Campbell, Jill Carter, Minnie Rhea Carter, Gail Cole, Kate Foster Connors, Sue Crannell, MaryAnn McKibben Dana, Kevin Day, Joe Evans, David Gregory, Arð-friður Guðmundsdottir, Chris Henry, Janet Tuck Hilley, Dana Hughes, Laura Jernigan, Julie Johnson, Lisa Larges, Kim Long, David Lose, Rob McClellan, Anne McKee, Carol Miles, Jean Morris, Damayanthi Niles, Rodger Nishioka, Kendall Pearson, Janie Spahr, Mark Shivers, Cathy Smith, George Stroup, Helen Stevens, George Tatro, Tandy Taylor, Jannan Thomas, Jay Thomas, Tricia Dillon Thomas, Vince Thomas, Casey Thompson, Rona Tyndall, Reggie Weaver, Brian Wren, LaShonda Yearwood, and (I am sure) others. Their insights have made this a better book and me a better person; I thank them for that gift.

I thank three wise women who have stepped in, these last few years, at pivotal moments: Deborah Botti, Stephanie Egnotovich, and Janie Spahr. Without their love and vision for an alternative way of being, this book—and its writer—would still be wild and wandering, somewhere; it is a blessing to be found and seen, and I am so grateful. I thank Gail Cole for her magical hands and a year of Mondays. I thank the Hosking/Diffin and Van Duys families for their friendship, and for being my children's second homes. And for faith and love beyond measure, I thank my sister-friends, these women of God, who are the family I choose: Janet Tuck Hilley and Julie Johnson, Arðfriður

Guðmundsdottir and Damayanthi Niles, Shira Lander and Judy Kim, and Liz Heller, the mother of God.

Finally, for the family I was born into—all variants of the Carter, Florence, Babson, and Herbert clans—there are no words. My beautiful mother, Anne Babson Carter, and my late father, David Martin Carter, gave me life so that I could have life; they are with me and for me, and I honor them. My grandparents taught me to love stories that begin *These are the names* . . . ; I am so happy that one of them, Joseph Martin Carter, will read the next chapter. My precious children, Caleb and Jonah, light the fire of inspiration in me each morning. My beloved spouse, David, makes our life together an adventure that I cannot wait to continue. More than anyone, David and the boys gave and gave and gave again, and then reminded me that no one ever *finishes* a book. Only God gets to finish; the rest of us just stop. They helped me know when it was time to stop, and I thank God for them.

My father, who is on another shore, knows why it had to be testimony. He gave me the missing pieces to sing. I give him this book.

Introduction

In Search of Testimony
and a Preaching Tradition

This is a book that asks you to rethink preaching in light of testimony. But it is also a book that asks you to rethink testimony in light of preaching, so let me clarify some terms. By *testimony*, I do not mean "telling your story" or "using personal illustrations," nor am I suggesting that the sermon is an appropriate vehicle for the preacher's memoirs. Instead, I am drawing on the classical definition of *testimony* as both a narration of events and a confession of belief: we tell what we have seen and heard, and we confess what we believe about it. A sermon in the testimony tradition is not an autobiography but a very particular kind of proclamation: the preacher tells what she has seen and heard *in the biblical text and in life*, and then confesses what she believes about it. Furthermore—and this is the troublesome part for preachers—there is no proof for testimony other than the engagement of a witness, and no proof for a sermon other than the engagement of the preacher. It is impossible to prove whether a sermon is true or false. One can only believe it or reject it.

The implications of relating our preaching to testimony may be setting off dozens of alarm bells for you, and indeed they should; this is serious talk, with the potential for serious misuse, particularly in our tell-all-and-bare-all age. History shows us that testimony can be appropriated for good and for ill, and that the pulpit is both a powerful and susceptible place. If you are cautious, then, about reading any further, I am glad for it; if you are dubious, I understand. So was I. But testimony has a way of unfolding itself across a life, and so it is that I have a story to tell—a testimony, if you will—of how and why this book has come about in the first place. If you can hold off the alarms for a few pages, I invite you to read and then judge for yourself.

The story has two parts: two testimonies.

FIRST TESTIMONY: THE TALE OF
THE ANXIOUS PREACHER

While We Were Sleeping

By now it is generally accepted that humanity in the late modern context has crossed some muddy and imprecise border dividing the *modern* from the *postmodern*, though how and why this has happened and what difference it makes for the pulpit, we cannot fully say. All we know is that one day we awoke to find ourselves living and preaching in different times. The old claims about power and knowledge—who has it, who defines it, and who gets to talk about it—were no longer valid. "Objectivity" had gone belly-up. "Certitude" was about as fashionable as a corset. And with these gone, of course, the houses of authority that had once sheltered preaching lay open to the elements, their original beams and trusses exposed. Whether those houses are facing major renovation or the bulldozer is endlessly debated; meanwhile, preachers have to rough it. We pitch our tents on the ruins of our former shelters and wonder if there is a wilderness metaphor at work, for surely, to quote John S. McClure's elegant phrasing, preaching in the postmodern context is "leaving itself in order to find itself":

> This is not to say that preaching has gone away or disappeared. It is not leaving the space that is constituted by the genre of preaching and going somewhere else. Rather, I want to argue that preaching has been *exiting those things that authorize its existence* and that this exit is designed, in part, to turn preaching toward its other(s) [that is, radical awareness of the "other" who is not like oneself] in such a way that *preachers may re-encounter something of the nature of proclamation at its deepest levels.*[1]

A wilderness holds within itself the promise of Canaan, and that promise keeps many of us going. But a wilderness also entails the hard work of exiting Egypt, and *this* is where the real wandering comes in. To leave behind the powers and authorities of a former existence, an enslaved and enslaving existence, is slow and painful and impossible to accomplish in a few months of committee meetings. It takes years— maybe forty of them—to leave yourself in order to find yourself. The process is not unlike the years of therapy that might accompany a recovery from depression. And this, I suspect, is probably why there is such resistance to postmodernism in some quarters: not all of us want to face Egypt, let alone leave it. We also do not particularly relish the exposure of our own homiletical fleshpots: if there is food in those pots, and we can count on it, so what if the price is remaining in slavery? Isn't the Egypt we know better than the liberation we don't?

The tricky thing about leaving and finding ourselves is coming to terms with our own peculiar and enslaved logic. Deconstruction, the most common postmodern method of reading and seeing "texts" (used in the broadest sense), can be quite helpful in this regard: ready or not, like it or not, when we deconstruct a thing, we *will* see ourselves more clearly. Deconstruction, like therapy, permits us to uncover the masked priorities and power dynamics of a text that may warp its authority structures, and so create ingrown systems that lead to oppression and suffering. Or, to put it another way: when we deconstruct something, such as preaching, we allow it to *show itself more clearly* so that we can see the things that make it what it is.[2] This may include exposing ways in which preaching, for example, appeals to its authority structures (the Scriptures, tradition, experience, and reason) in order to end discussion, suppress difference, and silence debate—and many of those revelations may be difficult and discouraging for us to swallow.

When something we hold dear, like preaching, is in the process of leaving and finding itself, it is hard on everyone. Critical appraisals take forever. Each new insight requires adjustment. Some days the insights take the form of accusations—or at least, it feels that way. We may get angry and defensive: Why is everything *our* fault? Why are *we* the ones who have to make so many changes? And why do we have to take responsibility for sins we never knew we were committing in the first place?

It helps, I think, to get a little perspective: reformations do not happen overnight. It also helps to laugh at ourselves: being paranoid and grumpy are part of the process, when change is happening, and some of us will turn in performances that are truly camera worthy. The thing is to get through this phase and move on. No one is "out to get us," or "out to get preaching" (certainly not in this book). Postmodern practices are not for the purpose of demolition. They are for the purpose of encounter; and with encounter, insight; and with insight, the chance to make right. In truth, such practices offer us a gift by opening up ethical space for us to make new decisions on behalf of the other. One could even say that the deconstruction of preaching is a kind of repentance, of turning around and looking again at our beloved practices of proclamation and seeing them as if for the first time. And awareness, of course, opens space for confession and, with God's grace, the time to amend (*re-form*) our lives.

In this book, I will be examining some of our long-held assumptions about preaching, and offering new ways to look at this practice to which many of us—myself included—have committed our lives. The examination process is not without pain, and it is pain I share. But I also firmly believe that the time to wake up and see *what we probably already know* . . . is now. To deny, retrench, roll over, and go back to sleep will only be at the expense of preaching itself, and with it, the One we proclaim.

The Authority Question: "Can I Really Say That?"

One of the most compelling signs of our transition into a postmodern era, in my experience, is the sheer number of preachers who report that they are no longer sure what the homiletical "rules" are. When church and society face challenges to orthodoxy, tradition, and leadership, preachers are continually forced to ask themselves by what authority they stand in the pulpit as interpreters of Scripture, and whether that authority "allows" them to speak openly. That is the crux of what I hear most frequently from pastors and students as they wrestle with biblical texts, listen to their people, and try to prepare sermons with integrity. They are always asking, *Can I really say that?*

> Can I really say that . . . if the commentary on my shelf says something different?
>
> Can I really say that . . . if it sounds totally illogical?
>
> Can I really say that . . . if no one will believe a word I say?
>
> Can I really say that . . . if it doesn't sound like "good news"?
>
> Can I really say that . . . if I believe it, but can't prove it?
>
> Can I really say that . . . if I'm only the seminary intern/a high school dropout/pulpit supply/a woman/a teenager/a layperson/a preacher?

Can I really say that? This is not a question we ask when the authoritative structures beneath us are set and strong, and we know where the boundaries of orthodoxy and acceptability are; when a system is closed, there is little need or even tolerance of questions. But when systems are in flux and structures wobble, closure gives way to something else: the possibility of construing authority differently. So when churches debate theology, denominations threaten schism, cultural norms shift, and personal experience ruptures prior claims, preachers cannot rely on the old and familiar sources in the same easy way. Those sources have to be tested for what they will hold and how far they will bend: *Can I really say that . . . without stepping out of bounds?* And this, of course, is the dangerous part. If the old structures give way, then new ones must be negotiated. If the old structures are rickety or rotted, yet not willing to give without a fight, then preachers will likely find themselves in the cloudy ranks of those witnesses whose words have cost them a great deal—perhaps even their lives.

Testimony: Open-ended Logic

Can I really say that? There are plenty of times when preachers decide that the answer to this question is a definite "No!" Maybe the time isn't right to test the situation; maybe they cannot summon the conviction or courage it will take to make that test. A vivid metaphor for this can be found in the so-called first ending of the Gospel of Mark (16:1–8): the women go to the tomb, see that it is empty, meet the messenger, hear his news, receive his instruction to tell the disciples . . . and run away in utter terror, without saying a word to anyone. It isn't hard to imagine why. *How could we really say that?!—when it sounds completely crazy . . . when we have no proof beyond our words . . . when we're <u>women</u>, for crying out loud, and no one will ever believe us!* The women are captive to old authority structures that would never permit such speech, and so the Gospel ends with an abrupt silence, a mute and terrified, "No!"

There is, however, a "second ending" of Mark (16:9–20) that goes rather differently. Scholars have suggested that this was probably added later, to smooth over the roughness of the first: in verses 9–20, at least one of the women, Mary of Magdala, goes on to change her mind and speak after all, and her witness is then followed by others. Thus the second ending makes plain what the first ending only implies: fearful first reactions are not the last word. We can look again, choose faith over fear, break silence, risk words—as indeed must have happened, since the Word is out! Some critics like the subtlety of the first ending; others appreciate the clarity of the second. But perhaps the point is not to choose which ending is best. Perhaps the point is to acknowledge that each is possible. Christian witness will always hinge on the question, *Can we really say that, even though we have no proof beyond what we have seen and believed?* Somewhere between the question and the answer is where Christian preaching locates itself—again and again and again.

Preachers who live in these conditions yet still decide to speak are choosing *testimony*, one of the oldest forms of Christian witness. Testimony contains both a narration of events and a confession of belief: we tell what we have seen and heard, and then confess what we believe about it. Therefore, testimony is not something that can ever be proven true or false; it can only be believed or rejected. The only proof of testimony is the engagement of the witness, and the only proof of a sermon is the engagement of the preacher: whether we are willing to seal our lives to our words.

More and more, it seems to me, preachers are relying not on outside authorities as the proof of their words (that is, ecclesial bodies that make decisions about leadership or orthodoxy), but on the authority of testimony: preaching what they have seen and heard in the biblical text, and what they believe about it. More and more, preachers are finding that what makes their sermons authoritative for their people is not the number of footnotes but the depth of the preacher's engagement with the Scriptures and life itself. More and more, preachers are asking themselves, "Can I really say that?" and deciding that *Yes, they can,* if they are willing to go all the way to hell and back to stand with their people in this text. *Yes, they can,* if they are willing to stand behind what they say and what they truly believe. It makes for an awkward and tippy pulpit, at least at first. But more and more preachers, and more and more people, are crying out for a deeper rootedness in the biblical text, a deeper embodiment—which is to say, *a living-out, in full view*—of theological questions. And these are the preachers who are adopting testimony as a homiletical model for uncertain times—which our postmodern context certainly is.

SECOND TESTIMONY: THE TALE OF
THE TRADITIONLESS PREACHER

The Void at the Intersection

Testimony first caught my attention when I was a graduate student in the 1990s, researching feminist homiletics and histories of women's preaching. I was frustrated by the lack of female role models in the standard histories of preaching; with a few exceptions, women were almost completely absent from these volumes. As if to underscore this void, I could find next to nothing about historical women preachers in the feminist homiletical literature at that time. Feminist homileticians, it seemed, were only interested in contemporary women—or maybe the standard histories of preaching were right, and there really weren't any historical women for us to study.

Partly as an experiment, partly out of desperation, I volunteered to do some exploratory research on women preachers for my History of Preaching seminar, fully expecting my search to come up empty. I headed to the library—and was utterly shocked. Women preachers were *everywhere*. Their autobiographies alone took up shelves and shelves of books, most written in the nineteenth century. And this wasn't all: womanist theologians had done some stunning work on histories of African American women preachers;[3] feminist historians were rapidly uncovering material on women who had preached in every age;[4] dissertations on the histories of women preachers were coming out every year, as steadily as clockwork; sermon collections were beginning to include preaching women from the past.[5] These historical writings were there; they were accessible; they were plentiful! So why did the fields of homiletics and feminist homiletics act like these women had never existed?!

I started to read. The history of preaching women in America, I discovered, is particularly rich. It can be traced as early as 1636 and continues through the struggle for women's ordination in the twentieth century. It includes a wide variety of pulpit practices, styles, theories, and goals. Despite such diversity, however, the women of this history hold some things in common with one another and even with contemporary women: they read and interpret the Bible differently from the men of their day; they hear in Scripture a different and liberating word about women; they place this word in the context of their own experience as women; and, despite lack of acceptance or even heavy opposition about women's right to speak or teach in church, they believe themselves to be called by God, after the manner of their biblical foremothers and forefathers, to witness to the truth of Jesus Christ as they have seen and believed it.

Then I found the linchpin: a difference between these women and contemporary women is that many historical women preachers described their preaching as *testimony*. There are some pragmatic reasons for this: in eighteenth-century and nineteenth-century America, "preaching" ordinarily referred to scriptural exposition by a member of the ordained clergy while "testimony" was the word for a public confession of faith in the context of personal experience that could be delivered by laypeople as well as clergy. Some women preachers ostensibly sought to avoid criticism by adopting the form of testimony, claiming that they did not preach expository sermons. The intense public reaction to their activity, however, suggested to me that testimony by women was seen as something new and powerful and dangerous. It was viewed, by supporters and opponents alike, as *preaching*, no matter what the women themselves called it. I began to speculate: Does testimony blur the boundaries of what a sermon is and who may preach it? Does testimony by women have a distinctive character?

Testimony: An Old Word in a New Key

Testimony is an old, old word for homiletics. We can hear it in Jesus' own preaching and in the witness of the women at the tomb on Easter morning. We can hear it in the apostle Paul's writings and in the *Confessions* of Saint Augustine. The history of Christian communities, from the earliest church martyrs to Puritan membership rituals to contemporary practices of faith sharing, are filled with this ancient Christian pattern for incorporating human experience into proclamation: through *confession* (of what one believes) and *narration* (of what one has seen), believers *testify* to their faith in Jesus Christ. Testimony was and still is a practice of the church open to all believers as a means of deepening faith in themselves and others through the passionate witness of life and expression. Yet it seems to be most alive among marginalized communities, where it functions as a powerful practice of proclamation that is often interpreted as preaching.

The very first Christians considered testimony a form of preaching every bit as important as the public oration. As church historian Ronald E. Osborn writes, the personal testimony of one individual to another, no matter how emotional or stammering, was "the leading edge of witness" and "the dominant form of speech to outsiders."[6] The testimony of martyrs such as Perpetua, Felicitas, and Eulalia held a particular place of honor and inspiration among the faithful; nothing was considered more convincing than the words of a witness willing to sacrifice her good name and even her life for the sake of the gospel. In fact, these martyrdom stories are actually the key to the derivation of the word: the word *witness* is derived from the Latin *testis* (a witness who testifies or swears on his virility, literally his "testes," as proof of honesty), and was later absorbed into the Greek *marturia* (the witness as "martyr" who swears on his or her life, thereby blending *testis* with the root *smer*—"to remember," "to deliberate with much care," and "to be able to tell").[7] In the most literal and corporeal sense, testimony is passionate truth-telling.

Many contemporary homileticians mention testimony in passing, but few engage it in any depth, perhaps because it carries an evangelical flavor and fervor that some find distasteful. In feminist homiletical literature, testimony is a virtually untapped resource.[8] These are curious omissions that need to be addressed, for at least three reasons.

First, testimony is a practice of the church with a long and vibrant history that in and of itself deserves greater attention. Yet the fact that testimony has been a practice of proclamation particular to marginalized Christians, including women, raises issues that homiletics and feminist homiletics would do well to explore. Why has the ancient practice of testimony survived and thrived in some churches while it has all but disappeared from others? Why is testimony recognized as a preaching practice of great power by marginalized Christian communities but so often ignored by homileticians who teach preaching in mainline seminaries? Why have women been allowed to testify when they have been forbidden to preach, and how have women negotiated the line between preaching and testimony? What is the nature of authority, power, and experience in testimony, and why is testimony a form of proclamation? As a practice, testimony raises many fascinating questions vital to homiletics and feminist homiletics—yet to date, these fields have shown little interest in raising them.

Second, testimony is appearing with greater frequency in the work of biblical scholars and theologians. Paul Ricoeur's seminal essay "The Hermeneutics of Testimony" (1980) was one of the first to explore testimony as the distinctive Christian hermeneutic; the witness character of testimony has always been a provocative and rich paradigm for New Testament studies.[9] Yet testimony is surfacing now in the work of *Old* Testament scholars as well. Walter Brueggemann's magisterial *Theology of the Old Testament* (1997), a work that draws heavily on postmodern scholarship, is organized around the concept of testimony: the character and mode of theological claim in the Old Testament, Brueggemann argues, is one of testimony, and the process of theological utterance and thought can be understood in terms of a testimony-dispute-advocacy model.[10] Perhaps sensing the void in homiletics concerning testimony, Brueggemann develops his idea further in a book specifically geared for preachers, in which he speaks of preaching as "decentered testimony" in times of exile.[11] Yet despite this biblical turn to testimony, the field of homiletics—testimony's family of origin—is silent.

Third, testimony is becoming more critical to the work of feminist theologians and scholars of all kinds. The word crops up with surprising regularity, in the work of literary critics like Elaine Showalter to that of poets and activists like Carolyn Forché.[12] You can find it in feminist theologians Mary McClintock Fulkerson (*Changing the Subject*, 1997) and Rebecca Chopp (*The Power to Speak*, 1989), who use testimony to wrestle with the place of women's experience in theological discourse and proclamation.[13] Feminists everywhere, it seems, are giving serious consideration to testimony as a practice that pushes the boundaries of women's subjectivity—everywhere, that is, but in the field of homiletics.

I have to wonder about this. Why has contemporary homiletical theory said so little about a practice so integral to the tradition of preaching? Why has feminist homiletical theory paid such scant attention to a theory that is making waves in other fields of feminist and theological inquiry? Could the marginal location and character of testimony have something to do with the silence? Does testimony challenge our assumptions about preaching in ways that are too disruptive, too dangerous, to explore?

A Preaching Tradition . . . *for Women and Men*

Testimony lies at the intersection of a conversation between homiletics, biblical studies, theology, and church history. It invites us to rethink proclamation as a marginal practice of the church, and to rethink our ideas about freedom, power, and difference. In short, here is what I hope to show you in this book: When we stand at the intersection of that four-way conversation about testimony, we can see the contours of a *women's preaching tradition*, part of a long history of preaching by marginalized Christians. And this tradition has enormous potential for our postmodern context.

But here is something else I hope to show you: Whether you are a woman or a man, this tradition is yours—and it matters!

Let me be very direct here. At first, I thought I was writing a book for women, that only women would read. I figured there might be a few sympathetic men out there who would read it in solidarity, or because they are related to me, but I didn't believe that testimony would hold much interest for men. That, of course, was before I actually talked to them about it. The pastors I have spoken with, both men and women, have taught me that testimony has everything to do with us. It is for all of us. I may have happened upon it at a particular historical and theological intersection, but that is certainly not the only place to locate testimony. Testimony springs up in marginal communities everywhere. Marginally located Christians have always known this. And as the so-called mainstream churches in the North American context get pushed farther and farther away from the power center they once enjoyed, these marginally located Christians will have much to teach their newly marginal sisters and brothers.

Testimony is not just for women. It is a way of preaching, a way of living out the preaching life, that the church desperately needs for its own survival and its own identity. It is the source of a different kind of power, a deeper vibrancy, than those in the center can ever know. And as my own blindness proved to me (what could be more stupid than not heeding your own words?!), testimony can be so threatening to our enslaved logic that we do not even notice how stuck in Egypt we are.

So now, let me ask the question that had me stumped, back in the early days of writing this book (before I had taken the amazing step of actually leaving my office and talking to real human beings about it): Why on earth should we bother to read the stories of a handful of obscure women preachers from the pages of history? What could they possibly have to do with us?

My response is, Everything.

Maybe you are a woman, reading this book in search of role models you never got in seminary. Maybe you are a man, browsing through this book for ideas about what to do with the women's Bible study. Maybe you are a solo pastor, praying that you will make it until your next vacation. Maybe you are a big pulpit preacher, wishing you had more time to prepare your sermons. Maybe you are a layperson, reading up on how to strengthen the quality of preaching in your congregation. Maybe you are a seminarian, fed up with colleagues who think "feminism" is an F word. Maybe you are a person whose denomination will not ordain you, asking where your authority to preach really is located. Maybe you are a tired seeker, wondering how it is that we live, and speak, and hold truth in these troubled days.

I believe these women have something to teach you, as they taught me. True, their life circumstances probably could not be more different from ours. Few of us preach regularly in our kitchens or living rooms, to standing-room crowds. We probably have not hiked twenty miles to give last Sunday's sermon, or written a dozen biblical commentaries in our spare time. Not many of us are hauled into court, excommunicated, or banished for something we have said in a sermon. Our preaching may aggravate the folk, but it is unlikely to topple the government.

On the other hand, many of us have known the agony of having a word to say and no place or (worse) courage to say it. Many of us have struggled with what it means to be called to preach, or to be a preacher. Some of us have fought for years for the right to be ordained in our own churches. Some of us despair at ever knowing or being a part of true Christian community.

What do we have in common with a bunch of obscure women preachers from the pages of history? *More than we know.* And they have wisdom to teach us that in my opinion is long overdue. In fact, I will go so far as to claim that these women bring into focus a preaching tradition that is of greater use and value to the contemporary church than many of those that currently hold sway.

A Preaching Tradition . . . *For Girls and Women*

I hope I have made it clear that preaching in the testimony tradition is not exclusively for women. It is a gift *of* the church, *for* the church; it is a part of our history and belongs to all of us, women and men. But I would be less than honest if I did not say that I hope women especially will claim this tradition with joy.

Some of you are mothers of daughters; you know the challenges of raising strong and confident girls who will grow into strong and confident women. As a mother of sons, I do not share that particular experience—but I am a woman, and a preacher, and a teacher of preachers. I know how hard it is to find your way in a preaching world that so often expects women to look and act just like men. I know how hard it is for some of my women students to physically enter the pulpit, after all the destructive messages they have heard about women preachers. I know how hard it is for teenage girls to really imagine themselves as preachers if they have never actually seen a woman preach (and amazingly, in my mainline denomination, I regularly find that fully a quarter of our young female and male leadership have never heard a woman preach a sermon). I know how hard it is for me to convince some of my women students that their tremendous pulpit gifts are truly a blessing rather than a curse.

When I compare the ministry to other professions, such as medicine and law, I am shocked, frankly, at how difficult it is to nurture strong and confident women preachers in a mainline Protestant seminary classroom. The preaching traditions that inform and shape my students are nothing short of exasperating. They feed the myth of women as perpetual pioneers—strangers and outsiders—in the pulpit ministry, by pretending that women have never preached without benefit of ordination (in my denomination, that would make our "women's preaching tradition" just fifty years old). Historically, of course, this is utter nonsense, but few of us—particularly women of European ancestry—know anything about our history: its breadth, its depth, and the resources (including some relatively recent publications) that are available to us.[14] Feminist homileticians, unlike our womanist and *mujerista* sisters, do not always appear to value a historical tradition, since much of the scholarship focuses on current preaching practices as they define a distinct feminist homiletic.

The result is nothing short of devastating. In my classrooms, I can detect chasms that divide the students from their history; men from women; and women from one another. The women, for example, believe that they are not part of any preaching tradition but have only recently been "included" or "admitted" into certain preaching "rights." They think they have to either preach like men or invent themselves from scratch. Meanwhile, the men struggle against some of the authoritarian, domineering role models that have shaped their ideas of preaching. They are looking for ways to embody strength and vulnerability in the pulpit that go beyond tired old stereotypes of femininity and masculinity. Everybody is sick of being from either Venus or Mars.

We need new preaching traditions. We need to actually name them, because they are real and they exist. Testimony is the key to one of them, but surely there are others that have been suppressed. And as the lessons of postmodernism continue to sink in (remember pluralism and diversity?), perhaps we will recall how simple it is, really, to keep turning, turning our eyes outward beyond ourselves, and to let go of the habit of privileging one set of experiences over another. The traditions, after all, are a gift; they are meant to give life, and they do give life. Stories of historical black women's preaching, for example, are honored and cherished in the community of black women preachers; they serve as sources of inspiration to share in a tradition of courage and resistance, creating a fuller picture of what preaching can be. In the same way, when we study the preaching practices of women who look nothing like the typical mainline Protestant woman minister (that is, women who are poor, uneducated, or not ordained), we broaden our understanding of "women's experience" and "women's ways of preaching," and we avoid the sin of universalizing only *one* set of experiences.

This is not to say that the preaching traditions that have nurtured many of us in the past are no longer valid; of course they are. But those traditions do not make up the whole story about preaching. And women in particular need to know it.

Finally Comes the Thesis

Perhaps you have been wondering when I would cut to the chase and write a clear thesis statement. Here it is.

Preaching in the testimony tradition provides us with a historical, biblical, theological, and homiletical memory of women's preaching: in short, a women's preaching tradition. This tradition is part of a long history of preaching by marginalized Christians that calls us to rethink our assumptions about what it is to preach and what it takes to become a preacher. For postmodern Christians, preaching in the testimony tradition is a vibrant and powerful way to proclaim the liberating Word of God into a new context. Yet it is also a way of being and becoming a preacher, of living in and living out the Word of God.

It works in the following ways:

1. Preaching in the tradition of testimony brings into homiletical focus a vast repertoire of women's sermons that have not been widely known or acknowledged as part of the preaching tradition. It changes the subject of preaching to include those who have preached and testified from the margins.

2. Preaching in the tradition of testimony shifts the locus of authority away from the ministerial office and places it with the one who testifies: that is, the one who has seen and believed the liberating power of God's Word and who then risks proclaiming the truth of the gospel. This shift locates authentic and authoritative preaching not in the ecclesial center but in particular situations of struggle and trial at the margins, in which competing worldviews

and even lives may be at stake. Yet testimony can also take "centrist" preachers—those whom the ecclesial center sanctions and supports—and reorient them, so that in their dislocation they see and speak of the biblical text and life in new ways.

3. Preaching in the tradition of testimony offers another view of the role of experience in proclamation. The preacher is called to engage the liberating power of God's Word in the biblical text and in life, and then to narrate and confess what she has seen and believed in that experience.

4. Preaching in the tradition of testimony offers us a view of what it takes to become a preacher and to be a preacher: by rooting ourselves so deeply in text and context that we embody the Word we proclaim—and must testify to what we have seen and believed. Preaching in the testimony tradition calls us to live in and live out the Word of God.

Road Maps and Synopses

I am sure there must be writers out there whose books have evolved deductively, their arguments lining up like ducks and their chapters falling into neat, orderly rows. That is not what happened here. Testimony appears to be a great resistor of straightforward logic, so this book—which turned out to be a search for historical, biblical, theological, and homiletical memory of a testimony preaching tradition—has had to move *in*ductively, through a lot of weeds and dead ends, sneaking around to backdoors and crawling through holes in the screens. It seemed appropriate (and very New Homiletic) to re-create that inductive process for the reader, so that the book might follow the same path as my own evolving thought. We are definitely taking the scenic route to testimony, as opposed to the shortcut, but sometimes the scenery is the thing. For those of you who like to know where you are going and why, here is a map and a brief synopsis to take along.

I first noticed testimony while reading histories of women preachers, so that is where the book picks up in part 1 ("Waking Up the Details: Stories of Testimony"). In chapters 1, 2, and 3, you will hear the stories of three women who are worth meeting: Anne Hutchinson (1591–1643), Sarah Osborn (1714–1796), and Jarena Lee (1783–?). It is important to begin with history, I believe, because testimony is empty without the story within which it unfolds, and the life through which it speaks. We cannot identify a preacher apart from that preacher's story—which includes the work of *becoming* a preacher. I encourage you, then, to read with an eye for detail and an ear for overlap, because you will probably recognize pieces of yourself in these stories; I hope you do. And if you are a person who finds history dull and dry, take heart: these women are anything but that.

From history we move to theory, or an attempt to address the questions raised by the details in these women's lives. This is where the plot thickens. Testimony raises issues—we might even call them "family secrets"—that the church and academy, it seems, would rather not discuss. Part 2, "Waking Up the Secrets: Theories of Testimony," will try to do exactly that. In chapter 4, Paul Ricoeur and Walter Brueggemann offer biblical perspectives on testimony, with special attention to Christian hermeneutics and biblical speech. In chapter 5, two feminist theologians, Mary McClintock Fulkerson and Rebecca Chopp, provide theological perspectives on testimony, with special attention to the category of women's experience and a theology of proclamation. I spend some time summarizing each theologian's work and then reflect from my own point of view as a preacher interested in testimony.

From theory we move to a discussion—okay, a *testimony*—of how preaching in the testimony tradition plays out in a preacher's life. Part 3, "Waking Up the Preacher: Practicing Testimony," offers some constructive proposals for preaching in light of testimony, and for the process of *becoming* a preacher, which is something every preacher must eventually face. In chapter 6, I make my case for testimony as a practice that speaks to many of the preacher's fears about authority and being "good enough" as well as the church's fears about biblical illiteracy, declining membership numbers, and conflict. There is no cure, of course, for everything that ails us. But testimony gets us in the habit of standing in our own lives (as opposed to the lives we wish we had) and in the biblical text (as opposed to the world's texts), describing what we see (as opposed to what we wish we saw), and confessing what we believe (as opposed to what we should believe). Testimony teaches us a closer reading of and a deeper grace for human life and God's Word. Those lessons can only strengthen our living and therefore our preaching. In chapter 7, we get practical—or at least as practical as testimony will consent to be—with guidelines, direction, and exercises for preachers, easily adaptable for your own context.

Waking Up the Author

A friend of mine pestered me until I finally bought Leif Enger's book *Peace Like a River* and read it. He knew I had to; it is about testimony. Here is a sample of Enger's exquisite prose:

> "Don't you ever doubt it?" Davy asked.
>
> And in fact I have. And perhaps will again. But here is what happens. I look out the window at the red farm—for here we live, Sara and I, in a new house across the meadow, a house built by capable arms and open lungs and joyous sweat. Maybe I see our daughter, home from school, picking plums or apples for Roxanna; maybe one of our sons, reading on the grass or painting an upended canoe. Or maybe Sara comes into the room—my darling Sara—with Mr. Cassidy's beloved rolls on a steaming plate. Then I breathe deeply, and certainty enters into me like light, like a piece of science, and curious music seems to hum inside my fingers.
>
> Is there a single person on whom I can press belief?
>
> No sir.
>
> All I can do is say, Here's how it went. Here's what I saw.
>
> I've been there and am going back.
>
> Make of it what you will.[15]

I have thought about this passage a great deal, because the process of writing is one of waking up. I cannot say if there is a connection between one's pace as a writer and one's pace in waking up each morning, but I would not be surprised to learn that there is. Perhaps those who wake up easily, bouncing out of bed as soon as the alarm goes off, are also those who write easily. Perhaps those who take longer to swim up from sleep and shake out dreams also take longer to wake up to what they really see and believe, and want to say. I do know that as a person who always leaves her bed with a certain amount of regret, wishing there were just a *little* more time before alertness were required of me, I have noticed the same tinge, the same urge to burrow down and go back to sleep, as I have written this book. Something in me does not really want to wake up—not right this minute, anyway—to the new-day implications of what I teach my students and ought therefore to write in all honesty and freedom. Something in me is reluctant to wake up the preacher I might become.

Then, to paraphrase Leif Enger, I walk into a classroom. I see the bare white walls and the institutional furniture and the faces of my students, waiting. I see the preachers they are becoming; I see the preachers that have awoken within themselves, because they trust God and one another. Class begins. Together we open our Bibles to the text of the day; together we start to read it; and *every time*, the text draws us out of our seats and into a world; and we then begin to move. We follow it across the page, out of the room, into the street, out of memory, through dreams, until something stirs. . . .

And once again, I am reminded of what I have seen and believed, and what I know I will believe again, once I crawl out of bed and enter the text's new day.

I defer to Enger. Is there a single person on whom we can press belief? I ask. And he replies, *No ma'am!*

> All we can do is say, Here's how it went. Here's what I saw.
> I've been there [in the text's new world] and am going back.
> Make of it what you will.

Are you ready?

PART ONE

Waking Up the Details:
Stories of Testimony

they ask me to remember
but they want me to remember
their memories
and i keep on remembering
mine
    —Lucille Clifton, "why some people be mad at me sometimes"[1]

Standing in Your Own Life

Some Words to Begin Part 1

I have been a knitter almost all my life. Recently I bought a knitting book by a young Norwegian designer named Solveig Hisdal, whose work is so admired that it often ends up in museums. There is a funny symmetry about that, since Hisdal's patterns for knitwear *begin* in museums: she repeatedly visits Norway's historical folk art collections in search of old textiles that will spark her interest, and then adapts the patterns for contemporary designs. Here is an excerpt from the foreword, written by the director of the Hardanger Folk Museum:

> A museum takes care of old things so that children and young people growing up can learn about what has happened and how things were done before their own time. Knowledge gives us roots and a sense of security, and it is with such a background that one can explore the world. But if no one uses the knowledge in a museum, it lies there dead, or at best sleeping.
> Solveig Hisdal knew that museums shelter knowledge, and she knew how to get hold of it. With the enthusiasm of one going on a

treasure hunt, she combed many of our country's museums. What was she looking for? Old patterns, techniques for textile production, rose-painted chests, cupboards, wallpaper, skirts, and the embroidered panels of bunad (folk costumes). But, perhaps more importantly, Hisdal was searching for inspiration and ideas that she could carry on and communicate through her work.[2]

In Norway, knitting is part of the cultural heritage. What's more, that culture is very much alive: every child (only girls, once, but increasingly boys as well) learns to knit in school; every knitter learns to identify the traditional patterns used in classic Norwegian sweaters. Hisdal understands herself to be firmly rooted in Norway's long knitting tradition. Yet she has also discovered how to live in it differently—by paying attention to details that others have missed or forgotten. In her hands, in her designs, those details live and breathe again. They wake from sleep. They speak to our times.

Our preaching tradition is a treasure: ancient, vibrant, and rich in detail. Like so many of us, I want to honor that tradition, to live in it with deep roots. But I also want to live in it differently, by paying attention to details that others have missed or forgotten. They are not so hard to find. They are simply sleeping in museums of books. And sometimes, there is a liberating word in the details, old knowledge that is waiting for a chance to wake up and speak.

Part 1 is my attempt to wake up some of those details. It contains the stories, which you may or may not have heard, of three women preachers: Anne Hutchinson, Sarah Osborn, and Jarena Lee. I selected them for a number of reasons.

First and most important, they are simply amazing people, with stories so remarkable that they would probably make good screenplays. If the average ninth-grade American History unit included narratives like these, it would keep the students awake better than a double latté, because there is just no way to doze through the Puritans once Anne Hutchinson makes her entrance.

Second, these women were more than fascinating: they were famous. On their home turf, they turned heads and stopped traffic. They preached sermons that left people speechless. They inspired devotion and resentment, elections and defections, revivals, dismissals, and even a war. Hutchinson, Osborn, and Lee were highly respected in their local communities; so respected, in fact, that they managed to avoid the public suspicion and hostility usually associated with preaching women—at least, for a while. When notoriety gave rise to public debates about women and religious authority, the powers-that-be quickly retaliated, and freedom turned to backlash. The women were denounced. Debate was silenced. Laws were passed to clamp down on women even harder, and the authorities themselves put the details to sleep and rewrote history. If you have never heard of the three women in this chapter, or if the only name you associate with Anne Hutchinson is "Jezebel," there is a good reason for it: some very worried seventeenth-century, eighteenth-century, and nineteenth-century officials did not want you to hear about them, ever.

Third, I selected these women because there are written documents associated with them that help to piece together their stories. We have trial transcripts, letters, autobiographies, and journals; from these, we can begin to piece together the women's stories as *they* told them. And clearly, they were eager to do so: each woman took tremendous care to explain and defend her actions in the words she left us. Each must also have known that whatever she said could become target practice for a slew of angry opponents and church authorities, any of whom had the power to deny, dismiss, or simply delete her story in one powerful stroke. The documents that still exist are therefore doubly precious for the simple reason that they have survived the ravages of time and censorship.

The narratives in part 1 are constructed in a particular way. I will not try to prove that these women were preachers: even their most vehement opponents agree that they were. I will not try to mainstream them by claiming that they preached just like men or were preachers just like men: they didn't and weren't. And I will not (I hope) be your tour guide through the Museum of Preachers (". . . and on our left, a special exhibit of the First Ladies of Preaching, with their lovely inaugural sermons . . ."), whisking you through the rooms so quickly and quietly that not even one detail awakes from sleep.

What I hope to show is this: these women created themselves, as outsiders.[3] They had no desire to be aligned with powers and authorities, or to preach like those who were. They did not necessarily campaign for ordination or admittance to the inner circles of power. Instead, they located themselves on the *margins* of power and authority, far from the center and its privileges. At the margins, life is a constant struggle to survive and thrive, let alone to preach the Word of God; these women knew that. Yet their struggles are no detour from the "real" preaching story that is recorded in our history books. Their struggles *are* the real story, as far as I am concerned. Preaching is not a right or a privilege reserved for those who locate themselves at the power center. Preaching, as these women remind us, is the slow work of standing in one's own life and in the Word of God and saying what one sees and believes, no matter the consequences.

So let me come clean. In this book, I begin with the assumption that, like it or not, legally or not, Christian women preach and always have, and our preaching history includes women. The numbers may be small, the details smudged or sleeping, but they are real, and they challenge the way we think about preaching. The story of Christian preaching is not just about the church's speech. It is also about the church's struggle, and the preacher's struggle, to *come to speech*: hearing it, naming it, attempting it, and embodying it.

Read carefully. In these narratives, you will hear echoes of our own conversations, the ones we cannot seem to finish or resolve, all these years later. And maybe that is the point. In these stories, unfinished and ongoing, lie the bright threads of an unmistakable tradition . . . of preaching women and preaching men, becoming preachers in America.

It is tradition that belongs to us. All of us.

1

Anne Marbury Hutchinson

(1591–1643)

In 1644, John Winthrop, charter member of the Massachusetts Bay Colony and governor of Boston, published a book titled *A Short Story of the Rise, reign, and ruine of the Antinomians, Familists & Libertines*, which began with these words:

> After we had escaped the cruell hands of persecuting Prelates, and the dangers at sea, and had prettily well outgrowne our wildernes troubles in our first plantings in New-England; And when our Common-wealth began to be founded, and our churches sweetely settled in peace, . . . Lest we should, now, grow secure, our wise God . . . sent a new storme after us, which proved the sorest tryall that ever befell us since we left our native soyle.[1]

The "sorest tryall" had a name: Anne Marbury Hutchinson. From 1636 to 1638, she and her followers challenged Winthrop and the local clergy in a struggle for power that came to be known as the Antinomian Controversy. The struggle was, as Winthrop intuited, the pivotal event in the early years of the Bay Colony, and his *Short Story* is told from the perspective of the victors. Winthrop's account includes his eyewitness report of Hutchinson's examination and trial, for which he served as prosecutor, chief judge, and governor. The document also contains his frank opinion of Hutchinson—"the head of all this faction," "the breeder and nourisher of all these distempers"—as a cunning, strident, and headstrong woman who very nearly destroyed the peace, unity, and purity of the colony with "the Plague" of her heretical views.[2]

For nearly three centuries, historians tended to accept Winthrop's version of things. None disputed that the Antinomian Controversy was a decisive turning point in the history of seventeenth-century New England, but few portrayed Anne Hutchinson as more than a religious fanatic and ringleader. Even contemporary scholarship, which grants that Hutchinson is essential to our understanding of religion and gender in early America, tends to overlook the obvious, which is that *women's preaching* is essential to that understanding. For it is remarkable, isn't it? The first European woman known to have preached in the New World almost toppled that world! No matter what most of us were taught in grade school (as we fashioned our construction paper headdresses and pilgrim hats), the biggest threat to the Pilgrims' survival, as they saw it, was not disease or starvation or Native Americans. It was a sermon series. It was Anne Hutchinson, preaching. When that woman stepped into the pulpit, she became the Godzilla of Massachusetts Bay.

This might sound crazy to many historians, especially those who seriously doubt that a sermon could ever exert such power. Indeed, how could one Puritan woman in a pulpit be such a threat?! Because she was a woman? Because of the preaching? Or because she was a *woman, preaching*?

These are questions that need to be sharply contextualized. Anne Hutchinson was extraordinary, all right, but so were the people and forces around her: women enthroned and reduced, clergy rebellious and compromising, the Word of God interpreted this way and that. It was a time when politics determined religion in a deadly game of musical chairs. Every time the crown changed hands, the church in royal favor did, too—and no one wanted to be sitting in the wrong seat when the music stopped. In these circumstances, it was not easy to *define* authority, let alone *locate* it. Yet both were crucial to survival, as Anne Hutchinson knew. In her story, we can trace exactly what was at stake in those definitions and locations: a woman's place, a man's place, and with them, the whole social order.

BEHIND EVERY STRONG WOMAN . . . IS A VIRGIN QUEEN, A REBEL FATHER, AND A PREACHER ON THE "MOST WANTED" LIST

Strong women abound in every age. Many of them, by choice or necessity, take up work that might be considered unusual for a woman. Anne

Hutchinson, however, saw nothing at all unusual in her decision to preach. For her, good doctrinal preaching was simply a way of living, and a necessary one at that. If the parish clergy either could not or would not provide sound preaching, Hutchinson was perfectly willing to step into the void; she had complete confidence in God's favor and her own abilities. That assurance undoubtedly came from an unusual constellation of role models who taught Hutchinson that authority was not something to blindly accept, but to carefully, prayerfully, studiously consider—and, if necessary, to re-image. Of those role models, I want to highlight three in particular.

First, and perhaps most overlooked: Hutchinson grew up in England in an era when a *woman* ruled England. Elizabeth I, the only surviving Protestant heir of Henry VIII, enjoyed one of the longest and most successful reigns (1558–1603) of any British monarch. Brilliant, educated, victorious in battle, Elizabeth managed to secure the love and loyalty of her subjects while breaking every rule concerning women's place. This was an unusual situation, to say the least. It also required some fast rhetoric. Elizabeth and her promoters had to find a way to explain how the fixed hierarchies of the universe that governed every other aspect of British society appeared not to hold in the case of Her Majesty: if women were truly inferior to men, how could a female monarch be Head of the Church and Queen of the Seas? The answer, they reasoned, was that Elizabeth did not completely blast the cosmic order by virtue of her womanhood; she was merely a *kink* in that order. She was the Virgin Queen, appointed by God as the earthly equivalent of the Virgin Mary. And while men were still undeniably superior— well, only an idiot would still take part in the old sport of deriding women, in public and in print. Instead, politicians and poets (dubbed "Elizabethans") switched to praising the virtues of the fair sex and its fairest Queen instead.[3] Female literacy rates rose, reaching a level not seen again until the nineteenth century. Anne Marbury (not yet Hutchinson) was only fourteen when Elizabeth I died, but fourteen is old enough to see that "fixed hierarchies" is really code for "fixed . . . unless it suits us to be flexible." She was also old enough to notice that if a system could be made to tolerate a female monarch, then other aberrations must be possible.

A second major influence on Hutchinson was her father, the Reverend Francis Marbury. Marbury was an Anglican priest who campaigned loudly for Church reforms in the areas of preaching and clergy education, and so gained a reputation as a troublemaker.[4] He gave his daughter her first lessons in church reform and resistance. In 1590, when Marbury rebelled against the Queen's bishops, he was turned out of his parish for insubordination. This left him with nothing to do for twelve years but write his trial memoirs (a scathing and clever exposé of inept church authorities, later published) and tutor his twelve children at home. Somewhat unusually, Marbury believed in teaching even his daughters the unfeminine disciplines of theology and Scripture, and by his own admission, his best pupil was his oldest daughter, Anne.[5] For most of her childhood, Anne studied daily with her father. Eventually, the economic strains of a large family led Marbury to seek and receive a new appointment to a prestigious church in London, but only after he assured the bishops that his youthful days of rebellion were long past. No doubt his daughter learned the high cost of resistance and compromise when powerful churches demanded allegiance.

Hutchinson's third major influence was her pastor and spiritual guide, John Cotton, the great Puritan preacher and theologian. In 1612, the same year that Anne Marbury married William Hutchinson in the town of Alford, Cotton came to fill the pulpit of St. Botolph's in nearby Boston. He was something of a phenomenon. Brilliant, popular, possessed of a maverick blend of Puritanism that could flaunt or taunt orthodoxy, Cotton was hard to label and even harder to arrest. For more than twenty years he slipped in and out of the hands of would-be Anglican accusers, always managing to avoid persecution by outpreaching or outreasoning his opponents. In 1633, however, the climate for Puritan Separatists in England had grown too dangerous even for England's most celebrated preacher, and Cotton accepted the invitation of the Massachusetts Bay Colony (newly named "Boston" in his honor) to join them in forming a Reformation Community in the New World.[6]

The Hutchinsons were staunch and avid supporters of Cotton through these volatile years. Cotton's influence on Anne Hutchinson is inestimable. His sermons were the topic of discussion at the women's group she led in her home. His rejection of Anglican doctrine matched her own conclusion that the Church of England was spiritually corrupt. His theology taught her to search for a personal experience of divine grace (she called hers an "immediate revelation"[7]) and to speak of it publicly. His scholarship inspired her to formulate her own theological position through intense Bible study and reflection. His departure to the New World was a major incentive for her and her family to do the same. And lastly, his example of courage under interrogatory fire encouraged her to follow the strength of her own convictions, even when those convictions veered sharply from Cotton's—as, in fact, they were to do.

Hutchinson always claimed Cotton as her theological and homiletical mentor. If she had been a man, maybe he would have claimed her as his protégé—but she was not a man. She was a woman, and a controversial one at that. Cotton may have argued bravely and brilliantly on his own behalf, but he was not known for doing so on behalf of others who might threaten his status and reputation. Hutchinson, of course, was a threat of the worst kind. Not only was she his parishioner; *she was his rival.* She could match him, intellect for intellect, sermon for sermon, crowd for crowd, debate for debate. When the student began to surpass her teacher, it became clear that the teacher was not about to give up the title of "Most-wanted Preacher" without a fight. Hutchinson had grown into a preacher that only a rebel father could love and a Virgin Queen could understand.

THE END OF THE WORLD (AS WE KNOW IT)

Elizabeth I's reign was noted for longevity and prosperity, but with her death in 1603, stability abruptly gave way to turmoil. James I was not nearly the monarch his predecessor was. He failed to build consensus or inspire loyalty, and almost overnight, England seemed to fall apart. The signs of national decay were everywhere: a weakened military, a sagging economy, soaring taxes, religious persecution. Furthermore, James hardly endeared himself to half of his constituency, since some of his first acts of legislation were aimed at crushing women's influence. These included stricter penalties for witchcraft, the elimination of schools for girls, and a declaration that woman's place was not to engage in politics but to obey her husband. Anne Bradstreet, a contemporary of Anne Hutchinson who also immigrated to New England, mourned the changing climate with these lines:

> Now, say, have women worth, or have they none?
> Or had they some, but with our queen is't gone?
> Nay, masculines, you have thus taxed us long,
> But she, though dead, will vindicate our wrong.
> Let such as say our sex is void of reason,
> Know 'tis a slander now, but once was treason.[8]

There were other causes for alarm. One of the worst of these, according to religious and political authorities, was that *women* had begun to preach in great numbers—a calamity worthy of John's Revelation, as far as they were concerned.[9] All over England, women of every class and rank, from the most educated elite to the illiterate poor, were claiming a prophetic voice and the right to use it. A flurry of writers hastened to address the issue using every means at their disposal. A 1641 London tract, titled *A Discoverie of Six women preachers, in Middlesex, Kent, Cambridgeshire, and Salisbury,* gave the names of six infamous women who claimed to have experienced "immediate revelation" and who, the author surmised, would be better off in Bedlam:

> Is it not sufficient that they may have the Gospel truly and sincerely preached unto them, but that they must take their minister's office from them? If there had been such a dearth of the Gospel as there was in the reign of Queen Mary it had been an occasion somewhat urgent. But God be praised it was not so, but that they seemed to be ambitious, and because they would have superiority, they would get upon a stool, or in a tub instead of a pulpit.[10]

If Hutchinson had a reputation in London and its environs as yet another woman responsible for apocalyptic decay, we have no record of it. We do know that her 1612 marriage to the wealthy merchant and sheep farmer Hutchinson kept her occupied with the private world of family for some years, and, by all accounts, it was a happy marriage. Anne Hutchinson had inherited her mother's constitution: in eleven years, she gave birth to nine children without losing one and continued to find herself pregnant with regularity and without incident until well into her forties. Considering that in those days (indeed, until relatively recently), one out of three women died in childbirth, these were awesome statistics. Somewhere around the mid-1620s, however, the Hutchinsons suffered their first tragedy when their eighth child, William, died before his second birthday. Then, in 1630, their daughters Susanna and Elizabeth succumbed to the plague. And as she was later to tell it, Anne Hutchinson's world collapsed for a time.

She sank into a deep depression. Despair is a textbook reaction for any parent who has lost a child, but this was a time in which children's deaths were blamed on the spiritual or moral lapses of their parents. Families who had lost children—and during the years of the plague, most families had—were required to hang a sign emblazoned with a red cross and the words "Lord, have mercy on us" outside the house.[11]

Horribly, predictably, Hutchinson's despair evolved into a spiritual crisis. She no longer had faith or confidence in the church of her upbringing. Even its Puritan reformers did not seem to her to go far enough, and while the Separatists appealed to her theologically, to join with them was as good as signing a warrant for her own arrest. In desperation, Hutchinson did as all good Protestants were conditioned to do: she searched the Scriptures for answers, relying on the inspiration of the Lord to "open the Scripture to me," and "be the Prophet."[12] So she searched and studied, prayed and fasted, waited and listened, and waited some more.

It took many months, but as Hutchinson later described it, God finally spoke to her—directly. She had an "immediate revelation" that lifted her up and out of the pit of her despair and returned her to the world, whole and strong. Her depression broke. The spiritual crisis dissolved. Hutchinson felt liberated, and her captor, she now knew, was a false covenant of works. Only a covenant of grace could save one from despair.[13] And now she longed to share that joyful certainty with others, earnestly believing that what had come of her spiritual crisis could defeat that experience in others. Besides, Hutchinson was certain that her "immediate revelations" authorized her to make three claims for herself: the assurance of divine guidance on all important life decisions, the ability to recognize true and false preaching in the church, *and the authority to preach and prophesy herself.* She was ready.

By this time, the Old World was fast becoming too dangerous a place for such theological ideas, and the Hutchinsons began thinking about immigrating to the New one. The literature they had read about New England impressed them. On the most basic level, it offered a plague-free climate, no small thing for a large and closely knit family. Economically, too, the move made sense: William's once thriving business could scarcely survive the heavy taxes, and Massachusetts Bay had made it clear that he would be welcomed rather than burdened there. In a bid to attract women, the colony had also begun to advertise itself as a model Reformation community of equals, in which wives were treated as the equals of their husbands; then, in 1633, the Hutchinsons learned that the pastor they most trusted, John Cotton himself, was no longer safe in England and so had been invited to be the spiritual head of Massachusetts Bay (which had been hastily renamed "Boston" as a tribute to Cotton and his English hometown). Finally there was the matter of Anne's certainty that God had ordained a special role for her in the New World. She later told of how the Lord directed her to a passage from the book of Daniel, assuring her "that though I should meet with affliction yet I am the same God that delivered Daniel out of the lion's den, I will also deliver thee."[14]

Hutchinson was never one to let a challenge or the cup itself pass. On June 4, 1634, she and her family boarded *The Griffin* and sailed for New England.

THE WOMAN WHO *STEPT OUT OF HER PLACE*

It took less than three years after the Hutchinsons' arrival in Boston for the magistrates to bring Anne Hutchinson to trial and, when she showed no signs of remorse or repentance, to banish and excommunicate her. In retrospect (Governor Winthrop wrote in his *Short Story*), the signs of her future insubordination were there: Anne Hutchinson had left a trail of deceit in her wake.

First, there were reports of sinister prophecies on the ship's crossing, irregular enough to delay her membership in the church for two weeks.[15] Then there were the visits to every childbearing woman in the Bay, cementing Hutchinson's place in the female community as a religious confidante and leader and prompting even Winthrop to admit that she was "a woman very helpful in the times of child-birth, and other occasions of bodily infirmities."[16] The twice-weekly women's meetings she led to discuss Cotton's sermons were "winked at, for a time," by the magistrates, as relatively common practice.[17] But when these meetings drew almost every woman in Boston—and then some men, as well—so that a standing-room-only crowd was gathering at the Hutchinsons' home on a regular basis to hear Anne "set forth her own stuffe," as Winthrop put it, alarms went off all over the Bay.[18]

There had been individual troublemakers in Massachusetts before, some of whom had had to be banished (Roger Williams was the most famous of this group), but none had attracted followers in these numbers; none had created such political disturbances. None had proven as resistant to authority, either. On September 7, 1637, a synod gathering condemned eighty-two opinions of Hutchinson's followers and published this pointed resolve:

> That though women might meet (some few together) to pray and edify one another; yet such a set assembly (as was then in practice at Boston), where sixty or more did meet every week, and one woman

(in a prophetical way, by resolving questions of doctrine, and expounding scripture) took upon her the whole exercise, was agreed to be disorderly, and without rule.[19]

It did no good; the meetings continued, as irrepressible as ever. Anne Hutchinson continued to testify about her religious experiences, to interpret Scripture, to teach mixed-gender groups, to pass judgment on other clergy's sermons, and even to preach herself. The magistrates struggled to explain it and came up empty. What could account for the power of Anne Hutchinson and the devotion of her followers?

John Winthrop in particular was ravenous to know; Hutchinson's popularity and success seemed to him a direct and personal insult. In his historical writings, we can hear him puzzling it out. What made this woman so powerful in her preaching? Could it be her skill as a midwife? Like most men of his era, Winthrop was highly suspicious of midwives and their powerful role in the childbirth event when weak women were weakest and infants helpless.[20] Hutchinson, who had borne fifteen children herself, attracted her first following soon after she began visiting childbearing women; perhaps, Winthrop theorized, these visits had had ulterior motives:

> Shee easily insinuated her selfe into the affections of many, and the rather, because shee was much inquisitive of them about their spiritual estates, and in discovering to them the danger they were in, by trusting to common gifts and graces, without any such witnesse of the Spirit, as the Scripture holds out for a full evidence; whereby many were convinced that they had gone on in a Covenant of works, and were much humbled thereby.[21]

Winthrop supposed this might account for Hutchinson's devoted following among women, whose reasoning (in his view) was limited anyway. It could also account for the monstrous stillbirth of Mary Dyer, one of Hutchinson's supporters, whom she attended as midwife; Winthrop later seized on this tragedy as concrete evidence and exploited it with a grisly display of the exhumed body.[22] The only problem with the midwife theory, however, was that it did nothing to explain Hutchinson's popularity with men as well as women, something Winthrop could hardly fathom. And he could hardly deny that she had supporters in the business community and among the town's leading citizens—more supporters than *he* did, actually. Her religious meetings, once intended for women only, were attended by many men as well.

Could it be something about her interpretation of doctrine? Like other authorities of his day, Winthrop thought the people had been a little *too* empowered by their own biblical literacy; as a prerequisite for church membership, men and women alike were required to testify about their own experiences of God with an interpretive freedom that Winthrop found shocking.[23] A casual disregard for ministerial authority pervaded the air, and Hutchinson was one of the worst examples of it. Her interpretive errors could not be blamed on her pastor and teacher, Cotton; Winthrop and the Court had gone to great trouble to determine if Cotton was the source of Hutchinson's false doctrine or if she "cunningly dissembled" on her own. They concluded that the errors were hers, which was troubling, since it meant she felt free to make her own interpretive decisions and speak of them to others. And it wasn't just the dregs of society that listened. Winthrop would have expected the immoral and ungodly types to fall into step behind her— "Yea, many prophane persons became of her opinion," he wrote, "for it was a very easie, and acceptable way to heaven, to see nothing, to have nothing, but waite for Christ to do all,"—but it pained him to see that even upright citizens and the political elite were in her camp as well.[24] Even the new governor (Winthrop had lost the 1636 election), the twenty-three-year-old aristocrat, Henry Vane, was a follower of Hutchinson. Winthrop could not fathom how one woman's brash interpretations of doctrine could hoodwink so many intelligent men.

Could it be something as simple as her irreverence? Personally, Winthrop had never attended one of Hutchinson's meetings and could not speak to it firsthand, but she was, as he knew, "a woman of a haughty and fierce carriage, of a nimble wit and active spirit, and a very voluble tongue, more bold then a man, though in understanding and judgement, inferiour to many women."[25] She showed little respect for the ministerial office, which delighted her listeners and depressed Winthrop, but then, not many could remember a time when people *did* automatically respect their clergy: Winthrop blamed the turmoil back in England for that. And Cotton might not be responsible for Hutchinson's doctrine, but he was a bad influence all the same, sliding in and out of orthodoxy as it suited him. Hutchinson felt free to comment on any sermon she heard, an irreverence that reflected her teacher—unflatteringly, Winthrop thought. He especially resented how her comments exacerbated the awkward rivalry at the Church of Boston, where the two pastors (teacher and preacher, respectively) were not as accessible as they might be: John Cotton was known as one who relished his solitude and resented intrusions, and John

Wilson was known as one who bored his congregation to tears with unin-spiring preaching. Hutchinson filled a void in leadership, stirring the people up with her "mischievous opinions," passing judgment on every minister in the colony and comparing each one to the mighty Cotton.[26] Obviously, this would appeal to the religiously disgruntled. But did they not see, Winthrop fumed, that she was a *woman?* Did they not take that seriously? Could the need to flaunt convention be so strong that they could overlook it? Or had some seen an opportunity in the flap she cre-ated, and made it bigger, so as to divert attention away from their own plans for power?

Winthrop and his colleagues continued to puzzle, but they never got at the heart of the matter, perhaps because they could not allow of it. But others did. Edward Johnson, a chronicler of New England who arrived in the summer of 1636, told of his invitation (extended to him by a man) to hear Hutchinson:

> Come along with me, . . . I'll bring you to a woman that preaches better than any of your black-coats that have been at the ninnever-sity, a woman of another kind of spirit, who hath had many revela-tions of things to come, and for my part, sayeth he, I had rather hear such a one that speaks from the mere motion of the spirit, without any study at all, than any of your learned scholars, although they may be fuller of Scripture. . . .[27]

Johnson became an enthusiastic admirer of Hutchinson and her lead-ership, calling her "grand mistress of them all" and "this woman, who had the chief rule of all the roost."[28] He also saw her activity as some-thing more than interpretation of Scripture: he called it *preaching.* Winthrop used that word only to describe what Hutchinson claimed to do, never (in his view) what she actually did. She was not a preacher; she was "high-flowne in spirit and speech"; she was not a godly woman, she was "audaciously insolent."[29] Moreover, she was playing with fire. As one of her judges put it,

> I would commend this to your Consideration that you have stept out of your place, *you have rather bine a Husband than a Wife and a preacher than a Hearer; and a Magistrate than a Subject.* And soe you have thought to carry all thinges in Church and Commonwealth, as you would and have not bine humbled for this.[30]

The people recognized what the magistrates could not see: a woman was preaching the Word of God, and preaching to crowds greater than those in any church. The magistrates saw only the crowds, and the woman, and the sheer nerve of her, and the power. They saw the ruin that could come to all they knew and all they had, if a single person dared to step outside her place *and got away with it*—and this, they could not have. This, they could not even imagine. Who would they be, after such a thing? Who would *she* be? Where would it all lead?

The magistrates had reason to worry: in the system that ordered Puritan Boston, women were hearers and subjects. Women could not be husbands or magistrates or preachers, because husbands and magistrates and preachers were men; the lines were as clear as that. A woman could lead women's religious meetings; she could teach and speak to her own gender as long as her speech was not preaching. But if it *became* preaching, because others named it so and granted it that power; if her speech *functioned* as Word of God for the listeners, then she became their *preacher*—and that was way over the line. Her speech was blurring the boundaries and disrupting the order. She was stepping dangerously out of her place. And while the restless people of Boston may have been open to a little fluidity of boundaries, the clergy and magistrates were not. *A lay woman preacher*—a talking, preaching female—was an unspeakable corruption of God's divine order; by her very existence, she threatened everyone. She challenged men as preachers (in the church), men as magistrates (in the state), and even men as husbands (in the home), because she was usurping *their* role. John Cotton expressed this with cold dismissal, in his ultimate denunciation of Hutchinson: "And though I have not herd, nayther do I thinke, you have bine unfaythfull to your Husband in his Marriage Covenant, *yet that will follow upon it*. . . ."[31] Cotton stood firmly with the religious and political establishment, in this case. It was sheer lunacy to call women's speech "preaching" or to tolerate it in any way, shape, or form. To do so was to allow women to prevail over men, and chaos to triumph over order.

Once Winthrop was reinstated as governor with the power to select synod and Court members, action against the Antinomians and all other possible threats—including Native Americans, over two hundred of whom were slaughtered in the Pequot War of 1637—was swift and fierce.[32] Anne Hutchinson's examination at the General Court in November of 1637 resulted in her banishment from the colony. After a winter of house arrest, she was tried by the Boston Church in March of 1638 and excommunicated. The motives of the court became clear: the point of the trial was not to prove Hutchinson's guilt but to expose her own knowledge of error and make her repent. The point of letting her testify was not to give her a chance to describe the facts as she saw them but to embody her submission. If she did not, the Court meant to make an example of insubordination by banishing or excommunicating her; as Winthrop said, "Mrs. Hutchinson, the court you see hath laboured to bring you to acknowledge the error of your way that so you might be reduced."[33] Hutchinson's testimony, as far as the Court was concerned, was a public act of repentance and degradation—yet they could not make it so. Instead, Hutchinson spoke the truth as she saw and believed it. She embodied wit, intelligence (she was, after all, a highly educated elite woman), and spiritual power, rather than the meek submission the Court demanded. Her testimony smashed every intention the Court had for her, for the trial, and for the colony itself, simply by being *her* words, rather than theirs; *her* words, spoken in freedom and faith. It was an act so intolerable that it called for intolerable punishment: banishment and excommunication. Permanent separation from the community in life as well as death. Permanent separation from God. Or so the Court said.

In the summer of 1638, Hutchinson and her family—all of whom had refused to testify against her—settled in Rhode Island. They were joined by some of their closest friends, including Mary Dyer and her family, and were reported to be content. In 1642, however, William died, and Anne moved her family to a Dutch settlement on Long Island. There, in August or September of 1643, local Native Americans murdered and burned the bodies of Anne and six of her children; one daughter, Susanna, was taken into captivity and released four years later. This apocalyptic ending gave Winthrop the final image he needed to complete his *Short Story*. Claiming that God had vindicated New England through the providential deaths of the Hutchinson party, he closed the book on the controversy by which Massachusetts had nearly come undone.

2

Sarah Osborn

(1714–1796)

In the 1840s and 1850s, as bitter divisions between the North and the South threatened civil war in the United States and the issue of slavery continued to dominate discussion, New England abolitionists determined that what their movement needed was deeper historical and theological precedent. They went searching for early prototypes of crusaders in the fight against slavery—and found exactly what they had been looking for in the eighteenth-century theologian Samuel Hopkins (1721–1803). Hopkins, the protégé of the great Jonathan Edwards, was a brilliant scholar and pastor who publicly denounced the slave system as early as 1770. He seemed to be, as Harriet Beecher Stowe wrote in 1859, the quintessential Christian reformer:

> The only mistake made by the good man was that of supposing that the elaboration of theology was preaching the gospel. The gospel he was preaching constantly, by his pure unworldly living . . . and by the grand humanity, outrunning his age, in which he protested against the then admitted system of slavery and the slave trade.[1]

Samuel Hopkins was indeed an excellent role model with excellent connections; through him, the abolitionists could argue that their theological lineage extended to the mighty Edwards and beyond, which certainly helped the cause. But there was another role model waiting to be discovered that the abolitionists *didn't* find, someone who had also had a profound influence on Hopkins. In some ways, this person might

19

have had an even greater effect on all the ordinary, fence-sitting Christians—those uncomfortable with the idea of slavery but even more uncomfortable with the idea of joining a movement—because this person, unlike Hopkins, had not been a brilliant scholar with a first-rate education. She had not gone to college or seminary, or been mentored by theological legends, or served as the pastor of a congregation. This person was an ordinary woman, a teacher named Sarah Osborn. Osborn had not set out to be a reformer or preacher or town radical, but time and circumstance had led her to take those roles—which was a story that other common folk could understand. Had those mid-century abolitionists discovered Osborn, how many quiet, ordinary, uninvolved people might have given up fence-sitting in favor of a more activist life? In hearing Osborn's story, how many would have been able to rewrite their own?

The story itself is remarkable. Sarah Osborn was a longtime member of First Church in Newport, and the person largely responsible for Hopkins's call to that pulpit in 1770. She was also the person behind one of the most controversial ministries in Newport: the "Ethiopian Society" of free blacks and slaves who met every Sunday evening, in Osborn's home, for prayer, Bible reading, and exhortation. Osborn had not initiated these meetings and, in fact, was sharply criticized by Newport's wealthy slave owners for the part she played in them. But when approached for help by the slaves themselves, Osborn felt it her Christian duty to offer them what she could, which at first was only her living room. Soon, however, the meetings grew too big for her small house, and the group of nearly one hundred divided: free blacks began coming on Tuesday evenings, while the Sabbath was reserved for slaves—the only night, after all, that their masters would permit them to come. The slaves now asked Osborn to teach them to read and write, and she did. Two of those slaves, men named John Quamine and Bristol Yamma, studied so hard and so well that Osborn began to think them excellent candidates for Christian preachers: perhaps they might be missionaries to their native Guinea.

Meanwhile, Osborn's piety and the blacks' sincerity were making a big impression in Newport, and it wasn't long before scores of others—adults, children, teenagers, even "heads of household"—were clamoring to attend religious meetings at Mrs. Osborn's. There were so many, in fact, that she had to come up with a careful schedule in order to properly accommodate them; one could not, after all, have five hundred people passing through one's house each week without sorting them into groups by age, race, and gender. The success of the meetings launched a full-fledged religious revival in Newport between 1766 and 1767. They also empowered Osborn and the women of First Church to finally take charge of the dismal state of their own congregation: after years of idling under the shoddy leadership of an alcoholic pastor, the membership fired the man and issued another call to a promising young minister named Samuel Hopkins.

From 1770 on, Hopkins was heavily involved in the ministry to slaves that Osborn had begun. It was a steep learning curve for him: Hopkins was a seasoned reformer and missionary, but only in rural contexts, and primarily among Native Americans; before coming to Newport, he had never experienced firsthand the evils of slavery. But Hopkins's track record had been one of the first things that attracted Osborn and the search committee and convinced them that he was the man to provide vision for their congregation after the excitement of the revivals. So with Osborn's encouragement, Hopkins accepted the call and began work. He went down to Newport's docks and saw firsthand how this coastal town made its fortune; within a year, he was preaching against the slave trade and raising money to send First Church members Quamine and Yamma to Princeton.[2] He also forged a close friendship with the woman who was, unquestionably, the pillar of his congregation and remained so until her death in 1796. Three years later, as a Second Awakening blew through the new republic in 1799, Hopkins published the writings and spiritual pilgrimage of Sarah Osborn as a tribute to the woman whose life, he believed, was as eloquent a sermon as any ever preached—and every bit as eloquent as his.[3]

Of course, on paper, even a stunning example can look like a failure if the only sources of information are vital statistics and bank accounts. At first glance, Osborn's life looks like one disaster after another. But that is not the only way to see it.

FIRST GLANCE: SARAH OSBORN, PENNILESS SCHOOLTEACHER

Sarah Haggar Wheaton Osborn was born in London on February 22, 1714. Her parents, like thousands of others, sought the economic opportunity that had eluded them in the Old World by immigrating to the New, and in 1722 Sarah arrived in Boston at the age of eight. After several false starts, her family settled on Rhode Island as their permanent home, relocating to Newport when Sarah was a young teenager. Perhaps the Haggars found what they were looking for in their ocean crossing: they certainly did not starve. But they never numbered among Newport's elite, either, and maybe they hoped their daughter would achieve what they could not.

Sarah had spirit, even as a young girl. She also seems to have had a wild streak. As a teenager she used to sneak out at night, either to meet friends or to hear her favorite minister preach. Sarah's parents approved neither of the friends (one was a boy with "a reputation") nor the minister, but that never stopped her. At seventeen, she married a seafaring man named Samuel Wheaton, who died at sea two years into the marriage, leaving his nineteen-year-old widow with a baby boy and very few options. Sarah did not relish the prospect of moving back home with her parents, who had been firmly opposed to the marriage in the first place. Determined to remain independent, she spent the next nine years struggling to make ends meet by working various jobs. One of those was teaching school, a vocation for which she showed talent.

When she was not yet thirty, in 1742, Sarah married again, this time to a widower named Henry Osborn, who had three sons. It seemed her years of deprivation had finally come to an end. But trouble struck this marriage, too: within a year, Henry's business failed and he took to his bed, never to work again. Once more, Sarah was obliged to take on the role of breadwinner in order to support the household and pay her husband's heavy debts. Adding to her grief, her only son died in 1744, the same year she returned to work by keeping school. There was no question now about living into her parents' dreams of prosperity in the New World: Osborn knew she never would. For thirty years she managed to just eke out a living, only a step away from poverty, until her eyesight and health failed and she was forced to stop working. In her old age, with no savings to fall back on, she lived on the charity of friends until her death in 1796.

If anything, Osborn sounds like she just walked out of one of Jesus' parables, a case study for "the least of these." She sounds like Exhibit A for how widows and orphans fall through the cracks of society and the working poor are only two paychecks away from homelessness. How could such a person be a role model?

SECOND GLANCE: SARAH OSBORN, SPIRITUAL LEADER

Osborn may be one of those persons whose great losses send them down a path they might never have taken otherwise. Sarah Osborn did not set out to be a spiritual leader. She set out to be a spiritual *person*. That yearning sent her on a particular kind of journey, and along the way she discovered that others had fallen into step beside her. Soon these fellow travelers were looking to her for spiritual direction, referring to her as the backbone of her church, the leader of her Women's Circle, the teacher of slaves, and the spark behind the town's revivals. The poor schoolmistress of Newport had been transformed into the town's most beloved sage.

Hers was hardly a fairytale transformation. No flick of a wand could undo Osborn's humble beginnings, fix her bad luck with husbands, or turn the swamp of Newport into the land of Far, Far Away. Osborn's physical or material circumstances did not change as her reputation did, and she was not fool enough to pretend they had or would. What did change was how she and others saw those circumstances, how they read and interpreted them. The backdrop to Osborn's story is not the world of fantasy but *revivalism*, that expression of evangelical religious fervor that makes mincemeat out of stereotypes. Revivalism gave Osborn the freedom to see herself as more than a poor widow, and therefore to live as more than that, too.

Revivalism is a kind of contextual chameleon. It carries within it two conflicting impulses—a longing for the past and a desire to flaunt present conventions—and so it easily blends in with its surroundings, whether they are conservative or radical. This makes it hard to classify. The First Awakening (c. 1740), for example, might look like good-old-fashioned traditionalism, and with ample reason: the colonies' religious leaders, distressed about the rising numbers of unchurched persons in their parishes, hoped to revive faith in a drifting population through a return to the traditional values of their Puritan founders. Yet the First Awakening can also look as radical as any revolutionary vision: empowered by the experience of spiritual New Birth, laypeople broke the clergy monopoly on religious speech through new practices and even a new religious idiom. They testified and preached in public worship— and nothing like *that* had been seen among good Puritans since the days of Anne Hutchinson and the events of 1637.[4]

If we try to describe Sarah Osborn against the backdrop of revivalism, it can be just as difficult to draw any conclusions. Things are not always as they appear. On the one hand, Samuel Hopkins, in a burst of nostalgia, claims Osborn as the epitome of a forgotten Puritan ideal, even though she was doing things that would have been unthinkable for women in Puritan New England, unless their plans included Rhode

Island. On the other hand, when we compare Osborn to some of her more flamboyant eighteenth-century sisters in the faith, she looks downright conventional, since she never preached publicly, founded her own religious sect, dressed like a man, or got brought up on heresy charges.[5] She was never even disciplined for "disorderliness," as were hundreds of women of her time, for deliberately speaking up in church.[6] Osborn walked a fine line. She was poor, but not powerless; traditional, but not docile; radical, but not beyond respectability.

And this was surely the point. The beauty of revivalism, for Osborn and so many of her colonial sisters, was the freedom it gave them to be religiously subversive without "stepping out of their place." In the name of spiritual growth, laypeople adopted the spiritual practices of revivalism—some recycled from Puritanism, some altogether new— that were open to them: keeping spiritual journals and writing spiritual autobiographies, gathering together in small groups for prayer and Bible study, writing letters exhorting their friends, doing charitable works in the community, testifying and even preaching in public worship. Women in particular embraced these practices with enthusiasm. In the process, they discovered, as Osborn did, that articulating their faith was a powerful experience with radical potential. It propelled them into places that burst through the limits of women's traditional sphere or that pushed the limits without ever actually overstepping the bounds. Osborn rose to a leadership status that was certainly unprecedented yet easy to rationalize or defend in the context of revivalism: "An evangelical female told herself she was simply learning to live her Christian commitment to the full," historian Joanna Bowen Gillespie writes; "if that meant she overflowed her 'women's place,' she seemed not to notice."[7]

Osborn's writing is the best place to watch her transformation from faithful congregant to evangelical leader.[8] She wrote constantly, primarily in her spiritual journal but also in frequent letters to friends and former students, and a number of these documents have survived. The journaling practice was one she kept throughout her life, filling book after book with daily records of her spiritual progress (in prayer, Bible study, and works of charity) and reflections on spiritual matters. Each morning she rose early and wrote for two hours before her work day had even begun, yet over time, her journal became much more than a spiritual chronicle of personal trials and triumphs. Writing was Osborn's private form of testimony, a rehearsal space and testing ground for public words and actions; it was the place in which she, like other women, practiced the interpretive freedom to rescript her life and work. Because she wrote continually over the course of many years, we can trace her logic at work as she entertains the possibility of "overflowing her woman's place" at each new juncture. We can also follow her growing defense of her actions, as her testimony moves further and further into public forms and spaces.

OSBORN'S JOURNAL, C. 1740: THE TEACHER'S AWAKENING

Osborn's journal writing encompassed two distinct periods. The first spans the years between Newport's two revivals (c. 1740–64), a time when Osborn was busy teaching school and leading the Female Religious Society at First Church. Her reputation during this period had been firmly established, and her religious activities were well within the bounds of acceptability. Yet as her 1743 autobiography reveals, she had also begun to test the boundaries of acceptable behavior by experimenting, in her journal, with two interpretive practices.

One of these practices was a common one for women at the time and involves the use of the word "providence" as a flexible rationale for whatever life might bring. Evangelical women typically credited their "awakenings" of the spirit to God's providence, finding it both a comforting and convenient way to make sense of earthly troubles. It was providence that brought a meal to one's door at exactly the right moment, or that came up with the rent money at the eleventh hour. Sarah Osborn had so many earthly troubles and so many narrow escapes that she literally saw providence everywhere and recorded it in her journal with zeal and gratitude.

Providence also served an edgier function, however, and that was to help women sort through spiritual quandaries—including delicate questions of propriety. It would be unseemly, indeed, for a woman to organize a Bible study with the neighbors or exhort the local blacksmith. But a woman who felt *called* to such a thing, a woman who sensed God's providence directing her and authorizing her, could go forth in good conscience, secure in the knowledge that she had not so much *overflowed* her women's sphere as simply *enlarged* it. The distinction was important, and women were deadly serious about it: there was too much at stake in questions of propriety, and one flawed decision could result in loss of reputation, livelihood, or worse. But providence could give a woman confidence when the world did not. If ever she found herself in need of wisdom, direction, or justification, providence was an evangelical woman's best friend.

As a case in point, consider Osborn's dilemma about whether it was proper for her to pray out loud with her young students. She agonized over it in her journal, writing that she dearly wished to do so, but wondered if she might not be crossing some line of acceptable behavior. And then one day she had her answer:

> *Thursday, May 10.* [1764] I desire to record it with thankfulness, that God in his providence gave me an occasion last evening to advise with my dear aged pastor about praying with my scholars. He rejoiced much in the proposal; and advised me, by all means to proceed, and let nothing discourage me, and fear no scoffs; for it was God's cause, and he who put it into my heart to do it, would take care of his own glory.[9]

From then on, Osborn prayed out loud with every group she taught. Providence had led her to this moment of insight, and (she interpreted) given her leave to set her anxieties about "scoffs" to rest: if it was God who had put it into her heart to pray, then God would see to the outcome, for God's own glory. Since God was about to send her more students, and more kinds of students, than she could ever have anticipated, her confidence on this matter was vital and highlights just how powerful this interpretive practice was. In the context of prayer and Bible study, alone and in groups, evangelical women like Osborn were developing their own discernment process: to listen carefully, to share their insights with others, and to trust that God would provide what they needed in order to choose and live out their calling. They learned to trust the inner workings of the Spirit, even when those movements conflicted with rules set by their communities. In short, they learned to interpret their lives for themselves and to justify their interpretations to others.

The other interpretive practice that we find in Osborn's early journal writings is a bit more unusual. Like most of her journaling contemporaries, Osborn tended to focus her daily meditations on a passage from Scripture, using a number of common interpretive techniques (the use of allegory, for instance) to shed light on the text. She was particularly drawn to stories about women encountering Jesus and stepping out of their places in order to do it, which in itself is not so striking. What *is* striking is how skillfully she drew links between the text and her own life, so that in the telling of her own story, the text became a vehicle for her to interpret her experiences and decisions. This is especially evident in Osborn's journal descriptions about her childhood and early years, which contain numerous biblical allusions. One such entry, an allusion to Mark 5:25–34 (the story of the hemorrhaging woman), describes Osborn's desire as a child to touch people she believed to be "holy," in the hope that their goodness might enter and transform her. Another entry tells of her first communion and how she felt herself to be "unworthy of the crumbs that fall; yet, through free grace, compelled to come in, and partake of children's bread"; Osborn is pointing to Mark 7:24–30, the story of the Canaanite woman.[10]

These links are the kind of interpretive moves that we often find in sermons, particularly those that read Scripture typologically. But the interpretive complexity and sophistication found in Osborn's journals is not usually seen in other women's journals of the period (or we might say, "in other journals, period"). Perhaps Osborn was making the move from text to sermon before she ever started preaching. Perhaps she was girding herself, literally and interpretively, for a time when providence might again compel her to step out of her place to beg, bother, and even argue with Jesus—in order to receive the grace, the bread of life, the crumbs that fall to those who wait persistently. Perhaps she had begun to think, If I can engage Jesus in such a way, can I not, in Jesus' name, do the same with other men?

OSBORN'S JOURNAL, C. 1764:
THE PREACHER'S AWAKENING

The second distinct period of Osborn's writing began almost twenty-five years after the 1740 revival. Slowly, steadily, she had been growing in authority and confidence as a teacher and religious leader, gradually stepping into more masculine terrain as she felt the ground beneath would hold her. But in 1764, when a group of black slaves approached her to ask if they could meet with her on Sabbath evenings, Osborn found herself whisked into altogether foreign territory, with no precedents to guide her. It was one thing to find interpretive grounds for praying with your students. It was another thing to teach slaves to read. And these slaves wanted to learn to read the Bible; they wanted to go straight to the source. They had heard of Osborn's piety, they told her, and they believed that she alone, of all the church folk in Newport, would help them to learn what they needed in order to pray and read

Scripture. Osborn took some time to prayerfully consider their request, and then agreed, offering her home as the meeting place since none other was available to them.

What happened next was beyond anyone's imagination. It took no time at all for word to spread about the meetings at Mrs. Osborn's. Apparently, a houseful of enthusiastic slaves in that part of town was not something one saw every day; the enthusiasm turned heads, and it was contagious. It made people wonder what else besides the alphabet might be going on in that house. Soon there were others asking if *they* might come to Mrs. Osborn's, too; and if not for their ABCs, then at least for some of what the slaves were getting.

The layers of irony are thick and heavy here: white men yearning for what black slaves have; literacy as a code for salvation, and salvation as a code for literacy; people of all ages and races and genders recognizing truth that goes beyond any labels and categories, yet unable to speak of that truth together, in the same room. If Osborn had been a man, she probably would have been drafted for the revivalist preaching circuit; she would have addressed mixed audiences every day, under the same tent. But she was not a man . . . and protocol did not allow women to save souls in a diverse racial-ethnic environment.

So Osborn devised a meeting schedule to divide and segregate the folk, as protocol demanded. Sunday night was reserved for slaves and, in another room, young white men; Monday nights were for teenaged girls; Tuesday brought the "Ethiopian Society" of free blacks to her kitchen, and teenaged boys to another room; Wednesday was for her longstanding church women's society; Thursday and Saturday afternoons were reserved for children; Friday night was scheduled for "heads of families"; and Saturday mornings she saved for her oldest and dearest friend, Susanna Anthony.[11] Bear in mind that from Monday to Friday during working hours, her house was overrun with the pupils of her school, whose tuition paid her meager salary. The coming and going must have been something to behold.

As Osborn tells it, she was initially incredulous. Was there no one else in Newport to whom these souls could go?!—no pastor, or even a white Christian man, who was willing to take the risk of holding these meetings? Osborn recognized that for her, the risk was far greater than for a man. No matter how carefully she organized these meetings, she was always dangerously close to overstepping her "woman's sphere"; women were allowed to teach and exhort children, but not men or teenaged boys. And for a white woman to teach slaves and free blacks to pray and read and study the Scriptures—in her kitchen, no less!—was out of the question. Osborn knew she was approaching a heightened-security area that demanded to see more than appeals to providence and biblical linkages, if one wanted to enter. At the same time, she couldn't help but notice that the very thing she and her Female Religious Society had spent years praying for was actually happening: another revival had come to Newport!—and she, for one, was not about to get in the way.[12]

Osborn's writing during this period, therefore, takes on a very different character. After years and years of careful, meditative journaling about what God might call a woman to do and whether she ought to interpret Scripture in certain ways, Osborn was ready for more than theoretical case studies. It was time to put theory into practice, and her mission, she decided, was clear: she would teach any student who needed what she had to give. She would teach . . . any student. If skeptical observers wanted the theory behind the practice, she would be glad to show them the results of her years of diligent study. If they needed further proof, she would point them toward the obvious: she was not intentionally straying but merely filling a need that no one else would fill. Beyond those two modes of defense, Osborn had little patience for either argument or speculation. Her musing days were over; now, she had her hands full.

A fine example of this no-nonsense approach to defense is Osborn's correspondence with the Reverend Joseph Fish, the father of one of her pupils. Osborn and Fish were good friends who exchanged frequent letters on spiritual matters. In February or March of 1767, having learned of the meetings, Fish advised her not to continue them for three reasons: first, he said, Osborn's work with slaves and free blacks could violate the social order; second, he told her that others (men, or male pastors) were more qualified to do the work and that she therefore ought to let them do it; and third, he suggested that her leisure time should be spent in more feminine activities, as befitted a woman of her character and place.

Osborn responded to Fish deferentially but firmly. First, she claimed, her work with African Americans was in no way dangerous to the social order, because she never ceased to think of them as children, she set up clear conditions (such as the rule that they had to go straight home, after the meetings) under which they could come, and they willingly complied. Second, she pointed out that she had repeatedly tried to find a pastor to take on the work she was doing but had so far been unsuccessful. Third, she confessed that she hated needlework and other feminine pursuits and would "starve" without the invigoration and stimulation of the "Sweet refreshing Evenings my resting reaping times." "Would you advise me to shut up my Mouth and doors and creep into obscurity?" she inquired of Fish.[13]

The rest of Osborn's writings reflect her more immediate concern: every night—whether it was proper or not, whether she could defend it or not—the hungry souls arrived at her door, expecting to be fed. Every night, she was responsible for feeding them, since no one else could or would. Every night, she had to come up with a new lesson plan and another set of Scripture passages, since each group had a different set of needs and skills and rights and roles, and solid spiritual food for the goose was not necessarily solid spiritual food for the gander or goslings. With so much pressure to produce on a daily basis, who had time for private reflection?! Osborn began to use her morning meditation hours to prepare for her evening responsibilities. Her journal became a teacher's log of her lessons for that night; her prayers became fervent requests for the inspiration and wisdom to speak. Instead of ruminating on her own doubts and growth areas, she reviewed last night's meeting, reflecting on what had gone well and what needed to be improved. After one Sunday evening with the slaves, for example, she wrote the following:

> *Monday Morning, Jan. 26, 1767* . . . The house was full, no weather stops them. The Lord bless them! Lord, teach me what thou wilt have me to do. Let me be influenced by divine teaching alone, and not by Satan, or indwelling corruption. I want none of their influence or teaching. Make me quick to discern what is from thee, and what is not. And O God, I pray thee, make the path of duty straight and plain in this matter. And either spirit me to the work, and enable me to do it judiciously, in such a manner that will stand the test, or else to lay it aside, and do nothing at all.[14]

During these years, Osborn wasted little time in wondering whether she *ought* to lead. Instead, she prayed constantly for the Spirit to *bless* her leadership. She firmly believed that she was living in extraordinary times that required unorthodox methods. Like Joshua, like Ezra, like Esther, God had called her to "build up a house," "at such a time as this," using "what clay and spittle he pleases to open blind eyes, and cause the walls to fall, by what ram's horns he pleases."[15]

One other facet of Osborn's writings during this period deserves special mention. Because impoverished eighteenth-century teachers are not normally in possession of great libraries (one surmises), Osborn did not have shelves of biblical commentaries in her home. So she decided to write her own. A large portion of her post-1764 writing consists of commentaries on different books of Scripture that Osborn wrote herself. Her friend Samuel Hopkins was particularly impressed with this and made sure to include several excerpts from Osborn's commentaries when editing her memoirs. He also drew attention to the practice in the introduction he wrote to the memoirs, in the hope, as he put it, that others might wish to follow Osborn's example. He thought it an excellent idea for laypeople to read and comment on Scripture passages in their journals, for their own private devotional use.

Hopkins may have assumed that Osborn was compiling her own commentaries for private use, but the particular excerpts he chose to include in her memoirs date from the year 1767, a year when Osborn was fully occupied with the demands of teaching school by day and leading religious societies by night. In fact, given the functional nature of the rest of her writings of this period (her "private devotions" look increasingly like lesson plans), it seems highly probable to me that the "commentaries" were prepared to be presented at those religious meetings—as devotional *sermons*. There are simply too many compelling clues in the writing itself: the prose is more finished, and there is the assumption of an audience, with a shift from first to third person ("I" to "we"), as well as an emphasis on exhortation and conversion. Consider, for example, this 1761 excerpt from her memoirs:

> *Sabbath morning, October 1.*—Several christian friends visited me yesterday afternoon. And I was engaged in talking about the vices of the times, and the need there is of wise virgins awaking, trimming their lamps. . . . And in hopes of refreshing my friends, I read some of my own writings.[16]

An additional excerpt from her commentary on Matthew, chapter 25, the parable of the ten virgins, composed on Thursday, November 5, 1767, suggests that she had other purposes for it than her own private devotion. It was, perhaps, written in preparation for the children who would come that afternoon:

> *November 5, 1767.* O Thou great searcher of hearts, I fly to thee to search and try me now. I am one of these virgins who have taken a lamp, and am come forth to thy ordinances, the ways of thine own appointment, to meet the Bridegroom of precious souls. Show me

the truth *now*. Am I a wise, or am I a foolish one? Have I took my lamp without oil? . . . O arouse us before the midnight cry comes, that we may now arise and trim our lamps, while oil is to be had.[17]

If the commentaries really are devotional sermons, and if Osborn actually preached them without attracting attention as a preacher, then her courage and cleverness in interpretation are even more remarkable. Preaching in this era was expressly defined as the exposition of Scripture, from a public pulpit, by an ordained male pastor. For Osborn to bring women's traditional practices (private, devotional, testimonial reflection on Scripture) into the public sphere meant that she was pushing the definition of a sermon . . . and with that, the definition of a preacher, as well. For could a woman be called a preacher if she delivered what looked like a sermon? Could a woman be called a preacher if she did not claim that title herself?

"AN EMINENTLY GOOD WOMAN"

There is a reason that lawyers pay so much attention to character issues: the reliability of a witness depends on it. If we believe that what a witness *says* is consistent with who she *is*, we are more likely to trust her and to believe her testimony. We are also more likely to give her the benefit of the doubt, if her actions move slightly (or more than slightly) outside the bounds of her trustworthy, in-character behavior.

Samuel Hopkins obviously understood this principle. In an editorial comment to *Memoirs of the Life of Mrs. Sarah Osborn*, he wrote these words:

> Mrs. Osborn was esteemed as an eminently pious, exemplary christian, by all who knew her. And even the irreligious and profane had a degree of veneration for her, as a remarkably good woman. Few or none have obtained this character more universally than she did, among all sorts of people, who knew her or heard of her. . . . And this procured to her the general approbation of all, of every denomination and character, as an eminently good woman.[18]

Hopkins must have guessed how important it would be to emphasize Osborn's exemplary character: how else could one excuse such edgy behavior in a woman? How else could one explain why the usual rules never seemed to apply to her? And how else could one assure readers (and perhaps even Hopkins himself!) that this flirting with boundaries was not necessarily a trend, and not necessarily dangerous?

Certainly, anyone who had *not* known Osborn might come to any of those conclusions. They might examine her activities and wonder why she spent so much time lingering at the edge of acceptability. They might question her judgment, from the sheer numbers of people she allowed into her home (five hundred a week?!) to the bizarre range of them (slaves to professors?!). They might wonder whether she encouraged the near-fanatical respect and devotion people showed her (when British troops occupied Newport during 1778, they frequently harassed other citizens, but never "that good woman," as they called Osborn; when Osborn became blind and bedridden, her women's religious society promptly moved their meetings to her bedroom for the next few decades). Indeed, anyone who had not known Osborn might well decide that the woman was little more than a cultish figure: Jezebel, lately of Newport.

Hopkins was keen to avoid such quick dismissals; he wanted others to know and love this woman as he did. He wanted others to emulate her *character* rather than her edginess. So he continually drew attention to Osborn's piety, her faith, her eminent goodness. He declared that her character was the reason and justification for everything that might be deemed "unfeminine" about her: since Osborn's character was one of unquestionable goodness, then she could not have made a questionable judgment call, nor could she participate in a questionable activity. Her very nature would redeem whatever needed redeeming, lifting it into the realm of acceptable thought and behavior. Her character justified her actions. And since practically the entire community of Newport shared his assessment, Hopkins assumed the reader would as well. He assumed that the reader of *Memoirs* would be moved to follow her example through acts of piety, rather than acts of rule breaking.

Christian communities have always engaged in such lines of reasoning. Whenever a member of the community crosses a boundary, others have had to decide whether the action was justified; character issues have often played a major role in the community's deliberations. No (the argument goes), we don't *usually* allow persons of this (gender, race, ethnicity, sexual orientation, legal status) to do this particular activity, *but we know the individual in question*. We *believe* in her. We believe in her character; we believe in her motives. We believe God speaks to and through this person. And so while we might not be ready to change the rules permanently, we *are* willing to make an exception in this person's case; we *are* willing to allow her do this particular act. We trust in her character and therefore in her abilities. We trust her to lead us, in God's name.

The interesting thing, of course, is that character is often shaped by life's rough edges and the very act of crossing boundaries in the name of faith. We cannot emulate the character of another person without emulating her practices. In Osborn's case, this included responding to her Christian duty to teach others the Word of God, no matter what the law had to say about it. For those who read Hopkins's *Memoirs* and took Osborn as a role model, this inspiration would doubtless include a similar ethic of response—with similar examples of rule breaking. But the more one is known and loved in a community of faith, the more edginess and rule breaking that community is likely to tolerate. The more one's actions reflect one's character, the more trust a community is likely to place in one's judgment and witness. And this is probably why Osborn, unlike Hutchinson, was able to survive. It wasn't just the difference in these women's centuries, in their abilities, or in the respect others had for their talent. It was the difference in how their communities loved them and rationalized their "unfeminine" activities: was their preaching *with* others or *against* others? Did it tell others what to believe in Scripture, or did it teach others to read Scripture for themselves?

Osborn did not become the threat Hutchinson was because she was seen as a woman whose preaching reflected her character—and Osborn was a *teacher*. She taught others to read for themselves. She taught others to interpret for themselves. Her community knew her as a person who had suffered much and struggled more, who had erred and strayed and been lost and found, who had survived and thrived with none of life's comforts, and who had never failed to share what wisdom or courage or joy she had. Her community knew her as a person who was unafraid to examine her experiences openly, honestly, and intensely; a person who dared to talk about her faith; a person who would walk with you if you needed a witness along your journey, no matter who you were. Osborn was the people's theologian, the one who empowered you to speak of God, for yourself. She preached when others wouldn't, and she preached so that others could. This, her community reasoned, could not possibly be an *against-us* preacher. This was a *with-us* and *for-us* preacher—and a whole lot of "us," at that.

Maybe, since Osborn's impeccable character had already compelled them to reconfigure some of their boundaries (such as who gets to preach, and to whom), *maybe* they ought to reconsider other boundaries—such as who gets to *listen* with whom. Wasn't she preaching to five hundred of us, on a given week? Wouldn't it be easier if we could all be in the same place at the same time?

Funny how good preachers always make you think about more than you planned.

3
Jarena Lee
(1783–?)

In 1845, a fight broke out on the floor of the Annual Conference of the African Methodist Episcopal (A.M.E.) Church. The fight was about women, and books, or so it appeared, but really it was about the power to speak and read and write one's way into a new world. More precisely, it was about *who* may speak and read and write, and who gives permission for these acts, which meant that ultimately the fight was about a question at the heart of the A.M.E. Church itself, a question that had led to its very inception: Who gets to decide what freedom looks like? White people? Black people? Men? Women? Those who count the money? Those who measure respectability? Who decides what freedom looks like, and for whom?

The catalyst for the fight was a woman named Jarena Lee, an itinerant preacher, who was, in fact, the first woman licensed to preach in the A.M.E. Church. Lee had written a book, *The Life and Religious Experience of Jarena Lee*, which had already run through two privately financed printings in 1836 and 1839 and had sold extremely well; scores of church folk, women in particular, wanted to read it. This was hardly surprising, since Lee was a well-known and popular figure in many circles and had even been mentored by Bishop Richard Allen, the denomination's beloved founder. The A.M.E. "book concern"—the agency that had been promoting literacy and education among the faithful since 1818—thought Lee's book would make an excellent addition to its inventory.[1] Actually, Lee's book would probably *be* the inventory, since the only other titles the book concern published were a hymnal and a church discipline, neither of which sold. The African American community was far more interested in reading about A.M.E. saints than A.M.E. authority structures. They wanted stories about human lives and words to inspire and encourage them. They wanted books like *The Life and Religious Experience of Jarena Lee.*

The Reverend M. M. Clark, the denomination's book agent in charge of editing and marketing for the book concern, knew that books like Lee's were rare at this date. Only two A.M.E. autobiographies existed, as far as he knew: Bishop Allen's, which had been the first of its kind in the denomination in 1833, and Lee's *Life and Religious Experience.* Clark had made repeated attempts to broaden the book concern's inventory, but every time he proposed to publish a book that people would actually *read,* the book concern refused. So Clark got up at the Annual Conference and told those gathered that the time had come to seriously rethink their priorities:

> An incalculable amount of good might be done among our people in selling books, in encouraging them in the education of their children, in setting before them the sure and certain advantages arising from an enlightened education. . . . Inquiry is everywhere made [among the young] for books other than those now published by the book concern. . . . Could our book concern be made to meet all these demands [for biographies, histories of the A.M.E. church, "pocket-book style" Bibles, and scientific works "to be compiled and published by our own colored men"] it would prove abundantly useful to our race and Connection.[2]

Clark told the Annual Conference that if the book concern wanted to fulfill its mission and stay out of debt, it had to made drastic changes. His recommendation—the same one that the New York Conference had made, the previous year—was that the book concern publish two autobiographies, Bishop Allen's and Jarena Lee's, perhaps even as companion volumes. And *that* is when the fight broke out.

Whether Clark, the book agent, was making a calculated move to force an uncomfortable issue, or whether his impassioned plea for diversified reading material really was motivated by budgets alone, is not entirely clear. The debate about women's preaching had been simmering within the denomination for years; it would take a very naïve person, indeed, to raise the subject of Jarena Lee's book and not expect a furious reaction. But then, the issue touched on a number of sore spots for this growing denomination. Should A.M.E. clergy be men of education and respectability, such as other churches had? Would a female preacher, or an illiterate backwoods preacher without any education, ever gain acceptance among fellow clergy?[3] Did church members *really* need to be reminded of the bad old days when there weren't enough male clergy to go around? Was Jarena Lee a woman to celebrate, or was she best tucked away into some obscure corner of their history? And if *white* women were increasingly restricted to the private sphere, what was the proper role of an A.M.E. woman in society, anyway?

We do not know Clark's personal views on female clergy. Perhaps he, like many of the old-time country preachers (most of whom were illiterate themselves), supported women's right to preach as he supported the Spirit's right to blow where it would; perhaps he, like other forward thinkers, saw that times were changing and that book censorship was anathema to a people who needed exposure to the broader world of ideas. In any case, he must have been aware of what was likely to be the response of the conservative book committee and its chair, George Hogarth. In direct opposition to Clark's recommendation, Hogarth informed the Conference that the book concern would publish Allen's autobiography as soon as it obtained "the proper authenticated matter for preparation" but that Lee's autobiography was out of the question. "The manuscript of Sister Jarena Lee has been written in such a manner that it is impossible to decipher much of the meaning contained in it," said Hogarth; "We shall have to apply to Sister Lee to favor us with an explanation of such portions of the manuscript as are not understood by us."[4] With that, the matter ended, and the book concern continued to limp along.

The rejection of Lee's book, of course, had nothing to do with writing style, and she knew it. Jarena Lee, a woman who had spent three decades as an itinerant preacher, a woman who had once enjoyed the protection and support of the late Bishop Allen and who had preached as many as seven hundred sermons a year, had (according to her church's publishers) an *indecipherable* story?! Jarena Lee, a woman who had preached more sermons than most of the men at the Conference, needed to *explain* herself?!

Smarting from the rejection, Lee set about to revise her original narrative. This time, she determined to tell the truth about her treatment in the denomination she loved and served. She consulted her journal, wrote seventy new pages about her life on the preaching circuit— including explicit details about the people and places who had either supported or rejected her ministry as a female preacher—and, since she had no formal education, hired a publisher to edit and print her manuscript. The *Religious Experience and Journal of Mrs. Jarena Lee* appeared in 1849 to an immediate backlash in the denomination.[5] Clergy who had once encouraged Lee in her struggle for recognition now rejected both her book and her ministry, making it clear that women preachers, especially those who dared to criticize men in pulpits and in print, would no longer be tolerated in the A.M.E. Church. The A.M.E. Conferences refused to hear any lingering debate about licensing women to preach—an 1850 appeal to the Philadelphia Conference by a group of unnamed women known as the "Daughters of Zion" for permission to start their own Connection and appoint their own preachers in the circuit was rejected—and in 1852, the denomination made its definitive ruling: women were not allowed to preach.[6] Only three years after the publication of Lee's *Religious Experience and Journal*, women had been effectively removed from any formal religious leadership of the A.M.E. Church, and Jarena Lee herself disappeared from the historical record.

Jarena Lee's struggle to preach is a familiar story in nineteenth-century American Protestantism. The Second Awakening, usually identified as a period of intense religious revival extending from 1780 to 1830, ushered in a period of extraordinary religious freedom for women. Camp meetings were in full swing, new denominational offshoots sprang up in every direction, and the urgent need for preachers and evangelists created unprecedented opportunity for women.[7] The A.M.E. Church, like many other growing denominations, found it in its best interests to encourage female evangelists like Jarena Lee—as long as there were shortages of trained male preachers. By 1850, the fervor of the Second Awakening had cooled, and denominations like the A.M.E. Church, which craved respectability and acceptance in a society increasingly committed to "separate spheres" for men and women, closed their ranks to female preachers. Although many evangelical women continued to preach and press for formal recognition—A.M.E. women are a strong example—other women channeled their disappointment into the movement for women's rights. After mid-century, the debate about women's right to preach took on an increasingly political tone.[8] What makes Jarena Lee's story unique, however, is the way in which she managed to push the limits at every turn, even at an earlier stage of the evangelical movement. Her life and witness give us a new view of a women's preaching tradition.

HOME IS WHERE THE PREACHER IS

Jarena Lee was born in Cape May, New Jersey, on February 11, 1773. Although little is known of her early life, she was probably the child of free parents whose poverty forced them to break up the family; at the age of seven, Jarena was hired out as a servant—effectively, a legalized form of slavery—and sent to live sixty miles away. She was not to see her mother again for fourteen years, a tragically familiar theme for African American families of the period. In her narrative, Lee never comments on those years of separation, except to say that her parents had given her no religious upbringing to guide and console her for the loss of her family—which may be why she never mentions her birth name or the names of her parents ("Lee" was her married name). Whether Lee understood the choices her parents faced, she clearly felt the lack of kinship and identity that resulted: she was, literally, a child with no name and no way in which to hold onto her family. The experience left her with deep scars and little hope. Not surprisingly, Lee wrestled with depression and suicidal feelings throughout her youth and young adulthood, convinced, as she said, "that [she] could never be happy in this life."[9]

In 1804, at the age of twenty-one, Lee determined to build a new life for herself and moved to Philadelphia to make a fresh start. Her first order of business was to find a community of faith, a place where she could belong, and after several months of searching, she did. Richard Allen and the A.M.E. Church seemed to Lee to be the family she had never had. She declared, "This is the people to which my heart unites"—and indeed, that sense of belonging must have opened something powerful in her.[10] Only three weeks later, she experienced an ecstatic conversion in the middle of the Sunday service, just as the preacher (probably Allen) began the sermon:

> That moment, though hundreds were present, I did leap to my feet and declare that God, for Christ's sake, had pardoned the sins of my soul. . . . For a few moments I had power to exhort sinners, and to tell of the wonders and of the goodness of Him who had clothed me with His salvation. During this time the minister was silent, until my soul felt its duty had been performed, when he declared another witness of the power of Christ to forgive sins on earth, was manifest in my conversion.[11]

Although Lee does not refer to her interruption of the sermon as "preaching," this is the first time she records that she had both "the power to exhort sinners" as well as the "duty" to speak out. While she was clearly an awesome presence (no one, not even the minister, interrupted *her* speech), perhaps the most striking thing about this event is its timing. Lee did not preach until she knew herself to be home. She did not preach until she knew she *lived* somewhere. Her conversion from a mute child to a vibrantly speaking woman is unmistakably linked with a sense of identity, kinship, and belonging.

Lee settled into her new life with her new church family and continued to grow in her faith. Around the year 1811, however, she experienced an interruption of her own, in the form of a call to preach. She describes it as follows:

> On a certain time, an impressive silence fell upon me, and I stood as if some one was about to speak to me, yet I had no such thought in my heart.—But to my utter surprise there seemed to sound a voice which I thought I distinctly heard, and most certainly understand, which said to me, "Go preach the Gospel!" I immediately replied aloud, "No one will believe me." Again I listened, and again the same voice seemed to say—"Preach the Gospel; I will put words in your mouth, and will turn your enemies to become your friends."[12]

At first, Lee fretted that the voice was a figment of her imagination, or even Satan himself; but eventually she quelled her fears, summoned her courage, and went to see Allen. God had called her to preach, she reported. Allen listened carefully, and observed that "[their] Discipline knew nothing at all about it—that it did not call for women preachers."[13] Whether he meant to dissuade her with categorical statements ("There *is* no such thing as a woman preacher!—not as far as *we're* concerned!"), church polity ("You should know that the A.M.E. Church does not ordain women, at this time"), or the weight of precedent ("Gosh, we never *thought* about women preachers!") is not entirely clear, and neither is Lee's claim that she was actually relieved to hear Allen's words. At any rate, she returned home, resolved to let the matter go, only to find that she was more depressed than ever.

So in the classic tradition of frustrated women everywhere, Lee gave up the idea of becoming a preacher—and married one, instead. Her new husband, the Reverend Joseph Lee, was pastor of an African American Society outside Philadelphia; within a year Lee had left behind her friends and her church to join him. But she could not leave behind her sense of call. When Joseph Lee died after only six years, Lee could no longer avoid the thing that had been haunting her in dreams and visions for nearly eight years, until she was physically and spiritually sick. The cost of denial was too high for her to pay. She might be a widow; she might have a two-year-old child and a six-month-old infant to support; but it was time to face her call to preach.

Lee returned to Philadelphia and went to see Richard Allen with renewed conviction. This time, the new bishop granted her permission to hold prayer meetings and exhort "as she found liberty," but Lee was disappointed; the allowances struck her as conciliatory, and she did not believe they satisfied her call. So she—and the Spirit—took measures. During Bethel's Sunday worship, she leaped to her feet and once again interrupted the preacher, who had just announced his text from Jonah (and then, as she pointedly observed, "seemed to have lost the spirit"):

> I told them I was like Jonah; for it had been then nearly eight years since the Lord had called me to preach his gospel to the fallen sons and daughters of Adam's race, but that I had lingered like him, and delayed to go at the bidding of the Lord. . . . During the exhortation, God made manifest his power in a manner sufficient to show the world that I was called to labor according to my ability, and the grace given unto me.[14]

Lee sat down, fully expecting that she would be expelled for such an "indecorum," as she put it. But to her great surprise and joy, Allen rose and told the congregation that, although he had once discouraged Lee from preaching, "he now as much believed that I was called to that work, as any of the preachers present."[15] It was a wise move on his part. Women preachers may not have existed before in the A.M.E. Church, but clearly they did now, and any fool could see it, too: there she was, a *preaching woman*, right there in front of them, whether the "Discipline" saw her or not. What's more (as Allen undoubtedly realized), she didn't look as if she had any intention of moving until the family sat up and took notice of her—which is often the biblical way of things. A call is abrupt by nature. It breaks into the order as we know it and makes a fuss, until someone pays attention. To Allen's credit, he understood this, and his endorsement gave Lee all the support she needed.

It took her almost no time to mobilize. Around 1818 or 1819, she records that she had "broken up housekeeping" and entrusted her sickly little boy, James, to the care of friends and the supervision of Richard Allen. Whatever happened to her infant daughter, whether the child died or was adopted by another family, she does not or cannot say; perhaps the overlap between her daughter's life and her own unearthed a pain Lee could touch. We do know that for her, "leaving home" was a loaded phrase with complex associations: *home*, for Lee, was not so much about the constancy of blood family but the constancy of spiritual family. "Being home" was being in right relationship with God and God's people. "Being home" was knowing who one was. When Lee was home, she knew it: she could speak. She could preach. When she left home—something she had done too many times to make the same mistake again—she could tell immediately: the power to speak left her. She was Jonah, in the belly of the whale; Jonah, who could run but could never hide, until he obeyed God.

To the postmodern reader, Lee's decision to leave home in order to preach—and not just for a month or two, but for *thirty years*—may be profoundly shocking. It may bolster our worst fears about preaching's negative effects on the family and how children suffer for *our* sense of call. Certainly these are issues with which every preacher has to wrestle, and most of us come out limping. But to pass judgment on Lee without fully acknowledging her context is to miss one of the most powerful lessons of her story: preaching is a way of living and speaking in right relationship with God. It is a way of standing in one's own life, before God and others. A preacher who denies this denies her very self; she goes down into the pit. She gets swallowed by the whale. She gets tossed this way and that until she relinquishes false notions of what her life should be and submits to God. And God does not adhere to human articulations of polity: God calls whom God will. If the preacher is a poor black woman in antebellum Philadelphia in the year 1811, a woman whom no one will believe and for whom living out the call will be unimaginably difficult, so be it: God does not call preachers to *be believed*. God calls preachers *to preach*. Lee had tried standing in someone else's life; it hadn't worked. She was ready to stand in her own.

ON THE ROAD (AGAIN)

Life as an itinerant preacher in the early nineteenth century was difficult enough for men, but for a woman, and an African American woman at that, it was dangerous beyond belief. Lee, for example, was not ordained or even officially licensed; she could only preach by invitation. Her custom upon arriving in a new place was to make herself known to local African American churchfolk—Methodists and Presbyterians were often the most receptive—and request an "appointment" to preach, either to black or mixed-race audiences. If there were questions about her qualifications or authority, she carried a letter of recommendation from Bishop Allen and was prepared to show it. Lee earned no salary from the denomination as male preachers and evangelists did; occasionally she was the recipient of a freewill offering during one of her services. Most often, however, she was dependent on the charity and kindness of the people she met, never knowing the source of her next meal and shelter, or how far she would have to walk—twenty miles in a day was not unusual—to get it. Certain poverty, strenuous travel, broken health, exhausting pace: these were the rigors that defined itinerant life, and for thirty years, Lee lived with them.

There were other issues, deadly serious ones, to contend with; these mainly had to do with gender and race. As a rule, nineteenth-century "ladies" did not leave their domestic women's sphere by traveling alone or—God help them—speaking in public. Lee's race and class automatically excluded her from white circles of ladyship, but she nonetheless referred to herself as "a lady preacher," a distinction that drew attention to her dignity and respectability. It was a canny survival tactic, since African American women traveling in the North faced the perpetual threat of male assaults to both body and character. But venturing into slave territory as a black missionary, which Lee did several times, was beyond dangerous. Any free black who crossed the Mason-Dixon line—or who was carried across it without consent—could legally be forced into bondage, despite their status in other states. Even Richard Allen, a famous figure in Philadelphia religious circles of all races, was seized on the streets of the city one day by a slave catcher who saw Allen as easy cash; and such violations were common.[16] As every free African American knew, even "quasi-free" life in the North was filled with constant fear. And if church bishops were vulnerable, a poor black woman was even more so.

Lee measured her success as a preacher the way every itinerant evangelist did: large numbers of converted souls, the liveliness of a meeting, repeat invitations, a generous offering. Any of these were signs of the Spirit's favorable presence, and in that sense, Lee knew herself to be a very successful preacher. She took care to document it, too, in her *Religious Experience and Journal*. About an engagement near Philadelphia, she wrote,

> the Lord cut loose the stammering tongue, and opened the Scriptures to my mind, so that, glory to God's dear name, we had a most

melting, sin-killing, and soul-reviving time. . . . [In Woodstown, New Jersey] the minister got happy [and] we had a wonderful display of the spirit of God among us." . . . [At a camp meeting in Maryland] we had pentecostal showers. . . . [At Bethel Church in New York City] the spirit of God came upon me; I spoke without fear of man, and seemed willing even there to be offered up; the preachers shouted and prayed, and it was a time long to be remembered.[17]

Wherever she went, people of all walks of life—even "lawyers, doctors and magistrates"—came expecting fire, and they got it, for "the Lord gave his handmaiden power to speak for his great name."[18]

There were also negative reactions from time to time, but Lee tended to interpret these as prejudice against her gender rather than her race. In Portsmouth, Pennsylvania, she had to contend with novelty seekers: "It was altogether a strange thing to hear a woman preach there, so it made quite an excitement, which made my labor very heavy, as the people were all eyes and prayed none"; in Salem, New Jersey, "I walked twenty-one miles, and preached with difficulty to a stiff-necked and rebellious people, who I soon left without any animosity for their treatment."[19] In New Hope, New Jersey, Lee's femininity—like that of Sojourner Truth thirty-six years later—was even challenged: "I found some very ill-behaved persons, who talked roughly, and said among other things, 'I was not a woman, but a man dressed in female clothes.'"[20] Yet Lee wasted little time regretting these experiences. She usually outlived her opposition.

By 1839, as Lee approached her sixtieth birthday, the climate for women and lay itinerant preachers began to shift perceptibly, a change she especially noticed when she was back in Philadelphia. Bishop Allen had been dead for eight years, and without his support Lee's invitations to preach in the churches were limited, at best. After thirty years of service to the denomination, the irony and injustice were not lost on her:

In Philadelphia, N. York, Baltimore, and all the principal cities, from 100 to 1000 miles distant, as I travelled under the reign of the first Bishop Rt. Rev. Richard Allen, I have been instrumental in the hands of God of gaining many hundreds of dollars for the connexion, by raising societies where there never had been any, since which time they have grown to such a mass as to build large churches, and that in different places, and likewise have spent hundreds, but don't regret it, as I was about the work of Him that sent me, for which my reward is promised if I but hold out faithful.[21]

Part of the climate change had to do with a new educational sensibility among urban African Americans and demands for a different kind of clerical leadership. Lee was an old-style evangelical preacher, a woman with an iron-clad sense of call and no more than three months schooling; she belonged to a breed that remained popular in rural areas but was rapidly dying out in cities. Rising generations of increasingly educated, upwardly mobile blacks wanted their clergy to provide intellectual and moral leadership to meet the challenges of this life rather than the next. The A.M.E. Church, like other Protestant churches, stiffened its licensing requirements by stressing education as well as the Spirit's call; lay preachers like Lee found the urban churches to be less and less receptive to their leadership, especially as there was no shortage of clergy in the cities.

Lee's response to her lackluster reception in Philadelphia was to spend more time on the road. In 1843, the year of her sixtieth birthday, her health was poor but she wrote that she "commenced traveling again, feeling it better to wear out than to rust out."[22] The next year, the 1844 A.M.E. General Conference honored Jarena Lee with a recommendation that the denomination publish her *Life and Religious Experience*, an honor that was quickly withdrawn the next year. Lee felt that she had been publicly humiliated. Once again, to keep silent when her life and ministry were demeaned by those who had formerly welcomed (and benefited by) it was to deny the home she had made for herself through decades of constant travel. This time, however, Lee knew that there was more than one way to preach this sermon. She took her story to print, believing that she was still God's handmaiden and that the Lord "gave his handmaiden the power to speak."

BACK IN PRINT: TESTING AND TESTIMONY

In *Written By Herself: Literary Production by African American Women, 1746–1892*, Frances Smith Foster suggests that there is a nineteenth-century African American women's literary tradition that can be characterized by "testing" and "testimony": in their writing, these women *testified* to their existence, insisting that their experience opened up alternative visions for the world, and they *tested* the limits and power of the English language to bring those visions into being.[23] Foster argues that Jarena Lee, who is only the second African American woman known to have published a book (the first was Phillis Wheatley, whose

poems appeared in 1773), exemplifies this tradition. Lee, like virtually
all the African American women who were writing in this period, was a
practicing Christian who took seriously the command from the
prophet Habakkuk: "Write the vision; make it plain upon tablets, so
that a runner may read it" (Hab. 2:2). Yet Lee also took seriously the
power of the Word to shape that vision, and so did not hesitate to use
it as either sword or ploughshare. For example, she put words together
—"female preacher," "coloured lady"—that tested conventional white
understandings of genteel femininity and African American degener-
acy: no one had ever *heard* of a "female preacher" or a "coloured lady"!
The language provoked intense reactions, and that was intentional on
Lee's part. Her writing may have been an exercise in religious piety, but
it was also an act of political resistance.[24]

Foster's metaphors of "test" and "testimony" are helpful metaphors
to describe a women's preaching tradition. Preaching women such as
Anne Hutchinson, Sarah Osborn, and Jarena Lee offered a proclamation of freedom (testimony *for*), a prophetic critique (testimony
against), and an embodiment of each (a *testing* of systemic limits with
one's very life). The structures that bound them—racism, sexism, political and economic oppression—varied according to their different
social locations and determined the sort of freedom each imagined for
herself. White racism, for example, was never challenged by Anne
Hutchinson (an educated, wealthy, white woman and political dissi-
dent) and only peripherally questioned by Sarah Osborn (a moderately
educated, poor, white woman), while for Jarena Lee (a self-educated,
poor, African American woman), it was an unquestionable evil that
called for resistance. Yet on the lips of each of these women, the Word
was both sword and ploughshare, shaping their visions of life in their
time as it was—and as it could be.

In the nineteenth century, women's preaching and testimony
entered the public arena in ways that would have been unthinkable in
seventeenth- and eighteenth-century America. Female preachers spoke,
wrote, traveled, and also defended themselves publicly, often drawing on
the rhetoric of other mass movements—revivalism, abolitionism, women's
suffrage, social reform—as they justified their right to preach and testify.
Many of their arguments in favor of women's preaching were familiar
from Hutchinson's or Osborn's day: the evangelical call of the Spirit;
alternate interpretations of Scripture; exegetical skill; oratorical talent;
character and experience; the pragmatic need for preachers. Yet Jarena
Lee, a daughter of revivalist Methodism as well as of an independent

black church, offers a compelling example of how the conversation about women's authority to preach had shifted by the nineteenth century.[25] Lee's defense of her right to preach was empowered by at least three things: (1) the Second Great Awakening; (2) the separatist black church movement; and (3) the Methodist doctrine of sanctification.

THE SECOND GREAT AWAKENING: THE CHURCH GETS DEMOCRACY

The period 1780–1830 was a time of revolution and revival in both political and religious life.[26] The old order—characterized by a respect for tradition, authority, status, and education—was dying; in its place rose a new rhetoric of freedom and reform as more and more people gained confidence in their ability to think and theologize for themselves. The nation's population boomed; and with it grew the numbers of new denominations and preachers who were quick to pick up on the growing hostility toward orthodoxy and establishment religion. What these preachers offered the common people, in a time of profound uncertainty and restructuring, was a message of individual potential and collective self-confidence—and that message "democratized" American Christianity. The ideal clergyman was no longer an elite, theologically educated leader, but an ordinary person; the ideal sermon was not so much orthodox as it was vernacular. Common people were empowered by their own spiritual impulses (dreams, visions, bursts of enthusiasm—all signs of direct inspiration from God) as well as a limitless confidence about the power of religious outsiders to transform society. "The rise of evangelical Christianity in the early republic," writes historian Nathan Hatch, "is, in some measure, a story of the success of common people in shaping the culture after their own priorities rather than the priorities outlined by gentlemen such as the framers of the Constitution."[27]

The results were explosive. Preachers who might once have been overlooked as obscure, backwater prophets could, through the power of print and persuasion, command more attention and reach more people than Yale professors; while once they might have apologized for their "rough edges," now they celebrated them. The evangelical criteria for preaching lay not in educational polish and ecclesial authorization but in an experience of call and the demonstration of raw talent. Lorenzo Dow, the most intense, radical, and popular preacher of his day—a man whose straight-from-the-wilderness appearance and vulgar style mesmerized the common folk and horrified the clerics—declared,

> What I insist upon, my brethren and sisters, is this: larnin isn't religion, and eddication don't give a man the power of the Spirit. It is grace and gifts that furnish the real live coals from off the altar. St. Peter was a fisherman—do you think he ever went to Yale College? No, no, beloved brethren and sisters. When the Lord wanted to blow down the walls of Jericho, he didn't take a brass trumpet, or a polished French horn: no such thing; he took a ram's horn—a plain, natural ram's horn—just as it grew. And so, when he wants to blow down the walls of the spiritual Jericho, my beloved brethren and sisters, he don't take one of your smooth, polite, college larnt gentlemen, but a plain, natural ram's-horn sort of man like me.[28]

Once the walls were down, it was only a matter of time before women would rise to test the new criteria for themselves. Jarena Lee, whose pastor and bishop was himself a "plain, natural ram's horn sort of man," took it for granted that education and station did not qualify a person to preach. In her 1836 narrative, she used the "unlearned fisherman" angle to brilliant advantage, arguing that if the disciples could preach a simple gospel, so could a woman called by the Spirit. Her strategy was to take "preaching" through a series of progressively deepening associations until its link with "simplicity," "unlearned fisherman," "inspiration," "female," and finally "gospel," were clear:

> But some will say, that Mary did not expound the Scripture, therefore, she did not preach, in the proper sense of the term. To this I reply, it may be that the term *preach*, in those primitive times, did not mean exactly what it is now *made* to mean; perhaps it was a great deal more simple then, than it is now:—if it were not, the unlearned fishermen could not have preached the gospel at all, as they had no learning.
>
> To this it may be replied, by those who are determined not to believe that it is right for woman to preach, that the disciples, though they were fishermen, and ignorant of letters too, were inspired so to do. . . . If then, to preach the gospel, by the gift of heaven, comes by inspiration solely, is God straitened; must he take the man exclusively? May he not, did he not, and can he not inspire a female to preach the simple story of the birth, life, death, and resurrection of our Lord, and accompany it too, with power to the sinner's heart.[29]

In a similar vein, Lee capitalized on her "unlearned" status at the close of both her 1836 and 1849 narratives to argue that her lack of education was not contemptible but rather admirable; it gave her, she said, greater sensitivity and insight into the ways of the Spirit:

> It is known that the blind have the sense of hearing in a manner much more acute than those who can see: also their sense of feeling is exceedingly fine, and is found to detect any roughness on the smoothest surface, where those who can see can find none. So it may be with such as I am, who has never had more than three months schooling; and wishing to know much of the way and law of God, have therefore watched the more closely the operations of the Spirit, and have in consequence been led thereby.[30]

If for no other reason than sheer success, Lee concluded, she was "fully persuaded" that God had called her into a preaching ministry: "If he has not, how could he consistently bear testimony in favour of my poor labours, in awakening and converting sinners?"[31] These arguments in defense of her right to preach come straight from the "democratization" of American Christianity, but they also push those arguments one step further. Lee saw no reason not to include women in the new rhetoric of authority, experience, and transformation. Those who could not extend the logic should not appeal to *her*, she said; take it up with God, who never fails to offer a testimony of confirmation. And *she* had been confirmed: "I firmly believe that I have sown seed, in the name of the Lord, which shall appear with its increase at the great day of accounts."[32]

THE SEPARATIST BLACK CHURCH MOVEMENT: ABOLITION IN THE PEW

In November of 1792, Richard Allen and Absalom Jones, regular worshipers at St. George Methodist Church in Philadelphia, arrived for worship and took their seats in the congregation. It was the first Sunday following a major renovation at St. George's, a campaign financed by both blacks and whites; Allen and Jones, both African American, were as excited as anyone to mark the occasion. However, the growing numbers of black worshipers had begun to alarm the white membership, who chose this particular day to instigate a policy of segregated seating areas. When Allen and Jones sat in their regular places, they were hauled out of the "white" seating area in the middle of a prayer by two trustees. Outraged, Allen and Jones walked out of the service, followed by the other black members—and founded the first African Methodist Episcopal Church.[33]

The incident was part of a growing movement of religious independence among African Americans. Although Methodists were, as Allen put it, "the first people that brought glad tidings to the colored people . . . for all other denominations preached so high-flown that we were not able to comprehend their doctrine," white Methodists would not tolerate integrated worship any more than whites in other denominations; they invited blacks in and then sent them to the balcony. They encouraged blacks to preach and then refused them leadership. Once slavery had been abolished in northern states, African American preachers determined to create for their people free spaces for worship and self-governance. The struggle was usually bitter, for white ecclesial authorities actively opposed black separatist churches, which they (accurately) saw as communities of resistance. Black church leaders often had to take their cases to civil courts—as Allen did in 1816 in order to found the A.M.E. Church.

As a member of Allen's congregation and a pastor's wife herself, Jarena Lee would have been immersed in the struggles of the black separatist church movement's theology of liberation; as a woman, however, her experience would have been very different. Lee and her sisters absorbed and lived a prophetic religious tradition with roots in the black church, but as ethicist Marcia Y. Riggs has argued, their testimony of life and words shaped that tradition into something uniquely their own.[34] The very act of preaching itself, for instance, challenged the nineteenth-century patriarchal "natural order" (females subservient to males) as much as separatist black churches challenged the racist "natural order" (blacks subservient to whites). Female preachers like Lee could draw strength from their prophetic roots to meet the challenge but still had to reconcile gender identity with the call to preach the gospel.[35] Living in the nexus of these tensions required unprecedented survival and interpretive strategies. It made Jarena Lee a womanist: she did theology for herself.[36]

When the A.M.E. book concern declined to publish her book—suggesting, in effect, that her thirty years of service were as "indecipherable" as her manuscript—Jarena Lee took up her pen in resistance. Her revised 1849 narrative provided the names of dozens of African American clergy who had opposed her ministry and, as she saw it, stood in

God's way. In doing so, Lee invoked the prophetic religious tradition that had shaped her and led her to expect freedom in the church and pulpit. Those who refused her entry, thereby denying God's chosen servant, she did not hesitate to condemn as "enemies of the cross" (cf. Phil. 3:18)—and she contrasted them with the help she received from her "sisters" in the pew, women who dared, "like Esther the Queen," to approach grumbling men for the scepter of approval so that Lee might preach.[37] She let the contrast speak for itself:

> Rev. James Ward, a colored Presbyterian, assembled with us, although he was so prejudiced he would not let me in his pulpit to speak; but the Lord made a way where there was no way to be seen; there was no person to intercede until this sister tried to open the way: the men of color, with no spirit of christianity, remained idle in the enterprize, but we got possession and we had a large concourse of people. I spoke with the ability God gave me.[38]

When she met with opposition, Lee would often predict the overthrow of the mighty and misguided, and took it as God's own victory when her prophecies were fulfilled:

> It is to be lamented, that James Ward, colored, with his over-ruling prejudice, which he manifested by saying no woman should stand in his pulpit, and with all the advantages of a liberal education, was in a few weeks after I left there, turned out of the Church.[39]

For Jarena Lee, the right to preach was always a matter of religious freedom, no matter the race or sex of the preacher. She insisted on the right to define liberation for herself, which is to say, to do *theology* for herself.

SANCTIFICATION: HOLY WOMEN, HOLY ENERGY, HOLY RAGE

In his preface to the autobiographies of Jarena Lee and two other African American women, William Andrews writes, "We cannot understand the special sense of empowerment that [they] discovered in Christianity unless we examine the idea of 'sanctification.'"[40] Sanctification (also known as the "second blessing" or the "new birth") is the experience of being in complete harmony with God's will through the indwelling of the Holy Spirit. According to Methodist doctrine, it is the third stage of salvation (after repentance and justification) in which the sanctified believer achieves the state of "holiness," or spiritual perfection. Holiness is not sinlessness but rather righteousness; and in this sense, sanctification is a liberating experience of total identification with God—body, mind, and spirit.

It would be hard to overestimate the role that sanctification played for preaching women such as Jarena Lee. It was their primary experience of liberation, their basic source of empowerment, their one authority, and their ace-in-the-hole strategy for coping with church polity. It gave them amazing self-confidence and extraordinary self-worth. If a sanctified woman had recovered her "true, pristine identity in Christ" (as Andrews puts it), then wasn't it her duty to be faithful to that true self?—and if faithfulness meant that occasionally she had to disobey church law, then wasn't her disobedience really an act of *liberation*, through the power of the Spirit?[41] Preaching women like Lee were so buoyant, they were unsinkable. They fully believed that the Spirit would remove all obstacles.

This must be why Lee argues so passionately, in both her 1836 and 1849 narratives, for a woman's right to preach, and why her words sound so fresh and persuasive almost two centuries later. In both narratives, the pivotal argument comes immediately after the account of her 1811 audience with Richard Allen. Note well: Lee had not come to ask *permission* to preach; she had come to *tell* Allen that "the Lord had revealed it to me, that I must preach the gospel."[42] When Allen affirmed that this would be impossible for her to do among the Methodists, "since our Discipline knew nothing at all about it," Lee felt the "holy energy" within her "smothered." She then interrupts her story with a lengthy, careful, angry argument to prove her case:

> O how careful ought we to be, lest through our by-laws of church government and discipline, we bring into disrepute even the word of life. For as unseemly as it may appear now-a-days for a woman to preach, it should be remembered nothing is impossible with God. And why should it be thought impossible, heterodox, or improper, for a woman to preach? seeing the Saviour died for the woman as well as the man.[43]

These are confident, forceful, assured words, written with the sanctified conviction of a woman now too experienced to be easily discouraged. Twenty-five years later, she could look back on this incident and see that what had been at stake was not her reputation as a woman of propriety but the Spirit's reputation as the wellspring of possibility. It was Allen, not Lee, who endangered the "word of life"! Even if Methodist polity did not call for women preachers, the Spirit did. Lee knew in her bones the price one had to pay for failing to live out one's sanctified call. After Allen's rebuff, it had taken her nearly eight years of physical suffering to find her true identity as God's preacher—to find her way *home*.

Lee's belief in herself as a sanctified woman gave her the confidence to question her bishop and mentor—a man she deeply respected and to whom she even entrusted her child—as well as her theological tradition. Continuing her argument, she asks,

> If a man may preach, because the Saviour died for him why not the woman? seeing he died for her also. Is he not a whole Saviour, instead of a half one? as those who hold it wrong for a woman to preach, would seem to make it appear. Did not Mary first preach the risen Saviour, and is not the doctrine of the resurrection the very climax of Christianity—hangs not all our hope on this, as argued by St. Paul? Then did not Mary, a woman, preach the gospel? for she preached the resurrection of the crucified Son of God.[44]

Lee understands that the laws prohibiting women's preaching are grounded in ontological issues: If only men can preach, then Jesus died only for men, and he is only "half a saviour." But if Christ died for all, if he is a "whole saviour," then it is his wholeness—his humanness— that matters, and women as well as men are empowered to testify. She then argues that preaching is nothing more than the proclamation of Jesus' resurrection, an announcement made powerful by its very simplicity and first modeled for us by Mary, a woman. Yet for Lee, the ontological is ultimately a question of power and simplicity: once sanctified, we are identified—body, mind, and spirit—with the will of God, and nothing in heaven or on earth can change that.

And nothing in heaven or on earth can keep a sanctified woman from preaching a gospel of salvation.

Standing in the Details

Some Conclusions for Part 1

The details selected for these narratives are only a handful of those available to us. Others will want to tell the stories differently, or will come upon something sleeping in a book that will inspire a new appraisal of preaching. That is as it should be. From these renderings, however, what can we say about the preaching tradition that held these women as surely as it holds us? What do the testimonies of Anne Hutchinson, Sarah Osborn, and Jarena Lee have to teach us about what preaching is and who preachers are?

I offer four insights.

1. Women's preaching was disruptive

In the contexts in which these narratives are told, women's preaching didn't just challenge the system. It was far more dangerous than that: it actually disrupted the established order. It flew in the face of ruling hierarchies and then exploded them. And when a system is built on certain premises—linking "man" with preacher and magistrate, and "woman" with hearer and subject, for example—it cannot tolerate anomalies like *woman preacher* without collapsing. *Woman preacher* is about as anomalous as it gets. For rigid systems to accept such disruptions was the equivalent of ushering armed terrorists right through airport security: it meant imminent destruction. It meant the end of the world as we know it.

2. Women's preaching was liminal

It could be hard to classify. It might stay within some boundaries but sneak across others. It might push the limits but never quite cross them. This made it possible for women to preach even in the most rigid systems that neither condoned nor supported women's preaching; a woman's *speech* might be recognized by her community as a *sermon*— even if she did not claim it as such. And the converse was true as well: in systems that did (within limits) support women's preaching, women's speech was not automatically viewed as proclamation. These two premises gave women some leeway. Knowing this, many developed strategies for maneuvering within the system, one of which was testimony (narrating and confessing an experience of faith, rather than expositing Scripture; testifying to the freedom of the gospel and testifying against the oppression in human systems). Testimony was a kind of speaking that allowed women to preach without "overflowing their women's place." It also pushed listeners to recognize and name preaching when they heard it, regardless of what the (preaching) woman herself called it.

3. Women's preaching was proclamatory and prophetic

It was the preached Word of God, as irresistible and liberating as ever. Women claimed the freedom to interpret Scripture and their lives, and they also claimed the freedom to speak those interpretations, despite the structures that forbade them to do so. The words they spoke, therefore, contained *both* a proclamation of freedom *and* a prophetic critique of the order.

4. Women's preaching was embodied

Their bodies and lives were laid bare in the acts of preaching and testifying, relentlessly and dangerously so. They were literally on trial, in every sense of that word—but their communities were, as well. For every time a woman stood up to proclaim the gospel, her community saw, in its very reaction to her, a reflection of itself: what it believed, what structures ordered its life together, what views it held about power and privilege, who was and was not allowed to speak truth. In standing up to preach, these women stood in their own lives in such a way that the community could see the truth about itself, laid bare and exposed in the light of God's Word. Women embodied for their listeners the announcement that the Word became flesh and dwells among us— even in the flesh of women's bodies.[1]

The details are there, wide awake. But waking them up (or waking ourselves up to their existence) is one thing; actually *doing* something with them is another. I want to follow the example of Solveig Hisdal, my knitting heroine, who combs museums for the sleepy details no one else has noticed. What sleepy details do we see in these stories of preaching women? What lines and movements capture our attention and imagination? Which patterns speak to us most? Which do we want to explore further, or transpose, perhaps, into a new creation for our own time? And can we discern anything like a tradition in this particular collection of stories?

Pattern is really embedded and embodied theory, one might say. In part 2, we turn to some theories of testimony that might be shimmering, waiting, just beneath the surface of the details.

PART TWO

Waking Up the Secrets: Theories of Testimony

First, plain speech in the mother tongue.
—Czeslaw Milosz, "Preface," *Treatise on Poetry*[1]

Family Stories and Family Secrets

Some Words to Begin Part 2

I am a person who likes to hear family stories, right down to the sleepiest details. I like how they teach us to listen carefully and look below the surface, to honor courage and respect pain, to laugh at ourselves and face up to hard truths, to cherish and question and not give up until we find the thread of grace. Family stories help us to understand why things unfold as they do. They teach us to distinguish between a trend and a system and show us the cost of change and what it might look like to choose a different path. Above all, they teach us reverence, because listening to how another person stands as a human being before God is a holy thing.

Occasionally, in our listening, we trip over a gap in the story, details that are crazily out of sequence, and find that we have stumbled into a family secret. This is about as much fun as stumbling over a grizzly bear, because some details just do not wake up happy to see you. Family secrets do not aim to empower and connect us, as family stories do; in fact, quite the opposite. They are attempts to hide a wound, signs that something has gone horribly wrong and the system is gangrenous. Uncover the secret and you expose the wound, with its ungodly march of damage—and nothing fights more fiercely than a wounded system. But a secret held to the light quickly loses its power. Once named, it fills in the gap and settles back into sequence; it becomes part of the longer sweep of narrative. When we have searched it and known it, we can tell it as another family story of brokenness and grace, beautiful in its detail.

I did not go looking for family secrets in these narratives of women preachers, but they were there, and it would have been hard not to notice: puzzling gaps in the story, places that almost flinched when touched. For me, they indicate that something is not right among us, that there are places in our family story of preaching that would just as soon eat you as look at you. Those places need to be probed, and with as much light as possible. That is what we will do in the next two chapters, with the help of some theologians who are very good at this sort of thing: searching, naming, and discovering the sources of power. Once we do that, then perhaps the possibility exists of setting things right or choosing another path marked by common story instead of common secret. Maybe we will understand a little more about who we are and where we come from.

The search for theory is important. If we are serious about finding new models and traditions within which to preach, then we need to understand not only *how* they work but *why*, and which family secrets and family stories are operating below the surface. We need to locate our preaching models and traditions within both a historical and theoretical base. We need to see if testimony is both biblically and theologically sound, or if it runs afoul of everything we deem holy. In other words, we need theories to sustain our practice, and vice versa—or at least *I* do, since I dare to hope that teaching preaching is actually a theological endeavor, and that testimony can be more than "sharing my story."

Of course, some theories and practices do call us to rethink our orthodoxies. But that is one of the oldest stories there is, as any flip through the Bible will show. We are in very good company.

4

True Speech in the Mother Tongue

Paul Ricoeur and Walter Brueggemann

Because I stand in the Reformed tradition, and because I am a preacher, everything for me begins and ends with the biblical text: *sola scriptura*. The first place I want to look when it comes to testimony is to theory that helps me deal with issues of biblical interpretation and the character of the biblical text itself. In Paul Ricoeur and Walter Brueggemann, we have two theorists who provide exactly that.

PAUL RICOEUR: TESTIMONY AS CHRISTIAN INTERPRETATION

Paul Ricoeur's essay "The Hermeneutics of Testimony" is the classic starting place for scholars who write about testimony: you simply can't get to theories of testimony without passing through this work. Or perhaps you can, but you will have neglected a crucial philosophical base, which Ricoeur has already built for you—on solid rock, not sand. When the rain falls, and the floods come, and the winds blow and beat on my interpretive house, I want that house to be built on a foundation that Ricoeur has built, with a little help from Jesus.

What Ricoeur argues is this: Christian hermeneutics, or Christian interpretation, is not based in facts. It is based in testimony, which is an entirely different interpretive framework.

Basic Terms

To begin with, Ricoeur defines *testimony* as the act of testifying to an event and reporting on what was seen or understood. The crucial point, here, is that testimony is not perception; it is the report itself, or the narration of what has happened. We focus not on what is *seen* but on what is *said*. As an act of communication, then, testimony has two components: the one who testifies (the witness who has seen and who seeks to justify the report), and the one who hears the testimony (the one who has not seen but who hears the witness's report and forms an opinion about the testimony). Ricoeur stresses that it is only in the hearing that we can decide if the testimony is true or false, because testimony involves a movement from seeing to understanding, and, perhaps, believing.

Because testimony calls for judgment, it always exists in the context of a trial. This implies three things.

1. There is a *dispute* between two parties, or a struggle of opinion, although neither testimony can ever claim absolute certainty; only probability.
2. There will be a *decision of justice* between two claims, so that one of them will be invalidated.
3. There will be *rhetoric*, or speech that attempts to persuade.

We can see how complicated things become, with no certainty to rely on and a decision that must be made; everything, everything, hinges on the character of the witness. Remember that testimony is not the event itself but the report of the event; false testimony, therefore, is not an error in the report but "a lie in the heart of the witness."[1] Likewise, a true or faithful witness is not simply an accurate reporter but someone who "seals his [*sic*] bond to the cause that he defends by a public profession of his conviction, by the zeal of a propagator, by a personal devotion which can extend even to the sacrifice of his life."[2]

Testimony is risky business. It includes not only the witness's words but also the witness's acts, which are living proof of conviction and devotion. The difference between a true and false witness is in the engagement of the witness—"the engagement of a pure heart and an engagement to the death"—which must be why the Greek word for witness is *martyr*.[3]

Adding a Biblical Layer

Ricoeur sees testimony operating both prophetically and evangelically in the biblical text, each of which deepens and nuances the term. From his reading of Isaiah, for instance, Ricoeur notices the following prophetic aspects of testimony (Isa. 43:8–13 and 44:6–8):

1. The witness is not simply anyone who testifies but *the one who is sent* to bear witness to a testimony that comes from somewhere else.
2. The witness testifies not to isolated, pedantic, historical facts but to the *radical, global meaning* of human experience, or, in short, to God.
3. The testimony is *proclamation for all people* by a single witness.
4. The testimony calls for a *total engagement of words and acts*, even at the cost of the life of the witness.

The most striking thing, Ricoeur says, is that the testimony no longer belongs to the witness but proceeds directly from God. God initiates it! In the Isaiah text, God puts the people and their idols on trial, yet calls on the people as witnesses to God's mighty acts; they are the ones who must tell what has happened and confess its meaning. Their narration will always include historic signs, great acts of deliverance. Prophetic testimony fuses the confession of faith with the narrative of things seen.

For evangelical testimony, Ricoeur turns to the New Testament, where there is a new focus on eyewitness accounts. The Gospels stress that descriptions of Jesus of Nazareth are historical events; they actually took place. Witnesses testify to what they have seen and heard: a woman at the tomb, a disciple at Pentecost, the risen Lord, the apostle Paul. The eyewitness character of testimony therefore stretches to include a wide range of ideas about what constitutes an appearance of the Lord (such as Paul's encounter with the risen Christ on the road to Damascus, which is interpreted—as was common in the early church—as an eyewitness report no less valid than those of the disciples on Easter). Testimony about facts and events is linked to testimony about meaning and truth. This leads to an inevitable and surprising claim: faith is less about eyewitness accounts than about *preaching*.[4]

A Theory of Christian Interpretation

Ricoeur is now ready to show how testimony is grounded in a philosophy of interpretation. The crux is this: testimony *gives* something to be interpreted and, at the same time, *calls for* an interpretation.

1. Testimony gives something to be interpreted

God is not altogether hidden and silent. God is manifest in this world; God can be seen and known, here and now. God breaks into human lives and reflections and gives us an *experience* of the divine. And when this happens, we testify to it!

2. Testimony calls for an interpretation

No testimony can ever be taken for granted. There are false witnesses as well as true; we have to decide which is which. We have to judge between them. In this atmosphere of trial, there will always be tension between what is manifest and what is hidden, since we can never know for certain if what the witness says is true; we can only decide to believe it. This is the maddeningly dialectical structure of testimony, the tension between narration and confession, event and meaning. It is the same tension that led Jesus to the cross, making him the model of true testimony.

In the end, testimony is not just a story, a set of absolute truths. It is an *act*, and in that act, we recognize an expression of freedom—the freedom we would like to have, and to be. We recognize that the goal is not to suffer, but to claim the freedom of speaking what we have seen and believed, without fear of the consequences. Suffering and sacrifice may well be the result; the trial may indeed turn against us. Yet the distinctive witness of Christianity is that God is manifest in the life and resurrection of Jesus Christ. God shows us and calls us to share the news with others. God shows us and calls us to claim the freedom we would like to be. God calls us to testify. Christianity must always choose a hermeneutics of testimony.

A PREACHER REFLECTS

Preaching as Testimony: Into the Deep

This is one place in the book when I am wishing I could jump off the page and look you right in the eye, or hire Harry Potter and company to put a shooting-stars charm on this paragraph—anything to indicate that Ricoeur has just exploded onto our sleepy little preaching scene and *changed everything*.

If we accept Ricoeur's logic, that Christianity itself exists in a hermeneutics of testimony, and that testimony really is the distinctively Christian way of *speaking* and *knowing* (which is to say, *interpreting*), then preaching cannot be the proclamation of absolute truth; it never has been. There is no such thing as infallibility or inerrancy; there are no universal truths for us to own or access at will. There are only fleeting glimpses of the truth we see and confess in Jesus Christ, the truth that encounters us, in concrete human experiences, by the grace of God. Preaching is testimony: a proclamation of what we have seen and believed. It is claim and confession rather than absolute and certitude. And because the context for testimony is one of struggle and divergent opinions (which sounds a lot like postmodernism to me), a sermon, like any other testimony, must make its way in this world as best it can, through an invitation to believe rather than a command to obey. Who would have thought that the death of modernism is a *good* thing as far as preachers are concerned?! After all our fussing about lack of certitude and finitude, it turns out that postmodernism is actually the climate we are best suited to, and maybe even the climate that best reflects Christianity itself!

Because testimony is something we choose rather than something forced upon us, we are free to decide whether or not we wish to abide by a hermeneutic of testimony. That freedom is one of its most extraordinary features: *we have a choice.* We can choose to live by the rules of absolute knowledge or the rules of testimony. We can choose to live by certitude or by faith. We can choose to own truth or to incarnate it. We can choose the power that comes from having certainty and universalisms at our disposal or the power that comes from giving them up in freedom. Yet here is the inescapable logic: *Jesus himself consented to the rules of testimony!* Jesus himself chose not to wield absolute power. Jesus himself claimed the freedom of speaking the truth he saw and lived. In a world replete with manifestation and hiddenness, Jesus incarnated God. He embodied for us the essence of proclamation and the essence of Christian faith—which is to speak the truth we have seen and experienced in our own way, no matter what comes.

It sounds utterly shocking, like walking right over the edge of a cliff, and indeed it is. When we choose testimony, we throw certainty to the wind and trust to the Spirit; we *have* to! We trust that God will initiate encounters with human beings. We trust that we will have the courage and sensitivity and restlessness to interpret these encounters. We trust that we will find the words to testify to what we have seen and believed about it. And we trust that the community of faith and, ultimately, God will judge our witness as well as our own engagement with it. What we give up . . . is control. But I think the first family secret is that we never had it.

Testimonial Authority: The Engagement of the Witness

Once we take away absolute certainty, there isn't much for a witness to stand on except her authority. This is why the very first thing that must be done in a trial is to establish the authority of the witness, and why the very first thing that must be done in a sermon is to establish the authority of the preacher.

So what constitutes authority in a world governed by testimony? Is it a matter of being more convincing, more passionate, more biblical, more theological? Do we have to be more eloquent, more charismatic, more logical, more straightforward? Or should we concentrate on developing more entertaining sermons, more practical sermons, more cutting-edge, cut-to-the-chase, cut-through-the-crud sermons? Is that the ticket to authority?—just to *be more*?

Many of us are convinced that it is. Our congregations tell as much ("Pastor, couldn't you make your sermons more relevant?"). Our consumerist, expansionist culture advertises as much. Even our denominations encourage us to think as much, through constant pressure to increase our membership numbers. Everywhere we look, we get the message that *more is better*, and that if we just have more faith (or talent or skills or money or security or muscles or sex or beer), then we will finally have the right stuff to succeed. We can have bigger churches, bigger budgets, bigger programs. We can *have* more, if we are willing to *be* more.

Women feel this pressure in a particularly insidious way. Authority is a critical issue for female preachers, especially when they are still an anomaly (if not anathema) for many churches. Many women assume that they must simply be better than their male peers if they are to compete in the job market. Others believe the key is to smother their femininity by becoming more masculine: to "preach like a man," whatever *that* is. And there are certainly short-term gains to be had from this tactic. Anne Hutchinson proved herself intellectually superior to her accusers during her trial; Sarah Osborn's character made her religious meetings more popular than the local Sunday worship services; Jarena Lee's talent usually made her critics do a complete about-face and declare that—Lord have mercy!—*she* preached as well as a *man*! Women have in the past and will in the future establish their authority to preach by being "more than," if it looks like it will work.

But it never does, in the long run. To measure authority in terms of "more" does nothing to change the system itself. It does not fight consumerism or patriarchy or megalomania. It does not get women into head-of-staff positions or convince the pope about women priests or deal with the stained-glass ceiling. Worse, it does not sustain fragile human egos: if we must always have more and be more, then we never have enough, and we can never *be* enough. The pressure leads to a constant state of anxiety that only gets worse and worse. If we believe (counter to gospel) that there is not enough to go around, whether in terms of jobs or money or food or grace, we inevitably begin to hoard, to guard what we have, to suspect others of wanting to take it away from us. Brueggemann has called this "the myth of scarcity," noting its powerful hold on us. And it always backfires: we cannot preach God's generosity, abundance, and forgiveness if we are clutching to protect our hard-won place from outside threats . . . like other women, or other men, or other races, or other countries.

Hutchinson, Osborn, and Lee could have defined their authority in terms of "more" but didn't. Instead, they chose an authority that, by the world's standards, is hardly one to write home about, since the bottom line, in their cases, was less than spectacular: Hutchinson was excommunicated; Osborn was never credited with her role in Newport's abolitionist movement; Lee was never ordained a pastor. The authority of "more" never worked for them or sustained them. But the *authority of testimony* did. The authority of their witness convicted them and others. And their engagement with it—how fully they gave themselves over to their testimony—proved to be more powerful than any other skill or asset. In fact, the more engaged they were, the less they feared what would happen to them. Engagement is more threatening to an unjust system than any retaliatory force or action, because if what we believe engages us more than fear, the system and its deterrents have no power over us. Testimonial authority can bring down an empire.

I am guessing that one reason the church spends so much energy on the authority of ordination (who can have it, who cannot) is that the authority of testimony is so powerful—much more powerful, actually, than any authority conferred by a governing body. And *that* presents us with some very disturbing questions. Testimonial authority, by definition, cannot be restricted to a select few. It is open and available to anyone willing to pattern herself after the testimony of Christ. Testimonial authority also compels listeners to focus on what the witness says and does, rather than her right to say it; the focus, in other words, shifts to the truth toward which she points. That shift is often the impetus for change. But not everyone wants change.

Is it possible that all the debates about ordination that steer our focus to the person of the preacher, and "what the Bible says" about gender roles or homosexuality (for example) are really smokescreens to divert us from biblical discussions of authority? Is the authority of testimony another one of our family secrets?

Testimonial Experience: Encounter with God

Those of you who have worried that "testimony" is just code for narrative self-absorption, take heart: Ricoeur to the rescue. For starters, he narrows the term considerably, so that "experience" (as it relates to testimony) does *not* refer to every event that has ever happened to us and all that we have ever done and said. That is far too broad an understanding. In the same vein, "preaching from our experience" is *not* a recital or video or Web site of the minutiae of our days (riveting, no doubt, as it would be), including the cliffhanger of what we ate for breakfast and then how long we sat in traffic on Interstate 285. If we are to use the category of experience with any theological clarity and depth, we have to delineate it carefully, because the super-sized definition that currently holds cultural sway has brought us such civilization highlights as Reality TV, Internet blogs, and exhibitionist memoirs. Ricoeur suggests that we simplify things, as follows: *experience, as it relates to testimony, is an encounter with God.* It is what happens when God meets us, right smack in the middle of our lives.

There are several things to notice about this definition. The first is the word "when": experience is what happens *when* God meets us. The word is not "if." God will meet us; it is a given. Notice, too, that God is the initiator. We can count on God to come but not to call ahead, since it must be admitted that God shows very little interest in coordinating schedules, and apparently relishes the surprise factor. And finally, notice that although the encounter lodges in every portion of our being—body, mind, heart, spirit—we will never be able to describe it properly. No matter how deep it goes (and we are betting that it will go *very* deep), even if it gets under our skin, into our bloodstreams, and down to the bone, anything we try to say about an encounter with God is merely provisional. It falls way short but will have to do for now. To *meet God* . . . is simply too big for words. Our experience cannot contain it: we only see in the mirror dimly. All we can do is to *interpret* the experience through an act of imagination—which means that eventually, inevitably, we have to preach it. We have to testify to what we have seen and believed in the gift of this encounter. It won't be perfect; it won't say everything; but we have to try.

I find this reason to cheer: *Finally!—a decent way to talk about the role of experience in preaching!!* Honestly, there is no issue that creates more classroom headaches than this one. Some of us were taught to never, ever talk about ourselves in a sermon, lest we appear egocentric or manipulative. Others of us were taught that it is perfectly acceptable to tell stories about our children, our dogs, or our high school prom night. Still others of us worry about where the lines are between appropriate self-disclosure and inappropriate use of the pulpit to do our own therapy.

But Ricoeur totally reframes the issue. *Of course* we preach from human experience!—and not because it's flashy or entertaining or the height of cool. Not because *our* lives are so much more interesting than anything that ever happens in the biblical text, or because we have been told (falsely, I think) that our listeners are so attention-deficit that they need "illustrations" the way an addict needs the next fix: *No!* We preach from experience for one reason, and one reason only: *experience is where God meets us.* God is real. God is here. And not just theoretically: concretely. For real. God breaks into human lives in ways we can actually see and touch and taste. Each experience is so vivid that the scent of it lingers on our skin. The sound of it echoes in our minds. And it drives us *crazy!*—because from now on, every bush we see will remind us of *that bush*, the one that spoke to us from the flames, the one we keep trying to describe, the one we have to talk about or *bust.* . . . So, yes!—we preach from human experience. That is the natural progression of things, once God comes to meet us. And there is no benefit, none at all, to remaining silent; *we have to preach what we have seen and believed.* People are hungry for it. Lives depend on it, including our own.

Just one glance at our three historical women preachers shows us exactly what Ricoeur is talking about. These women's communities took it for granted that God encountered human beings. They expected it to happen to both women and men. They expected women and men to talk about it, to share their experiences of encounter as part of spiritual growth. They did *not*, however, expect women to share in "promiscuous" (or mixed-gender) groups, which resulted in a no-win situation: by faith, women were commanded to speak; by law, they were forbidden to speak. Notice the emphasis: it is not a woman's *experience* of God or her *interpretation* of it that most disrupts the order. The big problem is when she *talks* about it.

I wonder what is really behind the resistance to "preaching from experience" that many of us have inherited. Is it a reluctance to acknowledge that God *does* encounter human beings, no matter who they are? Is it a way to keep God safely "out there," cool and disinterested and beyond our reach, and therefore unlikely to bring about liberation or change for the oppressed? Is it a preventative measure to keep certain groups (women, for example) from speaking and testifying, since the testimonial understanding of experience leads inevitably to interpretation and speech? Is it a protective measure for clergy to safeguard their privilege of interpreting and testifying? Is it another smokescreen, to keep our focus on so-called external qualifications (such as education, class, sex, race, sexual orientation, nationality, morality) rather than the quality of the experience itself—which begs to be preached, heard, and judged on its own merits?

The resistance is very odd. And a sign, I think, that another family secret is just behind it.

Walter Brueggemann: Testimony as Biblical Speech

Walter Brueggemann begins his *Theology of the Old Testament* with a brisk and unforgettable comment. Basically, it goes like this. Yes, there is a profound "unsettlement" permeating Old Testament studies in these postmodern days, and yes, it is *very* sad that we are no longer able to make universal coherent claims about God, but get over it: *the very thing that unsettles us is "biblical" in the first place!*

Brueggemann tells us to take our cues from the biblical text. If the subject of Old Testament studies is God, and if God, by definition, *resists* definition (which is the essence of postmodernism), then the biblical text ought to be a gold mine of theological methods for us. In particular, we should be paying careful attention to what Israel says about God and how. And the really astonishing thing, Brueggemann says, is that Israel's speech patterns for God are in fact a model of how to go about biblical interpretation. Those speech patterns don't look anything like philosophical recitals of God's "being" or "substance"; they most closely resemble *testimony*, or telling about what Israel has seen and heard and received from God. In the legal realm, testimony is a public presentation of one version of reality offered by a witness for the decision of the court. In the theological realm, testimony is the process by which Israel's speech about God becomes revelation.[5]

Brueggemann notices that Israel offers four kinds of testimony: core, counter, unsolicited, and embodied. For the purposes of this book, I will focus on the first two.

Core Testimony

The main thing Israel wants to say is that God (YHWH) has no serious competition: *God is incomparable.* That's it, in a nutshell. Incomparability takes the form of God's solidarity with the poor (and with Israel, in its need), and God's power to intervene on behalf of the powerless, making possible what seemed impossible. So it follows: *God is great and God is good.* God is sovereign and compassionate, powerful and faithful. The hard part—and this is a *very* hard part—is that God does not always behave this way. God does not always stay in character for the duration of the scene; sometimes, inexplicably, God is absent and silent, hidden and inscrutable. Israel's theological task, its "massive Holy problem" (as Brueggemann puts it), is to come to terms with both these things, and this is its core testimony.[6]

Israel's core testimony is not so much the official royal portrait of God as it is a "study" or preliminary sketch, and on principle, Israel will never finish it. Lack of resolution is one of the hallmarks of its testimony: colons, not periods; additions, not conclusions: always another thought: ". . . and yet . . ." Two other hallmarks are detail and candor: for a sketch, it doesn't miss much. Israel pays careful attention to the concrete and the particular and can be embarrassingly honest. For example, Israel may testify that God is incomparable (no one else can create, promise, deliver, command, and guide as God does) and then in the next breath reflect about the brokenness it sees and experiences around it (in the wilderness, in exile, and so on). This can make for some odd reading, but Israel knows that God's sovereignty and God's solidarity do not automatically merge. Sometimes they intersect, sometimes they are in acute tension. God's order is "a certain kind of order" and God's power "a certain kind of power" that can be savage as well as gracious.[7] God is incomparable, yes—but also endlessly elusive.

This leads us to one more important thing to note about Israel's core testimony, which is that it *"yields a character who has a profound disjunction at the core of the Subject's life."*[8] The character, of course, is God: center of our lives, subject of our texts, hidden and manifest, gracious and wild. God, the massively problematic and disjunctive One. It seems so very strange, doesn't it?—that Israel would insist on God's freedom in any text to act out, bow out, or flip out. It sounds like an abused woman, defending the husband who beats her. But that is missing the point, because Israel does not defend God; *Israel describes God.* The Old Testament pattern of testimony will always favor honesty above closure, denial, and cover up. If there is any possibility of hope and truth, it is in the disjunction. But note well: that possibility is never resolution.

Countertestimony

This is Brueggemann's boldest contribution to his book. The work of any witness, he says, is to tell the truth. But the work of the court is to determine the truthfulness of a witness's testimony through a process of cross-examination. It follows, then, that Israel's core testimony must also be cross-examined to see how well it holds up against other evidence. This is not something that is done to the text by outsiders (like us); the process of cross-examination actually goes on within the text itself. Every Old Testament witness is subject to cross-examination. No witness has the last word. Core testimony and countertestimony belong together, in a continuing, mutual exchange, as a way of being faithful in the world.

Israel's countertestimony is sharp and impatient. It has to be: life in exile raises too many questions, and they all demand immediate response: *Why? How long? When? How?* Israel's cross-examination of the core testimony is relentless and ruthless, even to the point of endangering it. Recurring strategies include declaring God's *hiddenness* (God is "taken underground" into hiding as a way of interpreting God's absence or unavailability), God's *ambiguity* or *instability* (God is spoken of as unreliable, contradictory, and abusive), and God's *negativity* (God fails to keep covenant with Israel: the theodicy question).[9] The boldness of the claims may shock or even anger us, but there is an important reason for Israel's unflinching honesty:

> *Israel as witness knows that if Yahweh is not endlessly criticized and subverted, Yahweh will also become an absolute, absolutizing idol,* the very kind about which Moses aimed his protesting, deconstructive work at Sinai. Thus the deconstructive program in all of these dimensions is a characteristically Jewish enterprise of "smashing the idols."[10]

It may surprise us that the New Testament has the same dialectic as its predecessor in the Hebrew Scriptures—but it shouldn't. Christians might want to argue that Sunday resolves Friday, or that, in Jesus Christ, the new covenant and "core testimony" resolve the old covenant "countertestimony" of the Old Testament. And certainly this is true, in a sense—"except that liturgically, *both claims linger*."[11] We cannot resolve, because to do so would entail living in denial. It would entail living outside of our own history, our own story, which calls us to remember that we were once slaves in Egypt. As if to underscore this, the Christian liturgy makes it plain in "the mystery of faith": "Christ has died, Christ is risen, Christ will come again." Even Christians cannot rush too quickly to closure.

The beauty and even genius of the pattern, in my view, is this: *it needs everyone and makes room for all.* Testimony offers us agency and space to see the world as people of faith. It requires of us truth and details, no matter where we are. It will not allow us to choose between different views, different faith stances, but expects us to hold open. It puts God, the massive Holy problem, at the center of everything. It asks us to speak God's name . . . in every place and every situation. It is Godtalk in exile.

Brueggemann's closing plea is for faith communities to recover the "peculiar, distinctive idiom" of biblical witness in testimony and countertestimony. In the same manner, Old Testament theology cannot simply be analysis of ancient Israel's speech practices in the biblical text. It must also be an engagement with those speech practices. A community of interpretation has to learn to distinguish between what is and is not "true speech" by practicing these very concrete patterns from ancient Israel.[12] These practices are life forms. They enable a community not only to hear and host the testimony "in all its oddness," but also to live it, and with the living, to move toward true speech.[13]

In the end, my appeal to ecclesial communities, and especially to their leaders and pastors, is that there be a serious reengagement with this idiom, which is the *Muttersprach* of the church (as of the synagogue). It is my impression that the church in the West has been sorely tempted to speak in everyone's idiom except its own. Liberals, embarrassed by the otherness of the biblical idiom, have kept control of matters through rationalistic speech that in the end affirms that "God has no hands but ours," issuing in burdensome self-congratulations. Conservatives, fearful of speech that is undomesticated, have insisted on flattening biblical testimony into the settled categories of scholasticism that freezes truth. In both sorts of speech, the incommensurate, mutual One disappears. Neither liberal rationalism nor scholastic conservatism will yield any energy or freedom for serious, sustained obedience or for buoyant elemental trust. Old Testament theology is, in an ecclesial setting, an activity for the recovery of an idiom of speech and of life that is congruent with the stuff of Israel's faith. Where that idiom is engaged and practiced, openings may appear in the shut-down world of contemporaneity, openings for core testimony revisited and for counter-testimony reuttered.[14]

A PREACHER REFLECTS

Preaching as Testimony: The Recovery of Biblical Speech

Brueggemann takes Ricoeur a step further: testimony is not only the distinctive *Christian* way of speaking and knowing but also the distinctive *biblical* way of speaking and knowing. If you are part of a tradition that values Scripture, especially where preaching is concerned, this move is huge and probably impossible to overstate: now we have *biblical examples* for how this theory works. We have scriptural precedent. We have mandate. Ricoeur may have sent out the invitations for this testimony party, but Brueggemann gives us permission to go *and* the keys to the car.

Testimony is our oldest model for talking about God. It is the "mother tongue" of the church, and, as Brueggemann shows us, the Old Testament's primary players, Israel and God, speak this "mother tongue" fluently. They also have a lot to talk about. The biblical family story includes creations and floods, covenants and betrayals, enslavements and liberations, wanderings and homecomings. The people of God have seen it all. Moreover, they have refused to keep quiet about any of it, understanding that families need to talk to one another and to God, most of all. Not all of the talk is pretty, but then neither is life. Some days the only thing you can do is praise God on your knees; other days you just bow your head and cry. The only rule in God's family is that the talk has to be really and truly *yours*, which means that it's no good if you pretend to say *Thank you!* when the honest-to-God truth is that you are so fed up that you could spit. God's people do not hold back *anything*—not ferocious love or ferocious grief. "Restraint" is therefore not a word they use with much success. On the other hand, "intimacy" and "honesty" they do very well. They are also quite good at *disjunctions*, which is to say that they can hold together even the most out-of-sync and perplexing experiences without having to fold one into the other or ignore the bad stuff. They will simply talk about both, no matter how long it takes, and then pick up again tomorrow where they left off. After all, in this kind of talk there is always a next time. There is also room for revision, because there will always be another way to see a thing and another day to see it; and everyone knows it.

Testimony may be our oldest model for talking about God, but it certainly isn't doddering or old-fashioned. Testimony has all the chutzpah of an adolescent on a dare. It breaks rules and smashes idols. It could care less about playing it safe. It assumes that disjointedness and inconsistency are inherent to the life (and text) of faith, not to mention the character of the One we worship; it isn't remotely embarrassed to be caught holding core testimony and countertestimony in the same sermon. It is unhesitatingly honest and hopelessly naïve. It is bold, daring, concrete, and outrageous. I hate to say it, but if testimony were your date for the night, it is everything your mother warned you about.

I am pushing the chutzpah angle here not because I think preachers should relive their adolescence or get in touch with their inner rebel (both are highly inadvisable) but because testimony does require the kind of intensity that we do not usually associate with maturity. As mature persons, we learn to temper our words and passions: part of being an adult is realizing that you can't always get what you want. You can't always say what you think, or act on what you feel. Passions and desires have ethical consequences, and sometimes restraint is necessary and even beautiful. Yet restraint also has its downside. Too much of it creates a deadening of spirit and human beings who are so repressed or depressed that they *never* care passionately or speak boldly. Too much restraint leads to preachers so fearful that they never speak up, even when they want to and believe they should. Testimony, meanwhile, calls to the deep-seated human longing to be *real*, for once; to say what we believe and to be honest about what we see and where we are, without fearing what may happen.

When we testify, we weigh the costs of passion and restraint and *choose passion*—not because it "feels good" or "makes sense" or gives us an adrenaline rush, but because to stand in your own life before God, saying what you know and believe to be true, takes guts and tremendous passion. Furthermore, that is the example Jesus sets us. His passion for us led him to lay himself bare, to lay down his life for us. Our passion for him requires a testimony of nothing less: to lay bare our best and worst and fullest selves, in humility and freedom, and offer them to God, come what may.

To be quite candid about it, this way of talking is better described by *reckless* and *shocking* than by *genteel, well-mannered,* and *well brought-up.* That is bad news for those of us who were hoping that testimony would not necessarily entail snake handling, full immersion, or praying before meals in restaurants, because as far as polite society is concerned, testimony not only *sounds* weird; it *is* weird. But maybe this is one of those hushed-up family secrets: we come from very strange people. If they weren't your relatives, biblically speaking, you might rationalize them as amusingly colorful, but since they keep proudly claiming you as their own (and showing up unannounced), somehow you have to come to terms with the funny accents and uncouth imagery and embarrassingly loud voices. It would be a lot easier if they just stayed put between the covers of our Bibles, but every time we read Scripture, we have to come to terms with it all over again: *our mother tongue.* We can't deny it: *this* is the way our people from the home country talk about God. And truthfully, in our less guarded moments—when we are tired or stressed or scared or upset—we slip back into it without even realizing it. Just as if we never actually grew up, left home, and became fluent in so many other languages.

Testimonial Authority: Engagement and "True Speech"

Now we can get very particular about what authoritative engagement with the biblical text looks like. First, however, let's get one thing straight. We do not read Scripture in order to be "enlightened." We do not read it to be inspired or instructed, or motivated or moved, or a host of other excellent outcomes. We do not even read it in order to *preach*; not at first, anyway. We read the biblical text in order to *hear* it, in the fullest sense of the word, and then to *welcome* it and *host* it in our lives and bodies.

"Host" is the key word here, but not in a polite-society, gracious-living, southern-hospitality (my context) sense, as if we were inviting the biblical text for dinner or the weekend. We are talking about a radical kind of hosting, here: permanent, physical, and life-changing.

When we host this text, it goes in so deep that it gets imprinted onto our cell structures. It enters our bodies, but not like lemonade sipped on a veranda: it infiltrates us like a virus. It alters our routines like a new baby. We can't even go to the corner store without *implications*, for heaven's sake!—because once the text becomes part of us, we never go out unencumbered. Nor would we choose to; somehow, nursing mothers are programmed to keep loving that colicky baby, which is a miracle, when you think about the cumulative effects of constant screaming and sleep deprivation. Engagement is embodiment beyond thought. It is beyond intellectualizing. We may hold with Descartes ("I think; therefore I am"), but we can't very well "think without body."[15]

Engaging the biblical text involves one more step beyond hearing and hosting: *speaking*. Ultimately, our readings of Scripture push toward speech; we have to say what we see and believe out loud. And not in a random, stream-of-consciousness, thinking-aloud sort of way, because the speech we are talking about isn't idle chatter whose only purpose is to interrupt the silence. It is *true speech* (Brueggemann's term), whose sole purpose is to interrupt the order and bring about justice. True speech is an act of theological interpretation, with an unmistakable progression from hearing and embodying to speaking. It calls for deep and painful engagement. It demands that we take a hard look at what is not right among us. It insists that we flag down anything random or casual and replace it with something real. By definition, then, true speech will interrupt, critique, and reinterpret the community's life in relation to God, which is not always welcome and never easy. Empty words only satisfy in the moment, but true speech summons us home. It fills us with hope that we can live out what we believe.

Two important footnotes here. First, true speech summons us home, but not necessarily to the "home" we dream about, in a nostalgic or ambitious sense. True speech calls us to a home where everyone is loved and no one is lost—and *that* may look like a home we can scarcely imagine. True speech is for the realization and embodiment of *justice*, not the preservation of the community as is. It follows, then, that the community should not count on emerging from "true speech" intact. It may splinter into pieces. It may reject its own words. It may have to go home by another road. True speech, like the text itself, *changes us*, and there is something both frightening and challenging about that. Those in power are almost certain to reject it (and us) every time—which will not exactly encourage us to persevere. Inexorably, we will have to confront the question of whether true speech is worth exile from the "home" we had, or thought we wanted.

The second footnote is a direct response to true speech: we persevere, because exile is a surprisingly powerful place to be. Exile produces its own urgency and its own longing. Perhaps most intriguing, exile is a place where true speech thrives, as Israel's example shows: the postexilic literature is some of the most brilliant and daring speech in the Bible. There is a peculiar freedom, as Israel learned, in being as low as you can possibly go. You can retreat into silence, or you can decide that exile is an excellent place, even a God-given place, for speaking about the text. This is not to say that God wills or causes exile (we will leave those theodicy questions aside for the moment), but only that the *location* of exile is not God-less, or void of grace. Even exile has room for God and room for talking about God. When we stand in exile, claiming the right to imagine liberation and homecoming, it is an act of freedom. It is the act of standing and speaking in our own lives.

Hutchinson, Osborn, and Lee are beautiful examples of the way testimonial authority moves irresistibly from reading the text to hearing it, hosting it, and speaking it. None of these women set out to preach the Word. They set out to *interpret Scripture*, and in the process, recognized that there were things that needed saying. They didn't rely on some external authority like the act of ordination. Yet they became authoritative in their communities because they were seen as women who deeply engaged and embodied Scripture; women who heard, hosted, and lived the text. Their preaching seemed a natural outgrowth of their communities' "true speech" practices. Furthermore, each woman saw herself as part of an exilic community, a faithful remnant, deeply immersed in the task of resistance. For Hutchinson, it was New World Puritanism over Old World Anglicanism, with the ideal Reformation community of Massachusetts Bay; for Osborn, it was New Light evangelicalism over Old Light Congregationalism, with its spiritual revivals for all groups. For Lee, it was black separatist Methodism over white segregated Methodism, with its antebellum mission of liberation to the captives of slavery. Each woman learned that exile created unique opportunities for women's speech, because exile is always a context of possibilities. It is always a breeding ground for freedom. And maybe that is another secret: that the mainstream church's "decline," its fading influence in the dominant culture, is not something to lament but something to celebrate. It marks our clear differentiation from the empire. It signals an exile into new possibilities and a deeper access to authority.

Testimonial Experience: Speaking as God's Partner

Just to clinch the growing levels of passion, Brueggemann reminds us that when Israel encounters God, it does so as *God's partner*. This puts an entirely different (and passionate) angle on our relationship with God, as anyone who has ever been in a marriage or partnership knows. To encounter God *as a partner* nixes the possibility of remaining neutral or objective about this meeting. God is not a casual acquaintance. God isn't even a stranger, an enemy, or a close friend. God is the lover you have pledged your life and body to. God is the one you will grow old with. No matter how bad it gets, God is not going anywhere, and neither are you.

So there are at least four things we can presume, using Israel's example as our model. First, we expect that God will, in fact, encounter us; this is what partners do. God has a pattern and a habit of breaking into human life, so as God's partner, we are primed to keep our eyes open—and to be very vocal in our disappointment if God doesn't show up. Second, no one can expect us to be impartial when we talk about God. Partners have intimate knowledge of one another—the good, the bad, and the ugly; they have special insights and odd blindnesses, due to the sensitivity (and desensitivity) of long cohabitation, and they feel intensely about one another, always hungry for the next encounter.

Third, we expect that this partnership compels testimony, because you can't make a covenant with someone and then refuse to talk. It isn't enough to be kind and steady and handy with a box of tools. As God's partner, we have to say where we really are, and what we really feel. We have to really *see* the other, and allow ourselves to be seen. The meeting is a meeting of our deepest places, overwhelmingly intimate; and our speech with one another is the same, because that is how you honor your partner. You tell them the truth about who you are. You show them, in your words and actions. You don't mistake truth for mindless trivia or thoughtless facts, which only hurt more than they help. You testify, in true speech, knowing your life and relationship are on the line. It is even possible—Brueggemann barely suggests as much—that should Israel (or we) cease to speak and Israel's partnership with God be in jeopardy, God-in-relation would cease to be "in-relation" with Israel; perhaps, in some performative sense, God would even cease to be (for Israel, anyway).[16]

Finally (this is the fourth assumption), we have to expect that our talk will expose us. It makes us vulnerable. There is always the possibility of rejection; not even true speech is immune to it. Testifying to an encounter with God (with all the awkward, passionate, outrageous speech *that* entails) is terribly risky, putting us at the mercy of the community's judgment. Yet experience itself is not fragile. On the contrary: it is amazingly powerful. It is the awareness, and therefore the mark, of partnership with God. Within the community, it is the mark of authority. And the only way to silence it—and here, I am exposing another family secret that will probably make me persona non grata to every disciplinary body—is by taking the witness's life. Testimony is free. Unless the authorities are prepared to kill us, they cannot silence us.

5

Making Trouble and Making Good News

Mary McClintock Fulkerson
and Rebecca Chopp

Now we come to the explicitly feminist theorists, adding their insights to the layers we have accumulated so far. And maybe you are wondering why such a move is even necessary, given the wealth of material in chapter 3. Don't we have enough to go on without piling on more theories about testimony?

Admittedly, scholars do have a tendency to overwork things; it is an occupational hazard with us to think that we can create a water-tight defense of a theory by loading it down with more academic lifejackets than it can handle. I am as guilty of that as anyone else, and if you want to see a superlative example of lifejacket angst, you can read my dissertation. But in this case, because we are dealing with the stories of real women who really preached when it was against the law for real women to ever do such a thing, it seems safe to say that sex roles and power dynamics come into play here. A feminist analysis (that is, an attempt to reveal power imbalances based on sex and gender in order to liberate both women and men from oppressive systems) pays close attention to that and will pick up on family secrets of a slightly different sort. I think the additional layer is definitely worth the effort. Moreover, notice that while a feminist analysis and agenda will be the vehicles here for exposing family secrets, the issues they raise to the surface are by no means for feminists alone. They are for all of us who preach and all of us who care about the survival and well-being of preaching and people.

MARY MCCLINTOCK FULKERSON:
TESTIMONY AS THEOLOGY

Hometown sermons, as Jesus would probably tell us, are the hardest ones to preach. It is awkward and humbling and just plain dangerous to be a prophet in your own backyard, and I bet Mary McClintock Fulkerson, whose backyard is feminist theology, knows something about that. In *Changing the Subject*, she preaches what has to be one of the most difficult hometown sermons feminist theology has heard.

Fulkerson's biggest concern is the question of *difference*. She asks whether feminist theology, which happens mainly in academic settings, can really claim to be interested in the varied experiences and interpretations of all women when it does not appreciate these women and take them seriously. What typically happens, she says, is that academic feminists make room at the table for women who are "different" (nonacademic, nonwhite, nonfeminist) and then treat these women like quaint tourist attractions to look at briefly before moving on. They never really see or consider the "Other" woman and her wisdoms and knowledge. They expect the women who are different to conform to *them*—since in the academy, conversations move toward a single theory or viewpoint (such as coming to only one definition of "women's experience") in order to "produce" knowledge. And before you know it, feminist theology, which got its start by challenging male universal claims, is right back in the family business: "women's experience" means "white academic women's experience."

Fulkerson thinks the problem is methodological. If women's experience is used as a historical or political warrant for challenging male hegemony (that is, systems and ideas that are totally dominated by males), then nothing will change but the name of the oppressor: the male hegemony will become a white, academic, female one. Fulkerson does not want to make the category of "experience" foundational for anything. Instead, she wants feminist theologians to pay closer attention to the *place* where women's experience is processed: *women's words*, or what they actually *say*. This allows us to *change the subject* of that experience rather than universalizing it.

For example, Fulkerson makes the deliberate choice to study women in conservative Christian communities. These women live and even thrive in systems of economic oppression and patriarchy that look dreadful to an outsider. Even more befuddling (to an academic feminist, at least), they are uninterested or opposed to anything that smacks of "women's rights" or "feminism." Usually feminist theology looks at such women and shakes its head: if they only knew how ignorant and oppressed they really are!—which Fulkerson finds truly annoying. Because if we looked at how those women are interpreting Scripture, especially in cases in which their interpretations are in direct conflict to their community's interpretations, we would begin to see how women are *resisting*, right in their own hometowns. More women than we ever expected are actually "making trouble with their faith!"

The reason this is so important is that it prevents us from making premature judgments about things we have not taken enough time to really see. It gives us a deeper appreciation for how women adapt and survive in their own contexts, given the complexities of their situations. And since we have taken seriously our own locations as incarnate, limited, and fallible human beings (whose lives and perspectives seem just as befuddling to outsiders), we can stop being such insufferable know-it-alls. Our experience is not the norm.

Unstable Texts and the Women Who Read Them

Fulkerson obviously wants to avoid blanket statements at any cost. She would never say, for example, that Christian faith is *always* liberating or *always* oppressive. Instead, she might say, "When this particular woman in this context reads the biblical text in this way, it is oppressive for her—unless she resists it by creating a space for her own well-being (good news, gospel) to flourish." Fulkerson wants to get very specific about how different women actually read the Bible, so that we can see exactly when and where women "make trouble" with their faith. If we can do this, she says, it will be something new in feminist theology. We will be able to focus on resistance wherever it happens, even if it was never meant to be understood as "feminist."

In Christianity, the Bible is central to women's faith practices, so Fulkerson's first priority is to construct a theory of texts (by which she means the biblical text). She wants this theory to show how the Bible can be read in ways that are oppressive to women as well as ways that are liberating to them. She calls this the *instability* of the biblical text: the fact that it can be read and interpreted in so many different ways and for so many different reasons (not that it is inherently "unstable," which would be utter nonsense!). The thing that *stabilizes* the biblical text, she says, is a community's reading of it: what they are interpreting it *for*. Meaning emerges from practice. Meaning depends on "perform-ance." What is normative for one group (their "ideal regime of reading," as she puts it) may look like heresy to another, because communities read for different purposes and with different lenses—as anyone knows who has been paying attention. In fact, the biblical text can be read and interpreted so differently that we might think groups of readers are actu-ally relating to a different Scripture.

Fulkerson has done studies of middle-class Presbyterian women and poor Pentecostal women that illustrate her case. It will hardly surprise us to learn that these two groups read and interpret Scripture very dif-ferently. Yet we would never claim (and should never claim) that one of them is right while the other is wrong, or that one has interpreted cor-rectly while the other hasn't. Instead, Fulkerson thinks it is more accu-rate to say that these women are related to a "different Scripture" due to their different subject positions, purposes, and interpretation methods. In short, they "perform" the text differently. When we change the sub-ject (in this case, from middle-class Presbyterian women to poor Pente-costal women, and back again), we get a completely different—and faithful!—interpretation.

This reminds me of a friend who teaches New Testament at an interdenominational seminary.[1] My friend routinely flummoxes her students (a potent mix of Baptists, Methodists, Pentecostals, and oth-ers) by showing them how the same text can be faithfully interpreted in multiple ways—yet refusing to answer when her students demand to know which interpretation is "right." "My job is not to tell you what's *right*," she tells them. "My job is to show you what's *possible*. If you want to know what's right, check with your denominational authorities." Her students, for whom diversity and difference are a given in that setting, learn very quickly that different communities "stabilize" the same text in different ways, and that normativity depends on where you stand. In other words: changing the subject changes the meaning.

One very important reiteration: this does *not* mean that anything goes as far as Scripture is concerned and that we can mold the biblical text into anything we want it to say. It simply means that many possi-bilities for interpretation exist and that these possibilities depend on the location and interest of the interpreter's subject position. But we will never see how this is so if we do not nudge ourselves to keep changing the subject.

Getting Specific: Women Graf(ph)ting the Good News

The centerpiece of Fulkerson's theory of texts is the metaphor of "graf(ph)ting," a term she coins from literary and botanical creation.[2] In the horticultural world, a graft is a cutting that is joined to a rooted plant by means of a fracture or splicing. It redirects the sap of the host plant and creates a new plant, yet still depends on the host for its own life. In the same way, we can say that a *reading* of a text is a graft—or "graf(ph)t." We interpret Scripture from a particular place (that is, our subject location) and with a particular community. Every community has its own ways of interpreting, and every community exerts pressure on its members to learn and conform to those ways. And so we raise our children to believe certain precepts, teach our young people the ways of the community, and support adults in their continuing faith journeys, all in light of our reading of Scripture.

But sometimes, the way our community interprets a text feels crazy to one of us, and we just can't go there. Maybe the interpretation goes against everything we know and believe about God; maybe it asks us to deny ourselves or others. If we try to go along with the rest, it will break us. So what we do, either quietly or publicly, is exercise our subjectivity: we take liberties with the text by *making* liberty with the text. We deliberately or unconsciously shift the way we interpret it. We redirect the flow of meaning until it is no longer oppressive or corrupt, either to us or others. And in so doing, we find new paths—new ways of reading and interpreting—that lead to value and wholeness. Theologically, we might say that we have confronted sin by deciding not to take the path that leads to brokenness. A graf(ph)t, then, is a signal that *something is wrong*: for reasons that we can learn, if we pay close attention, the way a community interprets a particular biblical text is causing pain for someone. It is functioning as a roadblock for that person, and she is looking for a way around it, on her way through to grace.

For example, in Fulkerson's study of poor Pentecostal women, she finds two interpretive principles at work: a reliance on the Holy Spirit as God's empowering presence in human practice and the belief that Scripture is inspired and to be taken literally. The second of these principles would certainly appear to rule out women's preaching. The first, however, opens up possibilities that might override the second. Spirit-inspired preaching, without regard for race, class, or education, holds an honored and authoritative place among Pentecostals. Indeed, women have historically held positions of breathtaking power in the Pentecostal Church: women founded two of its denominations! The "ideal regime of reading" therefore *does* allow for women's preaching, even while it also allows for their subservience to men. The women themselves, who live in extreme economic deprivation and for whom survival is always an issue, have graf(ph)ted onto their fragmented subject positions a reading of a God who empowers them—with abundant strength and words and Spirit. This is nothing short of amazing: when everything about their circumstances tells them that they aren't worth anything, the women create sermons and song that give richly to others.

Testimony: A Theology of Affinity

From here, Fulkerson states her case. Feminist theology—indeed, all theology—needs to be reconstrued as *testimony*. We can no longer speak of theology as a series of absolute claims. The One to whom we testify may be absolute truth and grace, but our speech itself is not—and theology is speech. It is "an odd kind of truth," "ragged, not systematic or complete," with a future that remains ever open and undetermined; in my tradition, we call it "reformed, and always being reformed."[3]

Theology is a rhetorical practice, and its truth comes by persuasion. Yet it is hardly mere opinion, any more than a sermon is mere opinion. "Theology," Fulkerson asserts, "can be passionate commitment to God's work of redemption in the world."[4] Theology may be located, particular, and incomplete, but it is still passionate and important truth-telling from one place. It also does something far more important and honest than most speech: it can mediate difference. When we give up the practice of speaking for others, then we no longer have to tell what difference *is*. Instead, we tell who *we* are, through the process of our own testimony—which by definition leaves room for the Other.

Fulkerson concedes that this is a fragile theological position, at best. But if feminist theology is to resist becoming the oppressor itself (a real danger at present, she feels), then it can no longer participate in oppressive practices. It has to resist the desire to define what a "real woman" is. It has to smash some idols. It needs to practice testimony in order to pursue a *theology of affinity*. A theology of affinity, she says, admits that even love is not able to fully know the other; it can only tread a fine line between appropriating another's experience and delicately constructing "the just-barely-possible affinities, the just-barely-possible connections that might actually make a difference in local and global histories."[5] She leaves us with an awesome possibility:

> If changing the subject is to proceed beyond inclusion, it must go forward as a change that has no subject to ground itself in. I suspect that none of us can quite grasp that future. It holds the promise of kinds of joy that we miss under the reigning discipline. The terms of good news we might receive *if we were formed to receive from the other* will surprise even those of us who tell stories about the oppressed.[6]

A PREACHER REFLECTS

Preaching as Testimony: Changing the Subject

In some ways, I feel sad that a book like this needed to be written at all. Why should changing the subject be such a big deal? Why do we have to go to such elaborate lengths to keep ourselves honest about basic things, like remembering that everything is *not* about us and that more than one perspective exists? The reason, undoubtedly, has to do with human sin: our willful tendency to see the world as an extension of ourselves and our constant struggle to love our neighbors—or at least, to step into their shoes and look at things from their point of view for longer than thirty seconds at a time. Our inability to accomplish this is clearly what keeps marriage counselors in business and the nations' ambassadors scurrying to and fro. If each of us were able to do the comparatively simple act of changing the subject, we could probably do away with most conflict on this planet.

Meanwhile, we have people like Fulkerson to keep us honest. Her methodology may seem a bit labor-intensive for everyday use, kind of like bringing out the hand-painted china that has to be washed carefully and separately when all you really want to do is serve tuna fish sandwiches. But it is mostly a matter of downshifting into plain common sense: *before you make pronouncements, take a good look.*

When we do, there are certainly some surprising things to see. Most obvious is the number of preachers out there that we never thought to study or even dignify with the title "preacher," an especially important insight for those of us interested in researching women or other outsiders. Another is that we do not always find preachers in the typical preaching places; they pop up where we least expect it. It follows, then (per Fulkerson), that since preachers are difficult to identify by appearance or location, the best proof-of-preacher ID is to examine the words themselves: what the person is actually saying. We are looking for evidence of true speech but also more than that. We are looking for evidence that this person labored in a particular way to say these words because she wanted them to do something.

Here is the bottom line. Preaching is not just good news; it is *making* good news. It is creating something out of nothing, because there is nothing static about preaching. *Something happens.* Tombs open. Chains fall away. Preaching is creating a place to flourish out of a place that holds you prisoner. It is taking notes on resistance and hope and writing a new script for brokenness. It is tunneling a way through oppression to the freedom on the other side. And make no mistake: it is the power of God that does this tunneling, not the preacher herself, although the preacher has to be brave enough to believe it, to name it, and to claim it! The preacher has to be brave enough to testify to brokenness, as well as to the power of God to redeem.

Brokenness and redemption, however, look like very different things to different communities. One community's liberation is another community's sorrow. One community's good news is another community's heresy. Preaching, therefore, has to get very particular and contextual, because *freedom* is particular and contextual. There are also many conceivable trails that lead to freedom, and we are not all suited to the same paths. We have to choose our own trail as carefully as we name our own particular need for and kind of liberation, because preaching is not just announcing freedom; it is announcing a *way* to freedom. It is embodying deliverance, in the act of speaking the words. The preacher graf(ph)ts a new interpretation onto a worn-out one—and suddenly the community sees chiseled-out liberation, sewn-in good news. They see a way, and they can believe it. But only if someone lives it first . . . so that his words become preaching.

I have to be honest: this terrifies me. Can we really say that?—*You can't tell a preacher by her cover. You can only tell a preacher by her words, and whether they create good news for these people, here, today.*

If we do say it, we are taking a step away from Ricoeur and Brueggemann, for whom preaching is real liberation for real people *by saying something concrete and meaningful about God.* Fulkerson is less concerned with words about meaning. She wants us to backpedal to the act of liberation, before we start dawdling in theories about what liberation *could* mean, and lose the urgency and potential of the moment. And she is right to sound the alarm. When preaching loses its performative edge, when it stops *doing* things, it is nothing but hollow speech. It loses its common sense, as well.

We will need Rebecca Chopp and a theology of proclamation to help us bridge the gap before it becomes an impasse. Meanwhile, however, Fulkerson raises some very disturbing things to think about. What if plenty of preachers out there *think* they are preaching when their sermons do not give any evidence of it at all? What if those sermons only talk about good news without ever making any? What if the reason some preachers are barred from the act is that their communities are scared to death of chiseling out some liberation, even if it is the very liberation they know they need?

I wonder if it would be a relief to admit it and let the secret go.

Testimonial Authority: Who's Making Trouble, and How?

You have probably noticed that Fulkerson is doing away with labels, right and left. No more assumptions about a person (is he liberal? conservative? evangelical?). No more litmus tests for authority (is it located in the text? in the community? in the tradition?). Pay closer attention to the subject himself: listen to him "make trouble with his faith." We will learn what authority *is* by watching what it *does*. And that means we may very well find radical faithfulness in a person from whom we never expected it, because authority is never something we can learn from theological labels.

It was seminary that taught me about theological labeling. Shortly after we students arrived, scared and excited and fairly bursting with self-confidence and self-doubt, we were handed a student directory, known affectionately as "the fundy finder" or "liberal locater" ("fundy" was short for "fundamentalist"). At that time, the directory contained a picture of each student as well as that person's nickname, phone number, campus address, home address, denomination, and college or graduate school. It was a lot of information to get in one glance, especially if you were just flipping through to find out the name of that cute guy in Greek class. It also fed some rather discouraging tendencies among us. You could look someone up and make all sorts of assumptions about them. You could, as the directory rather lightheartedly put it, find the fundies and locate the liberals. You could sort students into categories: Californians (evangelical conservatives), Southern Baptists (inerrancy biblicists), graduates of religious colleges (campus ministry groupies), big-city residents (decadent snobs). You could find the right label for everyone, and we did, ruthlessly.

Of course, much of this labeling was a joke, but there was an insidious undertone to it that seeped into our classrooms and altered our dining-hall conversations. However unintentionally, our practice of labeling reinforced our habit of prejudging one another. It fed our insecurities. It interfered with our abilities to hear one another accurately or fairly. Soon, it defined how we actually related to one another—as church leaders who belonged to different and (we believed) irreconcilable theological camps, and who would soon be obliged to compete for members the way we then competed for grades. It was definitely dispiriting and bore no resemblance to the kingdom of God we all preached so earnestly, but try as we might, we couldn't seem to rise above what was happening. We had neither the skills nor the confidence that labeling could ever cease. This was life, we thought. This was church politics. Take it or leave it.

I think about that little student directory and see a parable in it that I never noticed at the time. The kingdom of God, I am fairly sure, does not look like a fundy finder. It does not look like labeling or competition or politics—the many masks of fear. For me, the kingdom of God, the *realm of God*, looks more like a preacher who catches you by surprise when you've lost your way. She shakes her head at all the labels stuck to your clothes and even matted in your hair, and then laughs as she brushes them off and pushes you gently in the right direction.

How much we miss if we stay stuck in the practice of labeling, and how many relationships we lose! How many preachers (I will speak for myself, here) we overlook! When I first went looking for historical role models, I was determined to accept only *true feminists* into my pantheon—let's say, women who had attended the 1848 Seneca Falls Convention, like Susan B. Anthony and Elizabeth Cady Stanton—and *not* some sentimental lady-like schoolteachers in headscarves. Thankfully, Fulkerson saved me from my own ignorance. Otherwise I would have missed Sarah Osborn completely; her concern for appearances would have struck me as pathetically timid rather than a strategic move to protect her very dangerous ministry with marginal groups in Newport. Jarena Lee might have seemed woefully bourgeois and patriarchy bound; Anne Hutchinson, just a power-hungry woman whose primary concern was to protect her husband's wealth. Interestingly enough, those very conclusions would have been exactly the ones these women's opponents would have *wanted* me to make and had in fact argued themselves. I suspect that the powers and principalities would like nothing better than for each of us to jump to hasty conclusions without bothering at all to slow down and change the subject.

And this leads us to some *very* intriguing issues about how we define orthodoxy and heresy. Hutchinson, Osborn, and Lee believed they were bearers of faithful Christian doctrine, preaching orthodoxy into the teeth of oppression and heresy. The graf(ph)ts *they* made were to set things right; their preaching *intended* to critique and resist those in power, and their communities judged it to be true speech. Those in power retaliated by calling the women deluded, deviant, and preachers of false doctrine. So who is right, here? Which party is orthodox, and which is heretical? How will those words be defined, and who will get to define them?

As history shows us, some "deviant" interpretations of biblical texts are not deviant at all but merely graf(ph)ts, and faithful ones at that. It ought to make us extremely careful when considering questions of orthodoxy today or flinging labels about. And since we know that history is most often recorded by the winners and insiders, we will have to look very closely in order to decide—which may dig up secrets that were intended to rest in peace.

Testimonial Experience: Encountering God, Encountering Ourselves

One of my favorite things about Fulkerson's work is the way it drop-kicks our understanding of experience. Preachers talk about experience endlessly and, in my view, fruitlessly. Ricoeur and Brueggemann have already given us some helpful ways to reframe the problem: "experience" is what happens when we live in and interpret the biblical text. Our experience of a text is what we see in it and believe about it. Fulkerson now ups the ante: experience is where the sermon begins and ends. If you haven't experienced the text, you can't preach. You haven't seen anything and you haven't earned the right to say a blessed word. And if *that* seems harsh, then go back and look at one of your sermons, because it is an artifact you can examine; it leaves traces of *you* everywhere. If you have had even the faintest experience of a biblical text, it will leave muddy footprints on every word you say.

Sometimes a student will come to me with a sermon in progress and ask whether he ought to "plug in a story" after paragraph three. I have to restrain myself (from either gagging or throttling) so that I can speak kindly and calmly, since I am only about to say the very thing I have to tell myself, over and over, every time I preach. No, I say, you do not need to plug in a story; that is the wrong idea entirely. You need to go back to the text and listen to what it is telling you. You need to have another experience of the text, so that you do not simply *talk about it*. And how long do we have to wait in order to "have an experience of the text"? Well, no one can tell you. Maybe a few minutes, maybe a few hours, maybe longer; maybe not. But you have to wait long enough until you are *living* in that text and it starts to make trouble with your faith. Stay there until it is keeping you up at night. Then come back and tell us what you saw and what you believe. Otherwise, you will start to plug in stories that ought to have been labeled "nonrecyclable" in the first place, since they only litter the preaching landscape with faded hand-me-downs that never will fit, no matter how you alter them.

It really is a deeper level of experience we are talking about here. Fulkerson calls it "ritual experience." The goal is not consensus but conversion: *our* conversion. The goal is not to "show" or "tell" our side of the story, but to be formed by the Other—or by the text. Preaching is a ritual space in which such a conversion may occur. And the best part—truly!—is that we preachers get to have the experience ourselves every time we preach.

Conversion, to be sure, is a humungous goal. Some of our denominations take to it more easily than others. For those of us who have been brought up to be wary of conversion (or any religious fervor), here is a family secret it is high time we heard: *preaching aims to convert*. It is unavoidable. And the first in line, every time, is the preacher herself—so we had better figure out a way to practice.

REBECCA CHOPP: TESTIMONY AS FEMINIST PROCLAMATION

Rebecca Chopp is one of those gloriously brave thinkers who only have time for huge ideas. She takes on projects that give other theologians panic attacks (such as constructing a theology of proclamation and the Word), and calmly goes about it as if she *weren't* the first person since Barth and Bultmann to do such a thing, and to do it well. There is a lesson for us here about not frittering away our time and sermons with shallow and trivial questions. Chopp believes the Word is central to theological reflection and that if contemporary Protestant theology were doing a better job of reflecting on it, the pulpit, not to mention theology itself, wouldn't be in such a sorry state. Another way to say this is that if we were attending to the things that matter, we would be speaking in ways that matter. As it is, however, Chopp thinks the Word has lost its power in the postmodern context: it is totally irrelevant. Christian communities see it as little more than a comforting tranquilizer to get us over the hump of unhappiness.

Chopp has no patience for this. She wants the church to stop crying over its lost members and get to the root of the problem. She wants us to engage in some serious reflection on proclamation—which is not the same thing as dreaming about how to lure the crowds back with snappy sermons or new sanctuary designs. She hopes we will return to what she calls "the Reformation insistence that God is revealed, experienced, and present in the proclaimed Word."[7] And yes, she promises that it will be hard work, much harder than just adding PowerPoint and stirring.

There are places where this work is already in progress, places where people of faith talk of freedom and therefore proclaim the Word to and for the world. One of the best examples, Chopp finds, is feminist theology. Feminist theology talks about freedom (she calls it "emancipatory transformation"), but this good news is not just for women. It is for men, too. It is for Christianity and the world. In fact, Chopp believes that *feminist theology has become proclamation to and for the world.* In *The Power to Speak*, she shows us how this proclamation may be interpreted as a testimony to and of God.

Once again, this is an extraordinarily complex and beautiful theory, which I have had to make quickly accessible to us in this book. Those of you who love to dive into the depths of systematic theologies will find Chopp's book well worth the investment of your time. It is about things that matter.

Testimony: A Feminist Mode of Proclamation

I imagine it may be a stumbling block for some of us to hear that feminist theology is proclamation to and for the world. If you are among those for whom this is true, then please hang in there until we get to the end of this. It's worth it.

Here is how Chopp lays out the pieces. In our "present order" (that is, our current system, which includes our ways of using language and power to signify hierarchies), we have one group that currently defines what it is to be fully human. This group consists of white men who have the privilege of economic solvency and a modicum of education; they are at the top of the food chain, so to speak, and so hold a unique place of subjectivity. In our present order, white men of privilege are, as Chopp puts it, "the universal human subject." All other persons fall into the category of *oppressed*, which means that their subjectivity (that is, their ability to speak for themselves, as "subjects") is denied; it is perceived as something less. And oppressed persons desire freedom. They desire subjectivity, to *speak for themselves*, which is the first act of survival; yet this seemingly simple act is unimaginably difficult.

In this present order, women fall into the category of the oppressed (and remember, we are using this term primarily to talk about *subjectivity*). Like other oppressed persons, they have no choice about it: that's life. Women cannot simply wake up one morning and choose to opt out ("Today I have decided: I no longer live in this system and am no longer oppressed!"); we are all here to stay. So if women want to stop being strangers or even prisoners in their own system, they have to do more than interrupt it. They have to change it, and this is what feminist theology, or feminist *theologies*, try to do. Obviously there are as many ideas about how to go about it as there are theorists and practitioners, but they do share some things. One is an honoring of multiplicity and otherness in both speaking and hearing. And another is a common goal: *the desire for freedom and for a transformation of the present order that goes beyond mere critique.* Therefore, Chopp says that feminist theology has become a model of proclamation that can save both contemporary theology and the present structure.

Of course, the oppressed—including women—do have a place in the present order of church and society. That place is not at the center of power and subjectivity but rather at the *margins*, that nebulous stretch of blank space that separates the center (of activity, of focus, of power) from its outer frame (edge, boundary, limit). The margin is not an easy place to be, but it does have its peculiar graces. It gives you a better perspective on the center, for instance. You get a clearer view of some things, while other things are blocked. Women listen and speak, then, "with both blindness and insight."[8] When women speak from the margins (and Chopp is clear that it can be only from *one* margin; we stand in particular places that must be defined), they are actually questioning the very boundaries of Christianity itself. This is much more than corrective speech; this is *proclamation of the Word*, for the purpose of liberating not only women but the whole of Christianity.

"The Word" Chopp describes is not a Word of order, or a Word of "the present order." That sort of word would only serve to keep women on the margins, where they already are. Chopp has to go outside the present order to describe the Word she imagines, which is one of creation, embodiment, and life. Chopp believes this Word has been hidden and imprisoned (and crucified) because of its openness to different ways of speaking and being. Still, she knows that even the margins have their graces—and one of them is the affirmation that *the possibility for change exists in the space between Word, words, and woman, or between women's speaking and the repression of that speech.*

This must be why Chopp calls the new Word she imagines *the Word as perfectly open sign.* The theological semiotics of this Word (to get technical for a moment) rest on the supposition that words are contextually understood and always open to new signification and meaning. The Word as perfectly open sign, then, is a Word of power. It is a Word that creates and sustains all other words. It is Word that opens up many voices, any of which can push and challenge and transform the present order. This Word is always open to new meaning; it is a perfectly open sign; it is God. It is also a bet against all odds that good news can still be proclaimed, even from the margins. It is a wager that women can speak of freedom.

At the same time, our scriptural and (for Chopp) Reformed heritage insists that Word/God is unnameable. Any words we borrow to name God, or this Word, must cross "an impossible gap, an abyss of meaning," even as they fall short of fully naming what is supremely holy.[9] What we have, then, is a mystery very like that of the Trinity, in which meaning depends on open relationships between the parts. Like the three persons of the Trinity, the Word and the words we choose to signify it are bound together in a relationship of meaning as well as chaos, presence as well as gaps. This will (big surprise, here) make our task of proclamation both exhilarating and infuriating. We will get meaning, and we will also get chaos. We will know presence, and we will also know gaps. This, in the very same sermon moment! Yet we can be sure that because the Word is in solidarity with words, is embodied by words, and anticipates words, it gives life and gives it abundantly. It is a Word of transformation.

The Word in Scripture

Now we must ask how Scripture might function in Chopp's theory of proclamation and the Word. How does the Bible speak to women of new freedoms and how does it empower them to speak freely?

Chopp has two governing insights for this move. First, *Scripture functions as prototype, not archetype.* An archetype is a fixed, eternal rule or structure, like a riddle that must be solved. A prototype, on the other hand, is an open-ended paradigm or model that guides action but is always open to transformation; we could say it is always moving toward freedom.[10] Elisabeth Schüssler Fiorenza's classic phrase—that Scripture is bread, not stone, and that it is for the flourishing of life—is Chopp's source here.[11] When we look at Scripture this way, we can say that it is *proclamation*, which is a reordering of relations. And just as Scripture itself is not fixed, so the Word as perfectly open sign is not fixed either; it moves through Scripture, prodding and pointing toward freedom within the words themselves. We find the Word as perfectly open sign in the play of images, in the language of poetry, and in singing and dancing and praying that express our deepest human hopes and desires.

Second, *women proclaim Scripture through a hermeneutics of marginality.* Chopp has already shown that women exist at the margins of the present order, and that they read and interpret Scripture from that marginal place. She has also claimed that women can and do find freedom in Scripture, despite their marginal place. Therefore, women have a "hermeneutics of marginality," which is to say that they interpret the text by bringing their ways of knowing in the Word (their experience at the margins and their new practices of speaking) to "an open dialogue about freedom" rather than an examination of the text.[12] A feminist reading of Scripture searches for freedom in the text and in life.

Here is where testimony enters the picture. When women interpret Scripture, searching for the freedom they know exists (because they have seen it and experienced it!), their interpretations are a testimony to what they have seen and believed in the Word and in their lives. "Proclamation moves through testimony," Chopp says, "relying on the power realized in speaking one's life."[13] That testimony (watch how Chopp is drawing on Ricoeur here) involves both a confession of the self and a narration of events: who we are and what we have seen. We proclaim the testimony with the involvement of our very lives. Yet our lives are not the testimony, and our lives do not prove the testimony; rather, our lives are *sealed* to the testimony, sealed to the narrated and confessed freedom the testimony proclaims—which is the Word as perfectly open sign.

Proclamation, then, is a testimony of freedom. Women have seen this freedom at work in their lives. They confess it passionately. They believe in it and labor for it from wherever they are. Yet the freedom women have seen and confessed is never for the sake of the present order, "keeping things as they are." If it were, our preaching would only be interested in trying to maintain the status quo. We would simply try to spread power around. We would try to help women become like men, blacks like whites, the poor like the rich—as if extending privileges through a heaping portion of patriarchal power were the answer to all our problems. But preaching, as Jesus taught us, is never for keeping the status quo. Instead, it is for the reordering of relations: for *jubilee*. It is for canceling debt and making all things new. It is for freedom.

Chopp has one more important insight about Scripture. Those who proclaim—even Christ himself!—are not in control of their own proclamation. They do not own it, and they cannot predict how it will be received. This is because "the passage produces a space between our meaning and our proclaiming," so that the "point" of a text "*is not sufficient to speak to what happens in the text.*"[14] Preaching a text sets the Word loose in the world, but the preacher is not the One in control! The moment we begin our testimony of the Word (which is to say, our narration of what we have seen and our confession of what we believe about it), the text may still break open upon itself, calling everything into question. The Word of freedom is so free, so *perfectly open*, it even resists us! This is a critical move, essential to maintaining the freedom of the Word of freedom. Without it, we might begin to believe that preaching can somehow direct or harness the Word—and from here, it is only a short step to melting down our gold and fashioning a calf for idol worship.

Don't despair yet. Chopp is not trumpeting our descent into nihilism and the death of preaching. The mystery of it, the incredible and beautiful mystery of it, is that somehow, preaching accesses a power that is altogether beyond us yet altogether through us: "Proclaimers' lives will cling to words of freedom and words of freedom demand the living of one's life, but all may be questioned, rejected, or crucified precisely when the meaning is grasped."[15]

The Word in Christian Community

Chopp sees the church as the embodied relations of Word and words. This is not, however, a sure thing. There is a "horizon" of freedom in the church, but the church does not always see it or proclaim it—and when it does not proclaim this freedom, it is not the church. Yet the possibility exists. Whenever the church makes itself a space and time of freedom, whenever it encourages new ways of speaking freely, it preaches good news; and whenever it preaches good news, the church is constituted yet again.

There is more, however. If women or any oppressed persons make for themselves a space in or outside the church to speak freely and proclaim freedom from the margins, then there, too, we find proclamation; we find the church.[16] There are seeds of this hope in every community. Sometimes it is more radical and pronounced; sometimes it is veiled in traditionalism. Yet whenever women do what they have always done in the traditional order of things—baking bread for communion, arranging flowers for worship, washing dishes after the potluck, serving tea at funerals, teaching children in the Sunday school, knitting shawls for a women's shelter—you can find grace, if you look. Every woman, no matter who she is, has dreams, longings, and desires to speak the Word. And women can; they can and do proclaim freedom wherever they are, even if they are not formally recognized or "ordained" or constituted as the church to do so! Whenever this happens, the space they create in that act of proclamation will be a community of faith: the church.

The Word in Proclamation

The last thing to say is that proclamation is never complete. It is always sketchy, always in progress. It is embodied and historical, which is to say that it exists in time and will be outlived or outgrown until it is finally fulfilled. So it lives in the cracks of things. It emerges from the margins where seeds of hope are waiting. It does not, however, simply float, suspended, accepting things as they are and never questioning. Proclamation has an aspect of critique, as well. It examines the order very closely to see how things work together to maintain the status quo. It aims to do away with any cover-ups. Proclamation is always for the purpose of transformation. Maybe it cannot actually do away with the present order—not until the moment of fulfillment, anyway—but it can resist. We can *always* resist. We can name how we have survived and describe what it is for us to stand in our own lives, there at the margins, looking toward freedom.

A PREACHER REFLECTS

Preaching as Testimony: A Proclamation of Jubilee

When I was thirty-five, I had my first mammogram, a rite of passage for women in our culture. Usually such screenings are preventative, but this one wasn't; my doctor had found something that needed to be checked out, and I was scared. Sitting in the enormous waiting room, too nervous to read and wishing I had brought someone with me, I looked around at the other women who were also waiting. There were at least twenty of us, as evenly spaced throughout the room as if we had been given assigned seats for the exam. We weren't *that* far from one another, but it felt like miles, because not one woman raised her eyes, or spoke, or moved. Overhead, a television was blaring, but we were still and silent. The message was clear, and I got it: we were not expected to talk with one another, just to wait, quietly, for our names to be called.

Finally I was summoned to the registration area, a row of semi-private cubicles where staff members took our information and entered it into their computers. A woman with kind eyes asked me the requisite questions—I think I barely whispered in response—and explained the procedure that was about to happen. But then she did an odd thing. Handing me my paperwork and pointing me toward the door where a technician stood, she suddenly looked me straight in the face, her gaze clear and steady, and nodded at me. "Be of good cheer," she said, and sent me on my way.

The mammogram turned out to reveal nothing worrisome, but I really don't remember much about it. What I do remember is that woman's proclamation to me: *Be of good cheer.* Words from Matthew 9:2, actually, spoken by Jesus to a crippled man and repeated to me by a faithful stranger who knew her King James: "Be of good cheer." Those words lifted me, just as surely as the crippled man's friends lowered him, into the presence of Jesus. They transformed a bleak waiting room into a tabernacle of hope, because that is what preaching does: it puts you in good news' way. It gives the present order a major design overhaul and reconfigures your living space. You look up to find the seating arrangements changed: you are among and beside, instead of separate and apart; your eyes meet faces, not blaring television screens. *Proclamation reorders everything* by showing us how words, Word, and life relate to one another—and indeed, how they *might* relate to one another if we dared to imagine it.

Chopp calls this kind of preaching "a proclamation of jubilee." It happens whenever and wherever preachers testify to those who need it, which will certainly throw a wrench into preachers' ideas about sacred space: if four words uttered by an office worker can transform life in a hospital waiting room, then why in heaven's name would we ever restrict our preaching to church sanctuaries on Sunday morning?! One of our biggest family secrets has to do with the *location* of preaching. Many of us have fooled ourselves into thinking preaching happens in church sanctuaries, when, as our historical women knew so well, nothing could be further from the truth. Preaching happens in kitchens and street corners and hospital waiting rooms. It happens wherever people are hungry for freedom and someone is given a Word of freedom to speak. The space itself matters only insofar as it is the space of encounter, the space where we meet God. And here is another uncomfortable little secret: we are much more likely to encounter the Word when we plant our bodies in marginal space, because the Word has a distinct preference for whispering liberation ("Be of good cheer"). It doesn't do us any good to sit in our studies and *think* marginal thoughts. We have to be there. We have to go marginal, if we aren't already. Which is something preachers have always known, actually; why else would we spend so much pastoral care time visiting our people in hospitals and crisis situations and life-and-death moments? We know the importance of being there, how sacred those moments are. The Word does, too.

But proclamations of jubilee do not just affect the *where* of preaching; they also disrupt the *when*. Jubilee, after all, implies a distinct *when*, since it is a regularly occurring insertion in time. For Israel, jubilee was written on the calendar in ink: every seven years, every fifty years, the old order had to turn over for a fresh start, and no reelections. All debts were cancelled; all captives released. Everyone began again in complete freedom. It was radical reordering, to be sure, and it was disorienting, too; no one would ever be able to do it without practicing long and hard. So the Sabbath became that chance to practice: a mini-jubilee, if you will. By engaging in the discipline (and it *is* a discipline) of rest and release, Israel got a taste, each week, of the extraordinary freedom that was coming and how much faith was required to enact it.

We get a similar taste when we pray the Lord's Prayer: "Forgive us our debts as we forgive our debtors." As far as Scripture is concerned, the existence of debt is reason enough to forgive it.[17] The existence of margins is reason enough to erase them. So everybody participates; everybody stands in need of beginning again. Each of us has both debts and debtors; each of us exists somewhere on the spectrum, either at the margins or nearer the center; each of us gets to practice jubilee and proclaim it: *Be of good cheer. There is a new order coming. Old debts will be forgiven, and old heartaches, forgotten. Old margins will be redrawn, and old powers, emptied. Good news is on its way.* Most preachers have regularly recurring times to preach, to "practice jubilee." But a big family secret, I suspect, is that the weekly rhythm is not the most important part of the *when* of preaching. The most important part is *when people need liberation.* We preach whenever we speak freedom to deep need. We preach whenever we claim the power of speaking our own lives, and God in those lives. There is a whole lot of preaching going on that no one classifies as preaching, and that will continue to happen whenever people need to hear the Word of freedom—as Hutchinson, Osborn, and Lee knew so well.

Jubilee also evokes a sense of joy, and a proclamation of jubilee does no less: it is *joyful* speech. How can it not be when freedom and speech are always possible?! The present order, of course, reckons we will never believe it; the order always bets on power. It does its utmost to drain hope and convince us that nothing will ever change. It builds walls to keep us waiting silently in our places, but here is another big secret: it happens wherever people are hungry for freedom and someone is given a Word of freedom to speak. But "something there is that doesn't love a wall, that wants it down," as Robert Frost observed.[18] That something is the Word, the Word as perfectly open sign. No matter how thick the wall, the Word dreams of freedom and whispers it to the bricks, until orderly rows topple over and light pours through the gaps. Power is no match for liberation, and liberation is God's constant wager. We are part of it when we find new ways of speaking, interpreting, and living, no matter where we are. We anticipate it when we proclaim a Word that never sends laboring women round the back to the stable, claiming with false apologies to be full. We welcome it when our inns always have room for another wayfarer; after all, we know that Christ and angels often go in the strangers' guise. Testimony as a proclamation of jubilee is *women preaching freedom,* men preaching freedom, narrating and confessing their faith in a Word that has been, for them, a perfectly open sign: an embodiment of the perfect freedom found in Jesus Christ.

Testimonial Authority: The Power in Speaking a Different Word

Chopp understands—rightly, I think—that if women are ever to have authority as bearers of proclamation, then they must have *access* to the Word; and if they are to have access to the Word, then they must not be forbidden to speak or represent it; and if they are to speak and represent the Word, the Word itself must be reconceptualized by closer attention to language and politics. We can no longer accept the traditional "masculine" imaging of the Word in terms of mind, law, governance, closure, and order—which is always (of course) depicted over and against the "feminine" images of earth, fluidity, openness, and chaos. Chopp is so convinced of the power of language that she is unshakable on this point: the Word is neither male nor female, but "a perfectly open sign" which is open to *everyone*.

This is a point that may cause some of us to yawn (inclusive language *again?*), but stop and think for a moment. Every culture that consists of males and females has very particular ideas about what it is to be "male" or "female." Those ideas are translated—sometimes forcefully and often intractably—into roles and images and qualities that are defined as "masculine" or "feminine" (so, for example, we go from the *biological* reality that females are mothers who nurture their young to a *cultural* association that links "nurturing" with "femininity"). The trouble comes when we make the mistake of saying that *male = masculine*, forgetting that "masculine" is just a cultural idea, not a biological reality, and that there are actually (obviously!) many different ways to be a man. Real men may, in fact, eat quiche. Real women may be quite good at nurturing or the thought of it may turn their stomachs. We are all amalgams of many different qualities, and thank God for that. As long as we can rise above the labeling that tries to shame us into being (or not being) stereotypically masculine or feminine—*and that incidentally has the fingerprints of an oppressive order all over it*—then we will not be slaves to language and its politics. We can eat our quiche. We can have our babies and read our books and fix our own cars, if we like. We can be, as the classic 1970s children's book put it, "free to be you and me."[19]

Except we aren't; we aren't free at all. Not in this world, with the words it dictates. Language is one of the most powerful tools of an oppressive system, and that is a BIG secret that no one, especially the present order, wants to spill or admit. I know this is a touchy point among us religious types, but please, if you doubt the power language exerts on your life, try, as an experiment, to spend a week addressing

God as "Mother" rather than "Father"; try, as an experiment, behaving in stereotypically masculine (if you are a woman) or feminine (if you are man) ways in public. You won't find it easy, especially if you live in a place where people rarely do these things. In fact, you may even find it dangerous, because oppressive systems are not at all tolerant of those who step beyond the bounds of "acceptable" masculinity and femininity (as any lesbian, gay, bisexual, or transgendered person can tell you) or who address God in "unprescribed" words. Chopp is only repeating what feminists and womanists and liberationists have been saying for years: if the divine is always represented by a particular human group (which is the group in power), then those who are not part of that group will have neither access to God nor authority in the community. The power of language *is* that strong.

Chopp's proposal of "the Word as perfectly open sign" is therefore critical, both for preachers and for preaching. Let me extend the secret further: *preaching will never change without new theologies of proclamation.* We will never revive the pulpit with a few fancy pulpit tricks and new preaching styles. We need theological support that goes as deep as the Word itself, because only a theology of a Word that resists idolatry will resist the idolatries of preaching. Why do we keep returning to Barth if not because of his insistence that the Word can never be a slave to some oppressive order? We do not return to imitate him as a preacher (although some have tried) but to follow his example as a theologian who preached the Word. Preachers who hope to gain access to better preaching are setting themselves up for disappointment. The first thing is to talk about our access to the Word and how such a thing can happen at all.

This is probably why Chopp's work is so shocking for some of us. She claims a theology of proclamation in which women have access to the Word. She also claims that we preachers are most authoritative *not* when we wear our clergy collars and display our degrees and showcase our skills; those signs of authority are granted by the center and so must always be held lightly and with a certain degree of suspicion. No, we preachers are most authoritative when we read our lives as *de*-centered testimony to what the Word of God has done and can do. We are most authoritative when we go marginal and look for God.

Is that not a completely backwards way to talk about a preacher's authority?! *When you are most powerless in the eyes of the world, you have the greatest authority to proclaim. When you are forbidden to represent the Word, you brush closest to its liberating power.* Surely that is a whopping secret that many religious folk would like to keep well covered; the implications (particularly to our ordination battles) are staggering. But the wider cultural implications are as well. Did the woman who registered me for my mammogram think of herself as a hospital worker or a preacher, or both? Did she know the power of her ministry—for me, at least, and I presume for others—to banish the weirdly marginal setting of that waiting room? What sort of ministry might others in our congregations have if "being a disciple" included looking for opportunities to proclaim jubilee? What sort of meaning might we lend to the explosion in Internet communication and testimonial self-expression—much of which, I think, is really a longing for freedom from oppressive systems, even computerized ones— if Internet bloggers, who surely sense the power of speaking one's own life, could grasp the source of that power?

What an extraordinary opportunity we have, as the church: to model testimonial authority by showing how the Word—a perfectly open sign—speaks and moves through human lives.

Testimonial Experience: The Word Goes Marginal and Comes Back Preaching

It is a nice touch (not a planned one; just a gift of the Spirit) that at this point we come round full circle. Chopp's view of experience, of course, has much in common with our three other scholars. Like Ricoeur and Brueggemann, she thinks testimonial experience is not simply a record of everything we have ever done or said, but an *encounter* with God/ Word and our imaginative interpretation of that encounter. Like Fulkerson, she thinks experience is not something we can either essentialize or universalize, but a *way to learn more about the subject herself,* including how that person sees and creates freedom from the margins. But Chopp is also a systematic theologian, which means she is interested in more than just the human subject; she wants to say something, however tentative, about *God.* By coming to experience through a theology of proclamation, she can bridge the various positions—through the act of *preaching.* We might say it like this: experience is what happens when the Word goes marginal and blesses us with the power to speak.

This is really an amazing insight on Chopp's part, because it allows us to do several things at once. We can think about what experience *is*, by focusing on the encounter with God. We can think about what experience *does*, by analyzing how women and men use it to create and even graf(ph)t freedom. Most important, however, we can simultaneously confess what the Word is for us and narrate what it has done with us *without ever taming or owning this Word!*—because God and God's Word resist idolatry in any form. The Word is not something we can predict. It is not something we can make an appointment to meet—at 9:00 a.m. on Tuesday morning, in the pastor's study, for example. It is not the automatic property of any one group, nor is it named or represented by one group. The Word is simply a free and gracious gift of encounter and communion, and it comes even to the most marginal; even to women. And when it comes, *it gives us the power to speak*. The outcome is always proclamation: *preaching*.

I have to say, it makes me think twice about why so many of us were cautioned about how dangerous and inappropriate it is for us to "preach from our own experience" rather than the always acceptable option of "preaching from the text." Clearly there *was* a "text" we were supposed to stick to—the acceptable orthodox interpretation. So *of course* it was dangerous to "preach from our own experience" . . . because that was to admit that our encounters with the Word might challenge or reinterpret our readings of the Word! That was to admit that we might have to reconstruct our prior understandings and golden idols of the Word, including the fact that it always blesses us for speech, for proclamation! And who would ever want to enter that breech?

I do not mean to suggest that the motives of our teachers and elders of yore were evil or insidious; not at all. For me, this is a case of historical hindsight and the wisdom that comes from waking up the details in those museums of books. We can understand why "preaching from experience" was viewed at one time as such a deadly and slippery slope; it shifted the focus from *orthodoxy* to *encounter*. It suggested that God was moving and loose in the world rather than eternally fixed. It challenged every boundary we lived by. It changed the subject of who was speaking and interpreting and, indeed, of who was preaching. Of course it was dangerous to preach from experience. It took our eyes off ourselves. It told us more about God than we wanted to know.

What gave Anne Hutchinson, Sarah Osborn, and Jarena Lee the power to speak? This is a question I have asked myself over and over again, and each scholar in these two chapters has helped me to form a response. Yet there is something about Chopp's theology of proclamation that brings us closest, perhaps, to a response. What gave these women the power to speak was the Word—

a perfectly open sign defying all that the order had taught them;

a Word which, to their utter amazement, encountered them at the margins;

a Word which they could confess and narrate in a testimony of freedom;

a Word which was not about them, but about God-transforming-the-world;

a Word which blessed them to speak . . . and preach.

In a world of such chaos, and in an order that is so oppressively disjunctive, experience has to create its own fire. You need courage if you want to speak a word about God. You need a sense of inevitability that there isn't any other alternative. You need the memory of your encounter with God to burn in you, as hot and bright as the bush that caught Moses' attention—yet was not consumed. The experience is not for the purpose of being consumed or even self-consumed. The experience is for the purpose of *preaching*, because you cannot encounter God and not talk about it.

Summing Up the Secrets

Some Conclusions for Part 2

Many of us preachers, at some juncture, were taught an old sermon form designed to enhance the listeners' retention of the message. It has three steps: you tell the people what you're going to tell them (the introduction), you tell them (the sermon body), and then you tell them what you've told them (the conclusion).

Preachers laugh whenever they talk about this form because it makes us sound like such plodding, one-dimensional idiots, with all the subtlety of a foghorn. I have to admit, however, that the form has its strong points, especially in a longer piece like a book. We can all do with an occasional reminder of where we've been and what we've covered so far.

The theories of testimony in part 2 have led us straight to some of the best-kept secrets of our preaching family. Reading Ricoeur and Brueggemann in chapter 4 has awakened us to these:

1. Preaching does not exist within an absolute interpretive framework. For preachers, there is no such thing as a correct interpretation of a text, and there is no such thing as control over the preaching process.

2. Preaching authority is rooted in testimony. The only evidence of authority is the engagement of the witness. Debates that focus largely on external characteristics of the preacher as a measure of authority are diversionary tactics that keep us from considering a deeper testimonial authority.

3. The resistance to "preaching from human experience" is a reluctance to deal with testimony as a hermeneutic and homiletic.

4. Our biblical heritage, as evidenced in our "mother tongue" of testimony and countertestimony, is a language of marginal resistance. That is not appealing to those who wish to gain more access to centers of power, or who already have it.

5. As a location, exile—or life at the margins—has its own gifts. It gives us deeper access to testimonial authority rather than false authority rooted in power. The "decline" of the mainstream church is actually something to celebrate.

6. The only way to silence a witness is by the taking of a life. But killing the witness does not kill the testimony. Testimonies can live on in the community. They can continue to resist the authorities that want to silence them.

And reading Fulkerson and Chopp in chapter 5 has awakened us to these secrets, as well:

1. Preaching is not just proclaiming good news; it is *making* good news, right here and now. The proclamation creates something.

2. You cannot identify a preacher by external things (her "cover"). You can only tell a preacher by her words and whether they create good news for these people, here, today.

3. In the same vein, you cannot identify a heresy or "deviant interpretation" by external things. A careful consideration of the subject and his words will often show us how "deviant" interpretations of biblical texts graf(ph)t good news onto oppressive interpretations, and that they do so in good faith and wisdom.

This ought to make us extremely careful when passing judgment on other preachers.

4. The goal of preaching is not consensus (the listener agreeing with the preacher). The goal of preaching is conversion—the *preacher's* conversion. The preacher models conversion by engaging the text at a deeper level ("living in it") in order to be formed by it (or by the Other, which is God).

5. Preaching will never change without serious engagement with the Word through theologies of proclamation. This includes theories of language.

6. You cannot tell a sermon on the basis of location or timing alone. Preaching happens *whenever* and *wherever* people are hungry for freedom. That may be in a church sanctuary on a Sunday morning, or it may not.

7. Still, the regular and repeated practice of preaching—every Sunday morning, for example—is important for preachers and congregations. It gives them regular experience with proclaiming jubilee so that they will recognize a *whenever* and *wherever* moment when it comes and stand ready.

8. The regular and repeated practice of dislocation is also important. The Word appears to have a distinct preference for encountering those on the margins who are hungry for freedom. When preparing sermons, preachers who do not know themselves to be marginal have to "go marginal." They have to plant their bodies in places where they and others are in need of liberation.

9. Preachers have the greatest authority to proclaim when they are most powerless and marginal in the eyes of the world. They brush closest to the liberating power of the Word when they are forbidden to represent it.

10. Everyone in the faith community is included in the call to preach *whenever* and *wherever* there is hunger for freedom. Everyone in the faith community is capable of proclaiming jubilee, either in the pulpit or out in the world. Our stories of encountering God are meant to be shared and *must* be shared. They must be preached. That is what the encounters are for.

What do you do next, after you wake up the secrets?
You wake up the preacher.

PART 3

Waking Up the Preacher: Practicing Testimony

I am a woman sixty years old of no special courage . . .
I am a woman sixty years old, and glory is my work.
— Mary Oliver, *The Leaf and the Cloud*[1]

Becoming a Preacher

Some Words to Begin Part 3

Testimony is . . .
A way of interpreting.
A way of knowing.
A way of speaking.
A way of preaching.
It is our Christian hermeneutic.
Our biblical mother-tongue.
Our only access to authority.
Our best mode of resistance.
It converts us, dislocates us, empowers us, liberates us.
It exposes our secrets, our preachers, our systems.
Testimony is . . . preaching the Word we have seen and believed.
Three chapters of history, two chapters of theory, and if you are anything like me, you are so steeped in testimony that by now even your eyebrows could preach. It is time for the "So What and Why Should I

Care?" chapter, as the teenaged practical theologians among us might aptly paraphrase. I will get straight to the point.

Testimony is what a preacher has left when everything else is gone. When all the searches for absolutes (the right texts, words, interpretations, techniques, sources, authorities) come up empty, and the preacher has nothing left to fill and empower and sustain her, then the preacher is finally ready to do the work of *becoming a preacher,* which happens with testimony. The work of becoming a preacher is seeing and believing that there is nothing that can separate you from God or protect you from God, and from what God's Word will do when it is spoken and heard—and then *saying it.* The work of becoming a preacher is living and preaching text and life, not as a response to fear but as testimony to God's freedom.

Perhaps this sounds like a lot of ivory-tower absurdity to you, as if "becoming a preacher" were the homiletical equivalent of reaching nirvana; let me assure that it is not. At the same time, I believe we preachers do not always set a very high bar for ourselves in terms of our preaching goals, or take the time to think through what those goals really say about us theologically. If we are primarily concerned with becoming more effective communicators—whether that means being clearer or cleverer, or more down-to-earth or creative—we subtly change the subject of our preaching to ourselves rather than the God we meet in the text. Yet one of the most magnificent things about testimony is how we are already hard-wired as Christians to speak it and live it. Testimony is structured into the text and into our very bones.

It is not so remote an ideal as we might think. Even the loftiest homiletical paths intersect it. Even the greenest, most inexperienced preachers recognize it. Even the fairest-of-them-all pulpit princes and princesses come around to it. Preaching in the tradition and pattern of testimony is always a choice that is available to us. Or maybe it would be more accurate to change the subject here and admit that it usually feels like the reverse: *testimony* chooses *us.*

And some of us take longer to realize this than others.

6

The Wide-awake Preacher

Living into the Tradition

In the introduction to this book, I shared a bit about how I came to be interested in testimony as a subject. An important addendum to that story is that when I first stumbled onto testimony and these histories of preaching women, I thought I had found the Golden Fleece: a dissertation topic *and* the long-lost key to my own preaching identity in one! What could be better?! Testimony looked like the answer to everything that ailed me as a developing scholar and preacher. Happily, I settled down to work—only to find that *it* was working *me*.

Critical distance is the first rule of academic survival, but I doubt I am the only one who finds it impossible to study a thing and remain unaffected by it. If, for example, you are going about your scholarly business and happen to bump into a historical vault (containing, shall we say, centuries of preaching women) that has been deliberately hidden, *anger* would seem to be a normal reaction. For my part, I was hopping mad. It struck me as a personal affront that I had never known these women existed, never heard their stories, never believed I was part of any tradition, never known the truth about the preaching women I came from. Clearly, my very identity had been compromised and possibly stunted: *If only I had known, surely I would be a different person! I would be braver, stronger, wiser, more self-assured! I would be a better person and a better preacher!*

I fumed for a while. There was a period of seething if-onlys, followed by a brooding melancholia that was hard to shake, mostly because the if-onlys had a point. I *would* be a different person if I had known about a woman's preaching tradition. I *would* be wiser if I had been given historical perspective and role models. I might even be a better person and a better preacher, but who could ever know? Who could say?

No one can brood forever, and I am here to tell you that if-onlys make terrible houseguests. Eventually you have to quit obsessing about conspiracy theories and what might have been and focus on what is. So one day I stopped reading these women's lives as the absolute missing link to *my* life (which, incidentally, had been a very convenient way to read them, since being deprived of my own history would certainly explain anything that went wrong in my life) and changed the subject. I looked at the women themselves instead of the woman I wasn't. I paid attention to the wisdom they showed me rather than the wisdom I had been denied. And suddenly, I saw: *I knew these women.* I may have been ignorant of the historical details, but I knew their lives. I knew what they faced, every time they got up to preach. I knew how hard it was, in every sermon, to keep spending it all without spewing it all. I knew why preaching thrilled them and exasperated them and would not let them go. In fact, you might say that when I finally changed the subject and stopped thinking of *them* in terms of *me*, I came to myself at last. I recognized patterns. I saw logic. These women and I, centuries apart, had had to learn the same thing: you cannot rely on others to make you a preacher. You cannot preach the text if you are trying to prove that you *can* preach the text. You have to change the subject and testify for yourself.

This insight gave me an important hermeneutic, or a lens, for understanding my own preaching life. Looking back, I realized how many years I *did* think that others could make me a preacher, and that they *would* if I did the right things. Ordination, for instance: it had seemed logical to assume that becoming a preacher was a by-product of that mysterious rite, the culmination of years of preparation. As soon as I was officially ordained, I told myself, *then* I would become a preacher—but the logic didn't hold. All the external things (a degree, a title, a job, an office, a clerical collar, a robe, a parking place at the hospital) were signs of my new authority, but they hardly granted it themselves; being ordained did not *make* me a preacher. This was abundantly evident every time I stepped into a pulpit and realized that my femaleness apparently trumped and even nullified all other signs as far as my skeptical listeners were concerned. (I like how the wise-cracking Reverend Geraldine Granger—a.k.a. "The Vicar of Dibley" from the BBC comedy series—sagely put it the first time she met her shocked parishioners:

"I know. You were expecting a bloke with bad breath and a Bible, and instead, you got a babe with a bob cut and magnificent bosoms.")[1]

If being officially ordained wouldn't make me a preacher, as it seemed to do for my male colleagues (including my ordained spouse), I wrote it off as an inevitable side-effect of breaking into a male profession: what could I expect, if I was still a pioneer in the field? This was the women's movement, I reasoned; this was what I signed on for, what we all signed on for. So I tried another approach: I consented to the rules of *more*. I worked harder, longer, faster, because obviously the way for a woman to become a preacher was to become a *good* preacher. I would have to be good enough to convince skeptics that women could preach as well as men did. I would have to be *so* good that they forgot I was a woman in the first place. Of course, there was a fatal flaw in this logic, too: my authority was now determined by others' perception of my performance, what *they* thought about *me*. Yet whenever the verdict came back that the sermon was "good," I didn't feel any closer to becoming a preacher in any identifiable way. The only thing *I* was becoming was identifiably anxious. I also had the distinct and painful sensation that every time I got up to preach, I was leaving parts of myself behind. In Harry Potter lingo, the term for that is *splinching*, "the separation of random body parts," and it occurs when the wizard-in-transit loses focus and concentration and inadvertently leaves a leg or an ear behind.[2] Splinching is not pretty to watch or to experience. When moving from one place to the other, the goal is to arrive whole and intact; no one wants to lose heart or mind or guts on the way to the pulpit. No one wants to be a generic talking head.

Two attempts to make it in the system on the system's terms; two strikes. My female colleagues could resonate, but interestingly enough, my male colleagues could, too. Some of them were beginning to realize that all the external sources of authority, so quickly granted them as men, had not automatically made them the preachers they hoped to be. Just because they had the power to speak didn't mean that what they said ever amounted to anything; in fact, to their chagrin, it often didn't. They were surviving by faking it, by hiding behind the façade of preacher. Months went by when they never said a word they truly believed themselves. They were dead preachers walking, but the most devastating thing was that nobody seemed to notice. Nobody seemed to care or hold them accountable. In workshops, I would hear these men joking about burn-out and workaholism. They would tell me they wanted to "revitalize their preaching" with whatever new-fangled stuff we were teaching at the seminary, but in their faces I could see the last-ditch effort to survive under the old system (*more* skills = better preacher). With a little *more*, maybe they could stop faking it and become the preacher they always knew they could be. If not . . . well, they would have to quit and do something else.

It finally hit me that we were all caught in the same vise, my anxious colleagues and I. Preaching was splinching us. It was showing us exactly how bankrupt and divisive the system was. It was showing us exactly how bankrupt and divided *we* were, deep inside. We could not go on proclaiming a Word of freedom if our experience was only one of slavery. We could not preach liberation if we no longer knew the liberating power of God for ourselves. The disconnect between what we said and what we lived was happening before our very eyes and in our very bodies; we were splinching ourselves right and left, and could barely locate our missing parts. Before the disease spread to our communities (God forbid) in the form of a preacher who was cracking up, acting out, or otherwise losing it, we had to do something, which really meant we had to *stop* doing something. We had to stop our endless searching for the fountain of authority. We had to give up the dream of the good preacher. Basically, we had to shut up for a while, be very still, and exercise our senses. Preaching had shown us how disconnected we were, from Scripture and from ourselves; now we had to watch and wait for God to appear and show us a way of becoming whole.

When we were little, my brother and I used to complain about waiting. Our mother told us that if we brought a book wherever we went, we wouldn't have to wait; we could read, instead. The lesson stuck. I still think the text is a good place to sit down when time feels heavy and there is nothing you can do to hurry things along.

WAITING FOR WORD

Annunciation

In Scripture, there are moments of truth that happen from time to time when God breaks into the story with a news flash, or appears with some divine update that helps to move the story along. The annunciations to Zechariah and Mary at the beginning of Luke's Gospel are good examples: each features an angel bearing some rather extraordinary news that most people would find ethically difficult, if not biologically impossible, to believe. For Zechariah, the word is that his elderly wife, in direct violation of the laws of infertility and menopause, is about to become pregnant. For Mary, the word is that she, in direct violation of the laws of Moses and high school Health class, is also about to become pregnant—with the son of God.

Zechariah and Mary are not at all sure what to make of these "moments of truth." Each asks the angel a question, but a very different sort of question. Zechariah asks, "How will I know this?" (Luke 1:18)—and gets zapped with a mute curse that will render him unable to speak until his son is born. On the surface, this seems odd: why should the angel take offense, when Zechariah is only asking for a sign to prove the angel's words? *That is exactly the point.* There *is* no proof for an annunciation. When God breaks in, the only thing you can do is believe it or not. You cannot ask for a receipt of the transaction or a sign to convince the dubious. God does not offer to cover your backside. Zechariah, however, would very much like some divine cover of his priestly backside when he conveys the news that old Elizabeth is in the family way. Without proof, he is uneasy, and his question reflects that precisely. "How will I know this?" is not about the in-breaking; it is about *him.* It is about his need for external authority. It is a question that reveals exactly how preoccupied Zechariah is with his own power, rather than that of the in-breaking Almighty. And the angel has an immediate remedy for the old priest's lapse: Zechariah will have to shut up and watch, for nine months, until he gets the message that proof has no place in preaching. You cannot preach God's Word without putting your own word, unprotected, on the line.

Mary's question is entirely different. She asks the angel, "How can this be?" (Luke 1:34). It is not a question about *her;* it is a question about the event itself and the all-powerful One who will bring it to pass: *How?!* The angel is laughably vague in response, as if mortified by Mary's directness (*How . . . if I am not having sex?!*). He cannot answer without resorting to euphemisms: "The Holy Spirit will . . . *overshadow* you." (Luke 1:35; emphasis added), but Mary seems to accept that it is difficult to describe exactly what is about to happen to her. She gets the message: *Honey, this is going to be impossible to explain, and if I can't do it, you won't be able to, either.* Some things are just beyond words. God breaks in; God overshadows. What else can you say, when the Word becomes flesh? Mary accepts this. Even better, she believes, and agrees to host the Word, as her extraordinary response makes clear: "Here I am, the servant of the Lord; let it be with me according to your word"

(Luke 1:38). For a girl who is about to be as unprotected as it gets in a society that sanctions stoning, this is astonishing. Who is going to need proof of her story more urgently than Mary? Zechariah's annunciation merely threatens his good name; Mary's threatens her *life*! When she tells her story, there is no way she will be able to reconcile her community's ideal of the good girl with her own experience of God! Yet she understands that there can be no proof that convinces in this case. There can be no fountain of authority that satisfies, absolutely. The only thing she can do is to let it happen to her, let the Word happen to her. Let the text overshadow her and come alive in her. *All right, then. Bring it on.*

Mary's words are preachers' words. When the search comes up empty, when the authority sources run dry, when the dream of the good preacher and the good girl dissolve, what is left but God's annunciation? God breaks into human life; we have seen it, time and again. Sooner or later, God will break into our experience and pause for our response: *How will I know this?* (the Zechariah Preacher), or *How can this be?* (the Mary Preacher).

The Zechariah Preacher focuses on proof. *How will I know this? How can I be sure? Who will back me up if I say it and no one believes me? And if it turns out that I was wrong, who will cover my backside?* Zechariah Preachers come to the text looking for orthodox interpretations, and they need to be right. They want certainty, absolutes, answers, explanations; they want proof texts. If they cannot find those things, they fear they will not be real preachers—or *good* ones, at any rate. Actually, the truth is that they will not be preachers, period. The text does not take orders, especially from humans; inevitably the day will come when it refuses to give them what they want. Things fall apart; splinching happens. The Zechariah Preacher will run out of certainty, run out of authority, and run out of words.

The Mary Preacher, on the other hand, focuses on the event, the in-breaking of God into human life and experience. Mary Preachers want to know *how*, but it is a different kind of *how*: *How can this be? How can God do these things? How will God bring it about?* Mary Preachers are curious about details because the text is fuzzy on details and no more forthcoming than it ever has been since Moses asked the burning bush for some ID. *Who? "I AM WHO I AM." How? "Overshadowing."* Asking for details, however, is not the same as asking for clarity, and Mary Preachers know the difference. They know the text itself is unclear for a good reason: it moves and shifts, resists closure, provokes new insights and then changes its mind, so that we cannot ever solve it definitively. This text refuses to be an idol. You cannot predict what it will do or explain what it does, but you *can* wait to see what happens next. You can become a witness to the event. And so Mary Preachers give up their innocent bystander status and agree to join in: *All right, then. Bring it on.* Let this Word happen to me. Let this text get inside me. Let it do its work, and I will tell you what I experienced. Let it be with me according to your Word.

Of course, there is this little matter of stoning.

The Logic of *Leiros*

Testimony elicits strong reactions. No sooner do you say, "Bring it on!" to the angel in your living room when an angry crowd appears in the village square outside, some of whom (you can practically count on this) will be brandishing stones or employment contracts. The Word is disruptive by nature; it threatens everyone in sight. People will be upset. Even those we love will be upset. We preachers have to come to terms with this, or we will spend our lives thinking that the anger is *always about us*—when that is not exactly true. Those angry little clouds of smoke are signs of the System's fear; they mark a spot where the Word has hit home and gone deep. It helps to remember that there is a pattern to this rejection, and even a peculiar and beautiful logic: the logic of *leiros*.

I have already said that if we were to chart it, testimony is the move from *He is risen!* (the Word) to *I have seen the Lord!* (our narration and confession of that Word), which is what Mary Magdalene announces in her testimony to the disciples on Easter morning (John 20:18). But to go the next step to *how testimony is received,* Luke's version of the same story gives us a better example. Early on Easter morning, as Luke tells it, the women go to the tomb, find it empty, hear the news about Jesus from the two dazzling men, and run back to tell the disciples: *He is risen!* Note well: the women do not make this announcement to perfect strangers. They do not rush out into the streets, shrieking the news to anyone in earshot. No, they save it for the ones who know them best and love them most: their own faith community. They save it for *family.* Who else would ever put two and two together, remembering all those Isaiah quotations about the Suffering Servant and Jesus' own predictions about his death and resurrection?! Yes, this story is pretty unbelievable, but it is not beyond the scope of the text itself, or of Jesus himself. The women have reason to expect that the disciples, their brothers in the faith, will at least *try* to believe them.

Alas. The disciples, I am sorry to tell you, are not as receptive to this news as we might have hoped. In fact, they are less than supportive. You might even say that for one wildly out-of-character moment, they forget their disciple manners and resort to the subtle cadences of a high school locker room: *Yeah? Well, that sounds like a load of ~!@#$?%^&!* to me* (Luke 24:11). Translators of Luke have clearly tried to play this down, with such game attempts as "These things seemed to them [the disciples] an *idle tale*, and they did not believe them" (RSV). But the Greek word in question is *leiros*, which means "nonsense," "drivel," "trash," "garbage," "crap," "bull," or, in its more vulgar form, "~!@#$?%^&!*." No matter how you spin it, *leiros* is just a locker-room word, a wet towel whipping through a chorus of jeers. Until adolescent boys start accusing each other of being full of *idle tales*, a more faithful translation would probably be "These things seemed to them like a lot of *nonsense* . . . a lot of *garbage* . . . a lot of *bull*," although you could obviously take the accuracy to much cruder levels. Furthermore, as if to underscore its shock value, *leiros* does not appear anywhere else in the New Testament, which suggests to me that Luke intends for it to make a strong impact on us. And it does, by actually inverting the narrative: instead of the women's testimony shocking the disciples, the disciples' response shocks *us*. Wait a minute—this is not how friends treat one another! This is not how friends receive one another's testimony! This is not how the church reacts to its own preachers . . . is it?!

Well . . . yes. It is.

The logic of leiros *is that our testimony will be heard as a lot of nonsense, even from the ones who know us and love Jesus most.* The gospel has always met with ridicule, right from the very first time it was preached. It has always sounded like a lot of *leiros*. It has always been more than the church can handle, even when it is the very thing the church prays for; not even the disciples, as much as they loved Jesus, could take the good news. They flung it back in the women's faces—and to be rejected by your closest friends, as Jesus might attest, is a crucifixion of another kind. When the people you love do not believe you, it kills the trust between you (*If you do not believe my story, then you are really saying you do not believe me!*). We are right back to the issue of engagement, which is the only proof a witness can offer, and the very thing that may break his heart and cost him his life.

On the other hand (and here is where the logic of *leiros* gets *really* infuriating, if you ask me), it isn't so hard to imagine why the disciples might be suspicious of the women's story. Maybe they were scared of resurrection. Maybe they were scared of *Jesus'* resurrection, after their behavior that weekend. Maybe they were terrified of preaching a gospel of inversion without a shred of proof. We could speculate on and on, because there are a million good reasons for yelling *leiros*, and they all make sense—more sense than the gospel, we might add.[3] But the logic of *leiros* is not about having good reasons; it is about having access to the Word. *Our testimony will be rejected, but it will also linger, because the hearers have to go and experience for themselves.*

Look at what transpires in the very next verse: "But Peter got up and ran to the tomb; stooping and looking in, he saw the linen cloths by themselves; then he went home, amazed at what had happened" (Luke 24:12). No matter how the disciples responded en masse, at least one of them has not completely dismissed the women's story; Peter, for his own reasons, decides to check out the scene for himself. He finds it just as the women had said. He does not, however, have the same *experience* that they do: no dazzling men, no divine updates. Testimony does not come with a rewind button so that we can duplicate another's experiences or absolutely confirm or refute their stories. Testimony merely sets something in motion, which is the impulse to go and see for ourselves—and Peter does. He sees enough to know that something has happened, something big. He may not be sure about it yet; he doesn't come home ready to testify, but he isn't whistling "*leiros*," either. The women's testimony opens up a space for possibilities, and Peter makes his way back to the community, wondering.

Eventually, we know, he will do more than wonder. But how would he ever have gone to the tomb himself, and why, if a preacher had not brought him the news?

PASSING IT DOWN

Preaching beyond Fear

The things that are most important to us—faith, wisdom, traditions, stories, languages—we pass down to our children, hoping that what we have lived and believed will somehow give life to them. This is how I have come to think about the preacher's role: as one who passes down a set of traditions about one way God's people read, speak, live in, and wait for the Word.

Not so long ago, if you had asked me what preaching traditions I would choose to pass down, I would have had trouble answering. It wasn't that I had stopped believing in my field, my mentors, or the wealth of wisdom available to me in colleagues and books. It was that I was unable to put all these pieces together in one body (mine), which made the thought of trying to put them together in anyone *else's* body a little ridiculous. How can you teach preaching until you have figured out what your own preaching teaches and whether it is actually viable for you, let alone others? (Note to self: if an examination of your preaching reveals a homiletic based on fear—evidenced, perhaps, in an abundance of strikeouts and splinching—you are in trouble, big time.) For me, the day came when I was tired of anxiety, tired of fear, and ready to change the subject. I sat down and waited for word, however it might come.

And it did; word, and even Word, came. It came from many sources. Some of them I have written about in this book; others are written into my life. They pointed to *testimony*, and testimony pointed to a preaching tradition, and before I knew it, all the issues I used to worry about had simply fallen away. All the fears that came between me and the sermon ("Can I really say that?") and pitted me against my listeners ("They will never accept this!") were gone. I was left alone with my people and the Word. I was free to be with them both, as deep into it as I dared. Nothing held me back anymore—but here is the thing: *nothing ever really had.*

I have come to believe that the fear that holds us preachers captive is an invention of the System, the Deceiver, the Powers and Principalities—whatever we choose to call that force, it is real and at work in the world. I think fear is intended to keep us and the Word apart. When fear succeeds in terrorizing and silencing us ("Are you crazy?! You'll get yourself killed if you say that!"), it also succeeds in its aim, which is to shift our gaze away from the Word and change the subject back to the preacher herself. It is a little trick with mirrors, nothing more—but it unnerves me to think how deadly and effective it is. Fear is a foil, but a clever one. It distracts us with our own reflections. If it can divert our attention with loud and insistent "threats" to the church and to our preaching, it will indeed tap into our fears, start the anxiety pumping, and make us lose sight of the power of the Word.

Testimony, in contrast, is the narration and confession of what we know and believe, which is that *nothing, not even fear, can separate us from the love of God.* Testimony is the opposite of fear-based preaching. It is confession based and experience fueled; it is a Word of liberation spoken in the face of fear. It is true speech that creates life, even at the margins. Testimony reassures us that fear is the System's favorite weapon, but groundless, and therefore powerless—as long as we do not fear the fear itself. Is it any wonder, then, that as a preaching tradition, testimony has been so neglected and subverted? How close to the Word it must bring us! And how dangerous *that* is, and always has been, in the eyes of the System!

In the months that I have been writing this book, the national forecast has been bleak, indeed. My country is at war. My denomination is in crisis. Every day I read of more "threats" to my security, my safety, my church, my financial solvency, my interpretive freedom, my rights, my body, and so on. To hear the press tell it, everything dear to me is in danger of collapsing because "they" and I have irreconcilable differences, "their" interests are counter to my own, "they" want to take over whatever it is I have and believe, and shape me in "their" image. Recently I have begun to wonder: who are "they," anyway?! Terrorists? People from other nations? People from other faith traditions? People from other denominations? People who disagree with me? People who read Scripture differently than I do, or think differently, or vote differently, or simply look different? Is *that* why "they" are such a threat to me—the fact that "they" are different?

As a preaching tradition, testimony is the enemy of "they." It does not allow "they" to exist as the System's henchman. Testimony insists that difference, conflict, mess, and uncertainty are part of life and faith; it insists that we tell one another the truth about this. Yet testimony also insists that difference and conflict, mess and uncertainty are no reasons to be afraid! None of these is a "threat" to us; none of these can separate us from God, as the System and Deceiver would have us believe. Testimony banishes those fabricated fears, compelling us to come together so that we each can tell and confess the power of God in our lives. It gives us the unbelievable grace of changing the subject—from ourselves, to the Word moving in another's life. It supplies us with the tools to deal with our own fear, so that we do not have to keep passing it down, from one generation to another.

I have begun to wonder if the dire warnings about cultural shifts, all of which (we are told) will require urgent and substantial changes to our preaching, are not also serving the System's purposes. Every year brings a new crop of books in which well-meaning authors gallop through the countryside, warning us of invasions (*Look out! The Gen X-ers are coming! The Fundamentalists are coming!—and the biblically illiterate are right on their heels!*) and offering strategies for how to cope by making our preaching *more* this and *more* that. These authors have a point: we can all do a better job of really knowing and seeing who our listeners are. But I am concerned, frankly, that all the warnings to change our preaching might be functioning as bids to bring the preacher in line with the System's values. A preacher who succumbs to the constant pressure to be "more entertaining," or "more relevant," or even "more biblical" (in the myriad of ways *that* phrase gets tossed around), eventually communicates that *unless it is entertaining, it is not gospel; unless it meets my needs, it is not good news; unless it is in my words, it is not Word.* The shift is profound and toxic, for his listeners and himself. Without even realizing it, and for the best of intentions, the preacher has slowly but surely changed the subject from the Word to *his* words, draining his preaching of any power—which is exactly what the System wants. The "threat" has succeeded in keeping preacher and Word apart, and fear claims the life of another preacher.

Fear-based preaching takes many forms. It slips into legitimate debates and infects them with the "threat" virus. It turns everyday challenges into code-red emergencies. It twists simple questions into fearful ones, so that we forget how normal it is to be imperfect, uncertain, broken—*human.* Like the serpent in the Garden of Eden, it manages to convince us that wherever we are and whatever we have is not enough, and never will be, until we have access to what is God's alone. I have noticed how fear insinuates itself into preaching discussions, couched as various "threats" to the church and its ministry. The "threat" then sets up a false dichotomy, which forces us to choose between our fear and our testimony. When preachers accept the threat as real, they take the bait, and get hooked into fear-based preaching—and oh, how shiny those lures are in the water!

To illustrate how fear-based preaching takes root, here are three typical examples—System standbys, apparently, since we keep falling for them. Each begins with an issue common to life in the faith community (how will we teach the Bible to our children? How do we interpret the biblical text in this community? How do we share our faith with others and invite them to join us?) but quickly escalates from open discussion to code-orange-level anxiety as the "issue" is recast as a "threat" to the community's security. Once fear takes root, discussion breaks down and the community becomes prey to wolfish absolutes in sheep's clothing. The pattern is a sadly familiar one, as the following examples show. I have dubbed them a fear of flying, a fear of failing, and a fear of fighting.

Fear of Flying: "Biblical Illiteracy" vs. a Love of Reading

There was a time, we are told, when preachers could open their Bibles to Genesis 33 and pick up the story of Jacob (who, as we *all know,* is about to wrestle with God and conscience on the eve of his reunion with his estranged brother Esau), confident that their listeners were tracking with them. No more. We are told that "biblical illiteracy" affects most congregations, in one form or another; preachers today can no longer assume that their listeners have even a rudimentary knowledge of the Scriptures, let alone the wherewithal to recognize who Jacob (or Moses or Mary) is. Obviously, this complicates things a bit. Our sermons have to make a lot of introductions and cover a lot of plot summaries. They have to get people up to speed, biblically and theologically, so that listeners don't feel as if they have dropped into the middle of a conversation with no clue as to what is happening. Meanwhile, pastors lament that their people do not ever read the Bible and that no one seems to be interested at all in attending Bible studies. Add to this the falling numbers in Sunday school attendance, and we can be reasonably sure that current trends will continue: more and more people are growing up without ever having heard the Bible stories some of us once took for granted.

Having said all that, I would like to back up and ask a different question. I wonder if the problem we face is really biblical illiteracy at all.

When a child learns to read in school, there is a great deal of practice involved, with drills in everything from phonics to spelling. Barring any preventative learning disabilities, most children successfully master the skill of reading in a few years. But just because a child *can* read does not guarantee that he actually *will.* Nowadays, parents are told that one of the most important things they can do for their children is to instill a *love of reading,* which is a very different thing from teaching the mechanics of reading. Schools, pediatricians, and even the backs of cereal boxes encourage parents to read to their children, to make that time of reading together a warm and pleasurable ritual, to create a home atmosphere in which children observe adults reading for enjoyment. These influences, we are told, are far more important than an endless supply of phonics workbooks. A child who associates reading with the cozy ritual of a bedtime story, cuddled up next to someone who cares for her, learns that reading is something you do with people you love; that books are filled with stories that can take her to exciting new places; that those stories are told in words she can understand and pictures she can follow; that until she is older and learns to decipher the funny black scratch marks for herself, someone else will gladly read them for her; that *not* understanding those marks is nothing to be ashamed of and that *learning to read for herself* is something wonderful to look forward to—as wonderful as learning to fly.

I do not believe that the real problem (or "threat") facing the church is "biblical illiteracy," in the sense of not knowing the biblical text itself. I think the System has used it to distract us from something much worse: an environment that does not encourage people to read at all. We have been duped into thinking that the issue is Bible drills instead of instilling a *love of reading the Bible.* We have been scared into sharing information about the text instead of our passion for it. And then, when our people cannot identify which disciple denied Jesus three times, we scowl and shake our heads—which is a little like shaming a three-year-old for not knowing her prepositions. We haven't shown our people flight; we have only shown them our fear of flying, which is anything but motivating and far from inspirational. Is it any wonder that our earthbound churches suffer from a lack of imagination?!

I suspect that the solution is not to offer more and more Bible studies. There is a prior task, which is to show our people our own love for reading Scripture. We have to communicate to them, through many different reading rituals, that the act of reading the biblical text is something wonderful and liberating (like *flying!*) that each of us can and will learn to do (fear not!). We have to create a loving and supportive atmosphere in which readers do not shame nonreaders for skills they have not yet learned or interests they have not yet developed. We have to have faith that the repetition of these reading-together rituals (such as weekly preaching) is doing the slow work of nurturing a love of reading. And then, when our people are up and flying on their own, we have to keep encouraging them by making sure our own preaching (among other rituals) continues to engage and challenge them. No one hands a kindergartner a copy of *War and Peace* or expects him to still be satisfied with *Green Eggs and Ham* when he is sixteen.

It strikes me that we preachers actually have a lot to gain from the "threat" of biblical illiteracy, and that perhaps we haven't fully come to terms with the advantages it gives us. Think about it: if we are the only readers in our communities, then we get to call the shots. We get to interpret as we see fit. We get to filter doctrine through our own readings of the biblical text. In short, we hold a lot of power—but it is not the Word's power. It is the System's power, which eats its own. As soon as we begin to anxiously measure Christian commitment and "literacy" in terms of Bible trivia, it isn't long until our sermons become games of Trivial Pursuit, so that what begins as a well-intentioned effort to raise literacy levels has ended up killing our own proclamation.

If, however, we try to instill a love of reading the biblical text, we are ensuring the eventual sharing of power—the Word's power. Our people will learn to read for themselves, looking for the Word of freedom in the text and in their lives. They will read not because they have to but because they love to. It is really such a simple shift to make. If we communicate that the act of reading and interpreting the Bible requires some special skills, yes, but *not* specialized degrees, we empower them to learn with confidence. If we communicate our happy expectation that the day will come when they will want to read on their own as part of the community, then we do away with false hierarchies that pit "readers" against "nonreaders." It is risky business, to be sure; once we are all readers, we all have a say in what we are reading and where we are flying. Anything can happen. But isn't that exactly the kind of freedom we hope for from the gospel? If none of us is afraid of flying, then there is nothing to keep us from soaring straight toward the realm of God.

One important footnote: this is not to say that the preacher, as someone who has likely been trained, educated, and/or set apart for a specialized role in the community, has nothing left to offer once the community learns to read on its own. We live in a culture of time restraints that force each of us to choose specializations for the good of the whole. Plumbers and accountants handle different sets of problems, and as one preacher put it, "When I need brain surgery, I want a brain surgeon to do it."[4] Preachers have a definite field of expertise to offer, with all kinds of scriptural knowledge that others will not necessarily have had the time to acquire. But there is a difference between being an expert who dispenses and an expert who engages. Preachers, I believe, are resources of engagement for their congregations. At their best, they are profound conversation partners and awesome flying teachers. Preachers in the testimony tradition pass down a love for God's Word, a growing maturity in the reading of and living in that Word, and a few snappy flying maneuvers (just for fun).

Fear of Failing: "Being Told" vs. Being Seen

The rise of religious fundamentalism has touched off all kinds of warning signals, and for good reason: whenever a system sets itself up as a rigid collection of absolutes, there is definitely cause for concern. History shows us that the clamor for truth at all costs usually leads to violence, and recent events have not done much to dispel that theory. Moreover, since we know that fundamentalism finds expression across all religious traditions, it would seem that no single nation or people is immune to or exempt from its effects. Interdisciplinary and interfaith studies of fundamentalism are probably imperative to the survival of our planet.

When the topic of religious fundamentalism comes up in my conversation circles, it is almost always cast as a "they" issue. *We* are open-minded; *they* are close-minded. *We* value education; *they* are suspicious of it. *We* read the Bible critically; *they* read it as the inerrant Word of God. *We* have diversity and pluralism; *they* have uniformity and rigid intolerance. *We* are postmodern; *they* are prehistoric. *We* are faithful. *They* are fanatics—which is clarifying, but hardly comforting, since *our* churches are shrinking while *theirs* are exploding.

What concerns me about *they* language is that it is code for stereotyping, which is absolutist behavior in itself. In other words: while it is certainly true that fundamentalist churches are increasing and mainline churches are decreasing, and while there are clearly many questions to ask about why and how this has happened, the situation itself is not necessarily a threatening one; it does not mean that one group is succeeding while the other is failing miserably. We have simply *interpreted* it that way; we have chosen to measure success in terms of numbers. We have also agreed to see *their* success as *our* failure, which creates an adversarial relationship as well as an environment of hostility and scarcity. The two traditions are now pitted against one another, unable to see one another clearly for the stereotypes that fly between them. They are competing for members, competing for truth, competing to *win* . . . but to win what, and on whose terms?

I suspect that the System has put its own spin on the number discrepancies in order to play on our fears of failure. If we can be convinced that success is measured by big numbers, then we will naturally evaluate preachers by how many people come to listen to them. We will assume that worship attendance is the key statistic. Low numbers will indicate a preacher who is doing a terrible job; high numbers (and listener satisfaction!) will mean that the preacher is succeeding. The "losing" church will also be driven to adopt some of the "winning" church's preaching strategies, such as offering more closed answers, more universal explanations, and very little interpretive wiggle room. The "losing" church will feel pressure to act like the "competition," since *they* obviously have a better handle on cultural realities; *they* know that life is now so stressful and complex that listeners yearn for absolute clarity in sermons. *We* (the failing ones) therefore need to imitate *them* (the succeeding ones) by preaching sermons that tell people how to succeed, both spiritually and materially. A good sermon will be marked by how directive it is: it must feature *being told* what to believe, think, and do.

I do not deny our human desire for clarity and answers, or dispute the tendency for stressed-out persons and cultures to be less tolerant of ambiguity and uncertainty. But I also firmly believe that the "reality" we are being presented with—that success equals big numbers and successful preaching equals big numbers of happy listeners—is totally rigged. It has the System's fingerprints all over it. It is also in direct contrast to the Word, which never measures "success" in these terms and certainly is not characterized by rigidity, closure, and absolutes. If we preachers take on the role of the one who gets to "tell" others what to do, then we are right back into power-swaps-that-lead-nowhere. We are right back into usurping the power that is the Word's. Besides, it is not at all a given that the happy listener is one who is "being told"; *that* is simply another of the System's sleights of hand. I think the happy listener, or perhaps the *met* listener, is the one who is "being seen." "Being told" means we have been given our marching orders. "Being seen" means we have been truly attended to, engaged, received, and known; it is *communion*.

The human need to *be seen*, really and truly seen, is so deep that each of us would probably do anything for it, even if we had to break covenants and denominational barriers. When we are starved, we probably will. *Being seen* is what a teenage girl is after when she gets into the backseat of a car with her boyfriend. *Being seen* is what a child is after when he starts the third tantrum of the day. *Being seen*—or the lack of it—is what drives families to church-shop, and couples to therapy, and countries to war. Sure, we may want to *be told* what the answer to our problems is. But if we have known what it is to be known, in the deepest sense, we have experienced communion; we have experienced the Word.

Preaching that is most concerned about the human desire to be seen rather than to be told is preaching that has no need of absolutes. It is preaching that is free to dwell in the power of the Word rather than the power of fear. It is also, I suspect, preaching that relies on testimony to communicate how human lives overlap and intersect. To tell where we have seen the Word in the text and in our lives, and to confess what we believe about it, is preaching that passes down the experience of being seen. It is also preaching that blows apart stereotypes as well as the false adversarial relationships that prey on difference. When one community chooses being seen over being told, the act has the potential to transform even the absolutist environment of the Other by opening up the possibility for communion—which ought to give the "declining" mainline churches many more options for relating to fundamentalist groups than reflexive fear. If we testify to what we have seen, we model another way, truth, and life than is currently available to our fundamentalist sisters and brothers. That is far more powerful than staring into mirrors and mimicking our own fear.

Fear of Fighting: "Entertainment" vs. True Speech

It takes no great leap of the intellect to see where I am headed next. Preachers who have gotten all worked up about biblical illiteracy and low numbers are probably also worried about whether their preaching is boring people to death: they have fallen for the "entertainment" threat. They have been convinced that institutional survival is dependent on worship that appeals to this electronic generation—which means worship that is at least as compelling as anything we might see on television. Preaching begins to take its cues from the entertainment industry, going for the big audiences, the big profits, and the least-objectionable subject matter. You give the people what they want to see and what they want to hear. You concentrate on getting them to worship. You avoid anything inflammatory that might alienate anyone and lower attendance. You aim for a middle ground, a PG-13 rating, a good family comedy or big-budget adventure, a feel-good message, and you leave the heavy and controversial stuff to small independents, who aren't really going for the big audiences, anyway.

The give-away words are "institutional survival" and "least-objectionable." Those words have nothing to do with gospel. Preachers who begin to equate sermons with entertainment (big audiences, no boredom, feel-good message) have been hooked by their own fear—of flying and failing, sure, but of *fighting*, most of all. Fear of conflict is one of the most potent forces in institutional life and human relationships. If we preachers can be convinced that conflict in the church is the worst thing that can happen to us, then we will steer away from reading Scripture with anything but an entertainment hermeneutic. We will not look for the Word; we will look for crowd-pleasing words and stories that may or may not bear any resemblance to what the text is whispering.

One of the saddest fallouts of this particular fear is that the community of faith does not learn how to engage in true speech. Preaching that aims to entertain is preaching that spoils, like a weak and indulgent parent. The church becomes a gathering of critics, evaluating the latest pulpit offering. Its members are those who feel entitled rather than those who feel empowered. They cannot speak truth to one another; their environment will not sustain it. And their preacher, whose love for them was never as strong as his fear, dies on the vine. He may even take the church with him.

Preaching that passes down the traditions of testimony is not afraid of conflict. It is not afraid of a fight, whether that fight takes place within the text itself—testimony and countertestimony locking horns, as always—or within the community. It welcomes the struggle that is ours: the struggle to read this text, to see and be seen, to speak and hear truth from one another. The struggle to get out of our own way. The struggle to become a preacher by being merely, miraculously, human.

Coming Back and Passing Down

The things that are most important to us, we pass down to the ones who come after us, and I believe a preacher passes down a set of traditions about how God's people read, speak, live in, and wait for the Word.

So here is what I want to pass down. It is something I had when I was born and something that took me years to wake up and come back to: testimony. Here is what I have learned.

Testimony has taught me to read the Word closely, to pay attention, to wait and watch for what happens next. It has shown me that making trouble and making good news are often the same thing. It has prodded me to change the subject and stop dramatizing myself. It has encouraged me to say what I believe before I say what I fear. It has nipped the splinching problem in the bud. It has offered me preaching ancestors where I had none. It has given me courage and joy and a really weird sense of humor, which is the best way I know to get through the *leiros*. In short, after a long hiatus of dancing around some golden words and thinking they actually had the power to save and create a preacher, testimony has given me back my mother tongue, my first language as a Christian. When I preach in this tradition, I feel like I have been born again. I *know* I have. All I can do when it is my turn to speak is pass on the tradition, which is really a language and access that is already ours. All I can tell is what I have seen and believed, trusting that the Word will take it from there.

Sometimes my students ask me if preaching gets any easier, the longer you do it. I tell them, "No." Why lie?! They are always crestfallen. "Well," I say, "there is one thing that does get easier. After your first sermon, when you realize that you have actually preached and *not died*, you know that it is at least possible that the next one won't kill you, either." The students look at me as if perhaps I were in need of a long vacation on a very deserted (and padded) island, and walk away, looking a little dazed. I try to stay nearby, for a while, because becoming a preacher is hard work, and I've been there; I still am.

What I don't tell them—not right then, anyway—is that *every* sermon kills you. For me, the act of preaching is really an act of dying. But it is also the act of being raised by the power and grace of God. This Word we preach takes us with it all the way to the cross and all the way back.

7

The Wide-awake Sermon

Preaching in the Tradition

Books about preaching are like preachers themselves: eventually, we all have to get practical. The time comes to actually *do* what we have been talking and thinking and reading and writing about, to see what practice itself has to teach us.

So how do we get started? How does a preacher interested in testimony go about practicing it and preparing a testimony sermon?

THE TESTIMONY JUMP START

The good news, here, is that preaching in the testimony tradition actually simplifies matters a great deal. It is practical theology at its finest, because testimony has distinct ways of reasoning, ways of speaking, and ways of being that lead straight into preaching. Testimony insists that we change the subject of preaching from ourselves and our words to God's Word as it moves through life and text. That one change is remarkably freeing.

1. *It keeps us focused.* We pay attention to our encounter with the biblical text and describe what we see, not what we want to see.
2. *It keeps us honest.* We confess what we believe about that encounter, not what we think we ought to believe.
3. *It keeps us grounded.* We testify to a particular people at a particular place and time, about one textual encounter: ours.

4. *It keeps us engaged.* We point to the Word, not to ourselves, because the encounter (not the office of preacher or the act of preaching!) creates its own invitation to the listener.
5. *It keeps us going.* Our preaching will never prove the Word, live out the Word, or live up to the Word. But it will seal our lives to the Word—which signals our desire to keep following, to keep practicing, to keep striving for one more day.

In short, testimony keeps us from trying to do too much or say too much so that we do not get lost on our way to the sermon or paralyzed by possibilities before we have even begun. It gives us clear directives for sermon preparation so that we can turn off all the background noise, sense the next task at hand, and settle into it. Even better, it jump-starts our intuitive reason by prioritizing those tasks: "how" questions (how should I say this idea? write that transition? use this image? speak that point?) play second fiddle to "what" questions (what I saw, what I believe, and therefore what I will say). "What" questions are testimony questions, and they always come first. They wake us up so that we can wake up the sermon.

And this clarification is critical. The preaching life is filled with distractions, all of them designed to turn our attention away from the Word (*what* we say) and focus it on ourselves (*how* we say it). The worst of these is the constant pressure to back our words and worth with some sort of absolute proof. Furthermore, when preachers resist those distractions and testify to the Word, we know what happens: they face the logic of *leiros*. Their listeners will not believe them. Even their closest friends will not believe them, because the Word that moves through lives and texts is utterly shocking. It explodes our systems, our structures, our traditions, our fleshpots. It makes fools of experts and preachers of fools. It even resurrects the dead!—and when the dead do not even stay dead, who and what is safe?! *The Word changes everything.* Preachers who testify to it will meet with resistance, and they will face it within themselves, because the urge to change the subject to something we each can manage is strong and real and terribly distracting.

So preachers need help. When the pressures begin to pile up, we need guidelines we can count on. We need clear, simple processes we can recall easily under stress. We need straightforward priorities that we can access through our own intuitive reason. And when all hell breaks loose (which it will, whenever the Word Itself is loose), we need guidelines for keeping focused, honest, grounded, and engaged. We need ways to keep going, because preaching is a cosmic struggle. Preachers have every right to ask for practical theology that works, both with them and for them. Testimony is exactly that. In my view, it is God's gift to the preacher.

The gift unfolds in three moves, or practices, which lead straight from text to sermon: attending, describing, and testifying. These three practices are really ways of living in the world as one who preaches. But they are also ways of *living in the text* as one who preaches.

Living in the Text

By "living in the text," I am reaching for words, however awkwardly, to describe a different way of engaging the text, one that aims for a direct experience of the text itself. Preachers in the testimony tradition do not go to the text for answers or explanations. They go to the text to live in it, to encounter it, to get inside the passage itself and experience what the text is saying to them. The sermon is the aftermath of that encounter: we tell what we have seen and heard in the text, and what we believe. We offer our testimony. And the testimony is not *about us*; it is not *about what happened to us* when we engaged the text. It is about *what we saw and heard in the text* when we engaged it deeply; it is about the view, seen from the vantage point of experience.

This sort of deep engagement is harder than it looks. For one thing, most preachers were not trained to do it; we were trained to talk *about* the text: to explain it, or solve it, or hunt down its one true "meaning."[1] We were trained to study and conjugate and translate into key theological ideas, and we can do it all day if you let us. We can keep talking about that text until the road is clogged with more information than one sermon can handle. What we *don't* always know how to do is get out of traffic, and this is where testimony-preaching practices can help. They push us to stop studying the text and start living in it.

There is another reason that this sort of deep engagement comes hard, however, and that is that talking about texts—a preacher's forte— is an excellent way to hold them at a safe distance. Keep talking about the text, and you can delay the moment when you might actually have to live it. You can pretend that the point is to be *enlightened,* not *changed.* But preaching in the testimony tradition is all about forced encounters, and the preacher is the first one in line. All the things we know about the Word of God—that it will shuck you like an oyster, ask the very questions you have been avoiding, rip off the KEEP OUT signs and turn on the flood lights—apply to *us*, first. Engaging the text this deeply calls for the preacher to live in the text first, not only to model the sort of encounter we hope our listeners will have themselves but to tell about what our own encounter has shown us.

Living in the text is exhilarating, but it has its excruciating moments, too. Shucking an oyster is not especially comfortable for the oyster. So preachers need a network of support and accountability, because no one can do this alone, week after week, without the love and friendship of persons we trust. Any preacher who is feeling especially singular and heroic should take another look at the prophets, none of whom could go very long without scheduling a small breakdown. And note well: Anne Hutchinson had Mary Dyer; Sarah Osborn had Susanna Anthony; Jarena Lee had Richard Allen. When these women first preached, they did it in the company of women's religious circles that supported them, encouraged them, and, one assumes, held them to loving accountability. Close friends and supports are not optional in this work, unless the preacher is looking to be served on the half shell.

A Word about Getting Practical

Preachers are all about getting practical; we are, after all, practical theologians. And books about preaching need to offer concrete suggestions. The challenge, however, is to offer guidance rather than formulas. There is a reason why so many Bible readers get bogged down in Leviticus, and why most of us find the building instructions for the tabernacle less riveting than the Exodus narrative. Explicit directions for anything have a way of seeming quaint and time-bound within a very short time—as evidenced by how few congregations these days feel compelled to install their own eleven curtains of goat hair (Exod. 36:14). They can also be boring and just plain uninspiring.

I teach preaching, and I walk students through the process all the time. But I have learned that giving direction is not the same as giving directions. Directions (notice the plural) can verge on the formulaic: follow these steps, and you will have a sermon. Direction (singular) is more akin to guidance. It implies that the one offering it and the one enacting it will discover together, in the process, the wisdom that they need in order to live truthfully in the text. It also takes seriously that each situation will have its own struggle for forms that work and structure that holds. Each sermon will have to work its purpose out afresh. Offering direction rather than directions honors the act of preaching without idolizing any portion of it. It reminds us that there is a difference between practicing testimony and dancing around a lot of golden words. I hope that in this chapter you find guidance for your own direction and even wisdom for your own preaching life.

1. ATTENDING: WHAT DO YOU SEE?

The first move toward the sermon, for a testimony preacher, is the practice of *attending* to the biblical text. Attending (like the practices of *describing* and *testifying*) is a way of being, seeing, and living in the text and in the world, and its primary task is to receive in openness. It reminds us that before we can be interpreters, we have to be witnesses; we have to pay attention. The question for this move, then, is, "What do you see?" Attending becomes even more interesting, however, when we shift the interpretive space of the preacher by changing his location or subject position. Where you stand, and with whom, affects what you see.

The Radical Art of Being Idle and Blessed

"Attending" is the art of paying attention, of *tending to*, and our tending can take many forms. We can tend a garden or a soup, a hearth or a baby. We can tend a flock or a ship, a queen or a business, or even, if need be, our *own* business.[2] Tending calls for watchfulness and vigilance; it calls for skill and care. It calls for relinquishment of our own agendas in favor of a different set of needs. More than anything, it asks us to stay awake, to keep watch, even when the night is long and we are sleepy disciples. Perhaps that is why we speak of "paying attention": our attending costs us something. It is a deliberate choice, not a default mode.

Attending to the biblical text encompasses all these forms of tending, and more. It is a different way of sensing: seeing, listening, touching, tasting. It involves physical sensation and visceral reactions, but it also involves feelings and emotions. It asks us to feel what we might not otherwise choose to feel; to stand where we might not otherwise choose to stand. It also asks for time and openness. Attending to the biblical text does not lend itself to quick decisions and speedy verdicts; those forms of closure serve human needs and desires, but they do not serve the text. The biblical text asks for a deeper and different kind of consideration, one that seeks out dissonance and disjunction when the initial harmonies have been played—and the text will not be rushed. It will revel in the stillness and slowness that deep attending requires. It will welcome yet another point of view. The time of attending is not a time of decision making or meaning making. It is time to soak, and dream, and receive what comes.

The poet Mary Oliver speaks of paying attention in the language of prayer. Attending, she says, brings us to our knees in the grass and makes us "idle and blessed," which is in radical opposition to the busyness of the world.[3] Attending prefers openness to closure, paradox to absolutes. In a culture of rampant consumerism, it interferes with our potential for consuming and the converting of our time into goods and services. Attending is simply an alternate way of measuring value— indeed, an alternate way of being. And that must threaten the System more than anything else, because this way of being exposes us, opens us, to the Word.

Preachers might as well accept the fact that their attending will indeed cost them something. They will pay in time that could have been spent differently—as all those distractions, minions of the System, keep whispering. They will also pay with their bodies and reputations, because there are powerful forces out there that will do anything to keep us from paying attention at all. Those forces will call us lazy and idle; they will insult our intelligence and skill. They will accuse us of incompetence and of not doing our jobs, because, really, who on earth has the time to just sit and listen?! Who on earth can afford to do nothing but *attend*?!

No one, of course. Which is why we must change the rules: attending to the biblical text is an act of resistance. It is the first step to opening us to the Word, with all its liberating, resurrecting power. We do not *have* time to attend. We must *take* it, and then *spend* it—on the radical art of being "idle and blessed," as Oliver puts it. Idle and blessed and open to the Word.

Sure, You *Could* Have . . . But *Did* You?

The practice of attending requires a particular state of being; before we can attend, we have to make time and space to attend so that there is room for us to be open and receptive to the Word in text and world.

But attending also requires a certain resolve—or maybe a better word is "resignation"—to be in that time and space differently. We have to put away our books (for a while, anyway) and leave our studies. We have to read the text in odd ways and in odd places. We have to try things with it that do not show us at our most dignified. When it seems to us that nothing is happening and we are not *seeing anything*, we cannot simply give up; it is not an option. We have to keep trying, keep going through the steps, keep practicing, keep trusting. Creativity, as the dancer Twyla Tharp has written, is not so much about inspiration as it is about habits: repetitive acts and disciplined routines that we do over and over until the Spirit moves.[4] Art does not just appear in a vision; it evolves, after a lot of sweat. As a preacher, I find this immensely reassuring. It reminds me that the hours we spend attending are not wasted hours; they are simply part of the process, and they do lead somewhere. The challenge for us is to build them into our routines, so that the daily discipline of attending is just part of our living.

Of course, the logic of *leiros* makes another entrance here: this work *will* make us foolish in the eyes of others. Some attending practices look downright eccentric, and the truth is, they are. They are foolish, as far as the world is concerned, but then so is the very gospel we preach. We preach Christ crucified, a gospel of repentance and liberation: what foolishness, what utter bunk!—and how fabulous to be *constantly reminded* of this in our very bodies, just by participating in some quirky exercise! In my view, that is the real gift attending offers us: a way to be foolish so that we can see gospel foolishness. The practices are a little loony (to the uninitiated, anyway), and they make *us* feel loony, which keeps our perspective slightly off kilter. If we do them regularly, we make a habit of dislocation. We get used to changing the subject, having our perspective reoriented. We also put ourselves in the way of the Word, should it suddenly leap across our path.

Preachers are not always in touch with the eccentric element at the heart of our calling; these days the pressure is to look professional, to blend. At the Rotary Club, we dress like the business community; at the gym, we wear sweats. We are so used to *not* standing out in a crowd that I wonder sometimes if we might benefit from a good dose of eccentricity, of actually looking as nuts as our calling truly is. Attending can get us back in touch with sheer craziness, the set-apartness of preaching that we might otherwise only access in moments of loneliness and soul-searching. And, it's *fun*. To be in the world as one who attends, one who is crazy enough, from time to time, to *be still and know that I am God, right here, right now!*—while the world goes about its frantic pace, is pure joy and freedom. It is like being a child again. It does us good to model this kind of craziness. It does us good to become accustomed to how odd we look. Eventually we get used to it and over ourselves, and we can concentrate on the Word we came to look for in the first place, which only makes our attending richer. Artists have much to teach preachers in this regard. To sit around thinking about what you *could* do (if only you had the nerve, or the time, or the insanely stupid idea) really *is* a waste of time when you might have done it and learned something—as Alex taught me.

Alex was my neighbor when I was growing up. She was an artist who worked in all sorts of media—paint on canvas, plastic sculpture, wooden box assemblages—and I spent hours in her studio watching her. She never minded as long as I sat quietly on my stool in the corner, which wasn't hard, actually; no one else I knew was painting cows hidden in abstract images, bending enormous sheets of plastic, or stretching black lace over fake peaches. No one else I knew could show me how to batik and silkscreen, or cut intricate paper snowflakes for Christmas and dip eggs in floating oil paint for Easter. No one else I knew would even think of showing me how to fill a crab shell with cement, stick the legs of the crab back in it, and make a necklace for my mother. But Alex told me to look beyond conventional surfaces because art could happen anywhere, with anything—which must be why it was always so exciting to repaint her kitchen (each drawer and cabinet was a different color), and why the incident with the doll's head has stuck with me.

I was in her living room when I spotted it: a plastic doll's head mashed into an empty tin can, perched on the mantle. It was obviously new and obviously hers, but for the first time, I questioned why this qualified as art. "Alex," I burst out; "*I* could have done that!"—to which she replied, crisply, "Yes. But you didn't."

There was a time when I would have rolled my eyes at the following exercises, none of which is particularly unique or original or earthshaking. I would have told you what a waste of time they were. I would have told you that I *could* have sat on the subway for an hour and read the biblical text; anybody *could* have, for heaven's sake, so if I didn't, what's the big deal?!

The big deal is that I didn't. And then one day I did.

It's a big, wild, beautifully foolish world out there, and it is too good to miss. Go for it. See what you find.

Exercises for Attending

Start with a biblical text.

1. Write it

By hand. In a journal—preferably one that is bigger than the standard 8½ x 11-inch page, and definitely one that is unlined. We all need help getting out of the box and off the computer screen. As you write out the text, notice how you are forced to slow down and really *see* it, *notice* it, *hear* it. If something grabs your attention, make a note to follow up on it.

2. Pocket it

Now write out another copy of the Scripture on a small piece of paper, small enough to fold and fit in your pocket. Get in the habit of carrying it around with you. You are going to be looking at it a lot. For example . . .

3. Memorize it

My students always balk at first when I tell them we are going to memorize our Scripture texts—but that's before they try it and become converts to the practice. The first rule is never to sit down at a desk and tell yourself, "Now, I will memorize." This is work that happens best when you are doing other things, mundane things, preferably with your hands. So take that Scripture text out of your pocket as you go about your weekly chores. Take it out when you're folding laundry, doing dishes, taking a walk, rocking a baby. Say the text aloud, over and over, until you've memorized it. Now live with it. (*Note*: Remember, you don't have to read the text as a memorized piece in worship. You aren't doing this for anyone but you, the preacher; you don't even have to advertise that you are doing it! The point is just to make sure that you turn your Scripture into the toddler that follows you around everywhere you go and never leaves you alone for even a single moment.)

4. Underline it

Read the text you've written out in your journal. Without stopping to edit yourself, underline/circle/mark words and phrases that stand out to you. Now look at the words or phrases you've underlined and write them out separately. Spend some time pondering and praying about those words. What do they suggest to you? What questions are you asking? Translate the underlined words into Greek or Hebrew. Keep asking, "Where are these words leading me?"

5. "Soccer Mom" it

I call this practice "soccer Mom-ing the text" because I *am* a soccer Mom (and a lacrosse Mom and a basketball Mom); it's how I spend a lot of time. So I have learned to read texts where I already am. If you aren't a soccer Mom yourself, think about where you do spend your time (the library, the coffee shop, the office, the carpool) and begin pulling your text out of your pocket as you frequent those places. Invite friends (strangers, if you're brave) to sit down and read the text with you. If they feel unqualified (you know, because you're the expert; you're a *preacher*), tell them you aren't trying to solve the text, you're just trying to hear it through many other ears. You'll be amazed at what they *do* hear.

6. Dislocate it

Take your text someplace that you wouldn't ordinarily go, someplace where you feel "dislocated"—either because of who you are (among others who are different from you) or because of what you are doing (reading Scripture in a place where such a thing isn't ordinarily done). It's important that the dislocation makes you feel odd, marginalized, or even nervous. Dislocate your self/body, and read the text from your journal (out loud, if you dare!). Now pay attention. How does the text look and sound different in this location? What do you notice that you might have missed before?

7. Subtext it

Subtext is nonverbal communication, and we all do it, all the time. Subtext is what we are *thinking* when we actually speak words out loud. (Example: to the question, "How are you, honey?" try saying the words, "Fine," while *thinking*, "I am having a miserable day," "I just aced that test!" and "Sometimes you make me so mad I could just spit.") One of the simplest and most evocative interpretive practices for a Scripture text is to play around with subtexts. Don't let yourself dwell on what the characters or narrators were *really* thinking when they said or wrote those words (who knows, anyway?!). Ask yourself what is possible. Then try some subtexts that actually sound *im*possible—and prepare to be surprised. This is fun to do with a group and hilarious to do with youth. It also might make an interesting change for lectionary groups; preachers could write various subtexts to try or take turns directing one another. The results are always rich.

8. Block it

"Blocking" is a theater phrase used to describe the physical movement and placement of actors in a scene: where they stand, when they are to cross downstage, when they are to drink from a glass, whether they say a line kneeling or lying down, and so on. Block your Scripture scene, first in your mind, then on paper in your journal, then (best of all) with some agreeable volunteers. Look at the physical movements of the characters; notice where they are in relation to one another. Are they facing each other? Is there eye contact? What does their physical placement communicate about their status, their feelings, and so forth? Again, this is good to do with a group of interpreters.

9. Body it

Some of us are kinesthetic learners: we learn best when we throw our whole bodies into a text. If you are this kind of person, try "bodying" the text by moving, dancing, gesturing, or whatever else comes to mind as you say or hear the words. You might try signing it (American Sign Language, or ASL, used in the deaf and hearing-impaired communities, is a beautiful language to embody and to see), or working with a group of children to come up with suitable gestures that tell the story (children have very few inhibitions about bodying). If the thought of bodying the text gives you hives, save it for a group exercise when you feel braver.

10. Push it

Try the ancient rabbinical practice of *havruta*, which gives you a way to explore the limits of interpretation. You need a partner for this. Sit down facing one another, each with a copy of the text in front of you.

Take turns reading the text aloud, while your partner listens. Then take turns reacting to the text: what do you each see and hear in it? Now get extreme: push your ideas and images as far as they will go, even to the point of the absurd or heretical, just to see what happens. If the listening partner feels the speaking partner has gone too far, s/he should communicate it calmly and nonjudgmentally. The point of this exercise is to find the limits of the text by crossing them, secure in the knowledge that your partner won't leave you stranded. Spend fifteen minutes engaging in *havruta*, then stop and reflect. Did the exercise give you freedom to push the boundaries of the text? Where are the limits of interpretation for you, now?

11. "Other" it

If you're a woman, read your text with a man. If you're a man, read it with a woman. Ask the other person to reflect particularly from the perspective of their gender (which you don't share). What do you each see differently? Talk about it. Now "other" the text for different races, ages, sexual orientations, nationalities, income levels, religions, or anything you can think of.

12. Counter it

Every text is a response to other texts, somewhere, in Scripture; they work together, talk to one another, agree with one another, challenge one another. What texts is *your* text responding to? Which texts do you imagine it might be countering? Another way to go at this is to ask what the countertestimony of your text might be and how that countertestimony keeps your text from becoming an idol.

13. Create it

Take your journal to a quiet place outside. Bring paints, pastels, charcoal, crayons, pencils, fountain pens, magic markers, or whatever else makes you feel like an artist. (You might bring one medium you know and one you've never tried before.) Read your text aloud several times. Draw whatever comes to mind, giving yourself time limits of two, five, ten, or fifteen minutes (to keep you from staring at the paper all afternoon). You can do one drawing or several. This works especially well with a group, since others often see things in our own art that we are blind to ourselves.

14. Study it

Yes, it *is* important to remember the world of scholarship! But now that you've had time to really *live* with the text, how do you hear the words of our biblical and theological colleagues? What insights seem especially truthful to you? What subtexts do you hear in *their* words? How might you continue this dialogue with them in the body of the sermon?

But How Long Will It Take?

My students sometimes ask me this, and the answer (naturally) is that I don't know. I suggest they try three exercises, one of which pushes them a little further in the direction of the foolish and undignified than they might ordinarily go and see what happens. The point is to get in the habit of stretching ourselves. Over time, we learn which exercises stretch us most efficiently and consistently, and we incorporate them into our routine; we make a habit of them. From there, we have to trust that by leaning into them, practicing them over and over, we will recognize the Word when it comes.

II. DESCRIBING: WHAT DO YOU BELIEVE?

The second move toward the sermon for a testimony preacher is the practice of *describing*, or finding words to express what we have seen in our attending. Describing asks us to narrate what we have seen and then to take it a step further toward the act of confession (Who did Mary Magdalene see? She saw *the Lord!*). It reminds us that we are *Christian* witnesses: we see what we see through a particular lens, which is a lens of faith. We will also speak in a particular language, which is testimony, the mother tongue of the church. The words we choose to describe what we see, therefore, come from a biblically colored lexicon, a biblically patterned grammar. We choose them in the company of other believers, who are narrating and confessing their own witness. The question for this move is, "What do you believe about what you have seen?"

Describing a Word You Have Already Described

"Describing" is the art of writing down or writing upon, so that others can see and understand our words. We can describe an object that exists or an image that does not exist. We can describe an experience that happened last week or an event that took place three thousand years ago. We can describe our homes and families, our jobs and plans, our loves and failures, our faith and dreams. We can describe concrete facts, abstract thoughts, theological concepts, and mythical tales. If we are good at it, we can help our listeners see and experience what we describe.

The biblical text is eager to describe and to be described. It is a Word spoken, a Word written, a commandment etched in stone, a law written upon our hearts. It is a vision we write down so they may run who read it. It is a prophecy of breath that we speak to dry bones. It is a voice we do not recognize, a dream we do not want, a message we can scarcely believe, and a call we cannot refuse. It is a burning bush and a burning coal, a wisdom we seek above silver and gold. We take it, keep it, recite it to our children, talk about it at home and when we are away, talk about it when we lie down and again when we rise, bind it on our hands, fix it on our foreheads, write it on the doorposts of our houses and our gates. We put it in an earthenware jar so it will last a long time. We set it as a seal upon our hearts.

The practice of describing takes these Scriptures seriously. We describe a Word that was first de-scribed, first written down, in *us*. We describe a Word that is already burned on our lips and sealed on our hearts; if we looked closely, we could probably find the marks. And others *will* look. They will look to see how this Word has affected us, whether our practice of attending has left any trace. They will try to read what is written in our faces and our bodies and described by our living. Whatever we describe to others about a text, whatever we try to say about it, is first de-scribed for them in us, through our engagement with that text—*because engagement leaves its own marks*. We are not just "seeing" something in the text; we are being affected, even changed, by what we see. Our attending moves directly into describing—and before we even say a word!

This is why the question "What do I see?" segues into "What do I believe about it?" The biblical text calls for our response. It asks us to follow, commit, repent, believe; it demands attention and then action. But it also demands *honest* action, which is why both testimony and countertestimony are available to us in our biblical mother tongue. If we do not describe what we really believe about what we see, we make an idol of the text and an idol of God; we refuse God's sovereignty as well as God's compassion. We deny the fullness of human life and the power of God's Word. The stone rolls back over the tomb and death wins. An honest description, on the other hand, is a true confession and an acceptance of our call to live in the text *as one who is in relationship with God.* An honest description comes from deep engagement that could easily have been otherwise if the preacher let fear and absolutes rule the day. "What do I see?" only separates from "What do I believe about it?" if we are ready to relinquish our mother tongue and lapse into silence—absolute silence.

Daily Themes

Describing necessarily involves words and the selection of words, because we want our sermons to *do* something. We want them to help our listeners see and experience and engage the text (rather than *us*) as deeply as possible, which means that we want our describing words to point to the Word—in true, accurate, faithful, vivid, fresh, poetic, evocative, and maybe even beautiful language. We also dare to hope that our describing words will proclaim (which is to say, "claim for" or "claim on behalf of") the Word that moves through life and text, the Word we met in our practice of attending.

This is a tall order for words. But it is not an impossible one, and testimony preachers do not need to be overwhelmed by it. We do not have to describe perfectly for all time and all people (thanks be to God); we only have to describe *one* attending of *one* text. And the best way to become a good describer, in my view, is to become a writer: someone who writes. Regularly.

Describing benefits from the discipline of writing, but like attending, it needs to be habitual. If we wait for the sublimely worded phrase to drop from the sky, we are going to wait a long time; sublimely worded phrases do not generally do this. They are more apt to show up in the daily grind of mundane writing exercises when we weren't expecting them. So it is helpful to get in the habit of writing, writing-down, de-scribing, every day, so that our muscles can flex and our scrap paper piles (replete with hidden sublimely worded phrases) accumulate. We might set aside the same time each day for this: perhaps the half-hour after breakfast, for example, or the same block of time each afternoon, or the same evening every week for group work. We might commit to trying a new exercise every week or repeating the same ones for a month. Whatever we choose to do, whether it is stream-of-consciousness journaling or a specific creative writing task, we have to remember: the time spent is never wasted. Even if we cannot see any obvious connections between our describing and the sermon that is waiting to generate, the point is to engage in the discipline, to keep up the habit, trusting that good (and inspiration!) will come of it.

Exercises for Describing

Take that same biblical text. Get yourself a large, blank artist's sketchbook, bigger than the standard 8½ x 11-inch pages that frame so much of our reading and writing. The blank pages unline your mind and free you up to write as big or small as you like. The size of the paper expands your imagination. The pencil or pen you will have to use literally gets you off the computer and slows you down. The physical motion of your hand on the paper taps into different parts of the brain that are underutilized in this Internet culture. The quality of the paper invites you to try painting or collage making within its pages (and probably takes you back to elementary school art). The thickness of the sketchbook lets you work on many ideas, exercises, texts, and sermons at once. The awkward size and heft make it stand out among your other books and folders, reminding you of the foolishness of your calling. Lugging this sketchbook about takes a little getting used to, and you will probably either love it or hate it at first. My students who initially hate it (but still have to do it, since I'm the teacher) get through the first sermon and report—with a great show of irritation and much heaving of sighs—that they still hate the stupid notebook, but they have to admit: it helps. I think their irritation is just splendid and excellent practice. The text can be irritating, too.

So get that notebook, and take out your text.

1. Image it

Make a list of images that appear in your text (light, water, salt, blood, seed, vine, etc.). Take one, close your eyes, and say it aloud. Let yourself "see" whatever words or pictures appear to you; then, after a moment, open your eyes and write down everything that came to you. Don't edit; just write rapidly, no matter how bizarre; your mind is telling you something, making a connection that isn't readily apparent to you. Now reflect on what you have written. What connections do you see?

2. Rewrite it

Many of my students have done this on their own out of frustration and found that it provided the seed to the sermon. Rewrite the text in your own words. You can try this from memory, checking later to see what you left out or added (what do those omissions or additions tell you?!), or you can start with a word in the text that is especially interesting or challenging to you—such as "blessed" in the Beatitudes. What does it mean to be "blessed"? Look the word up in a dictionary or thesaurus, or check Hebrew and Greek translations; rewrite the passage using each of the possible meanings ("Blessed are they . . ." becomes "Helped are they . . . chosen are they . . . happy are they . . . holy are they . . . set apart are they . . . prayed-for are they," etc.). What do your rewrites of the text say to you? Where do they stimulate you to go?[5]

3. Slang it

Youth ministry folks do this all the time. Rewrite the text in the particular idiom of the young people in your congregation, or some young people who are marginal to it. Put the youth themselves in it; imagine a present-day setting for the text (the church? a mall? a high school dance? track practice? a gritty street corner? the school cafeteria?). If you need ideas, ask some youth to help you. See where your imagination takes you.

4. Character-sketch it

Write a description of someone in the text, either a character or perhaps the author or narrator. Imagine what this person looks like, how she talks, what she ate for breakfast, what he picked out to wear this morning. What is he doing in this text? What does she want? What obstacles are before her? What strengths and weaknesses does he have? This is a good way to draw on our attending skills and take them further.

5. Monologue it

Pick a place to stand in the text. It might be in the shoes of a character in the story or a character on the fringes of the story who doesn't even appear in the text; it might be the narrator, or a young Sri Lankan woman as you imagine her reading the text. Write a short monologue in the voice of this person. Describe what you see in the text. Describe what you hear and smell. Tell what is breaking your heart or making it sing. This is an excellent exercise for getting some momentum going when you are stuck. The sermon may have nothing to do with the monologue in the end (and probably won't), but the exercise will likely begin to move you.

6. Dialogue it

Do the same thing, but this time write a dialogue for two people. If you want to take the exercise to another level, ask two volunteers to read the parts for you, so you can see how it actually plays. Make revisions to the dialogue if you like. Play with the subtexts. See where it takes you. This is an excellent way to involve people in your sermon preparation process and introduce them to new ways of interpreting the text.

7. Text-jam it[6]

Extend the monologue and dialogue exercises by writing a short scene or dramatic piece based on your text. You might try translating it directly into dialogue, or you might write an original piece based on the text with completely new characters and settings. Again, ask some people from your congregation or community to help you stage it, just to see what happens. This is fun to do on a regular basis with people who like theatre and like to experiment and might enjoy this phase of interpretation. Some of the students at our seminary have started a "text jam" night; they bring the texts they are working on and take turns enacting the material. The point here is not to come up with a finished performance piece (although you could!), but to see where the interpretive work takes you. A text jam could become another form of weekly Bible study, and it works well with all age groups, or even intergenerational groups (how about older women and young people together?).

8. Letter it

Write a series of short letters based on the text. They might be from a child who is writing to her pastor to ask questions about the text. They might be from a character in the story who is writing to another character, or to an imaginary one (what would Mary write to her high school teacher about this annunciation thing that has happened to her?

What would the Corinthians write back to the apostle Paul, either collectively or separately?). What makes this exercise especially interesting is to only write *one side* of the correspondence. Imagine that the pastor or teacher has written back but don't actually compose those letters. Stick with one voice. Again, see where it takes you.

9. Dream it

Keep a journal near your bed. Read the text before you go to sleep; pray in its words and images. In the morning, as soon as you wake up, write down what you can remember of your dreams, without editing. Don't worry if you forget parts; that's fine (this isn't psychotherapy). You will begin to notice two things: (1) how easily our unconscious minds free-associate, jumping around between scenes and characters and not bothering with the gaps; and (2) that dreams are powered by emotions, not logical narratives. The conscious mind constructs a narrative to *evoke* an emotion; the unconscious mind constructs a narrative *around* an emotion. Reflect on your dreams; ponder them; pray about them. They probably won't hand you your finished sermon on a platter, but they may (and often do) contribute, in surprising ways. Think of this as an experiment; be grateful for what comes.

10. Journal it

If dream work isn't your thing, try journaling on the text. This is a practice that many preachers swear by; they notice a depth in their preaching when they have given themselves the freedom to write whatever comes to mind, stream-of-consciousness style, for a set period each day. If you need stimulation to get your journaling going, try reading the newspaper each day with your text in mind; when you finish reading, start journaling immediately. Or find a poem that you like that reminds you of something in the text, and riff on it for a while in your journal. You can journal after visiting parishioners or as a means of prayer. The point is that it gets you writing and into the writing habit.

11. Change it

Write the text as you wish it were. Change whatever bothers you, upsets you, offends you, grieves you; write it the way you wish it had happened. Write it the way it should be, in your view. What does your rewrite tell you?

12. "If-only" it

Imagine what you would say about the text if you could. Imagine what you would tell your listeners, in the best of all possible worlds (for example, what would you say . . . if no one would get mad? if Mr. and Mrs. X wouldn't be offended? if the youth were the only ones listening? if the election weren't happening? if the building campaign weren't happening? if it would stop the war? if you only had the nerve? if you only believed it were true?). Start with the phrase "If I could, I would say _____," or "The sermon I wish I could preach would say _____." Write fast, without thinking. Put it away. Come back in a few hours, or the next day. Is it still true? Is it still the sermon you wish you could preach? Or has it become the sermon you can preach?

III. TESTIFYING: WHAT ARE YOU GOING TO SAY?

The third move toward the sermon for a testimony preacher is the practice of *testifying*, or finally saying what we have seen and believed. The contextual nature of preaching—that *we* are the ones saying *these* words to *these* people—has a strong bearing here as well, but with more urgency, as preachers come face to face with issues of relevance and love: Why are these words important to say to these people whom I love? What do I want to give them, with this sermon? Preachers also confront the fullness of the message itself and its implications in that suspended time between knowing what we *want* to say—and then saying it. The testimony move inevitably brings us to the authority question: Can I really say that? How can I, when I have no proof? How can I, when I am only _____ [complete sentence with some quality about you that makes you less than adequate and/or unqualified and/or marginal in this situation]? The question for this move is "What are you going to say?" but there is a powerful *why* that propels us through it: Why am I saying this? Because I saw it—and I believe it. I believe in this Word.

The Most Dangerous Question

There is no denying that this is the most dangerous part of the sermon preparation process. Testimony comes with a cost, for us and for our listeners, and this is the place where we decide if we are willing to pay it. And the matter is complicated, immensely so, because we are preaching to people we love. We do not want to merely *correct* them. We want to *liberate* them through the power of the Word we meet in the text. We want to give them hope, not hurt, for a future that liberates and redeems. The cost of *not* speaking is continued captivity, but the cost of speaking brings us all to the cross. There can be no resurrection without the events of Good Friday, and in the testimony move, we are painfully aware of it. We ache for the freedom that is possible, and we ache for the pain it will create on the way. We also see, in stark relief, that there is little comfort in being the messenger. Others' fears will backfire in our direction. We may become targets for a wide range of emotions: rage, grief, guilt, anxiety, numbness. We may become identified with the source of the problem when people confuse our subject position for a subjectivity that belongs only to God. This is the cost of speaking, and it is real and deep. The System is always stealthily at work, doing its best to undermine the Word and those who testify to it; right now, that would be us.

It is a moment of reckoning for the preacher, and two temptations immediately surface. The first is to back away, fast. We have a sudden, panicky urge to return to our attending and describing and second guess everything we have seen and believed. Maybe we didn't really see *that* in the text; maybe it isn't really there. Maybe we are reading too much into the text. Maybe we are forcing our own agendas on it, and then rushing to claims that are not ours to make. Maybe our testimony is simply wrong. Maybe it is too unorthodox. Maybe our listeners are not ready for it. Maybe we are not the ones who should say it. Maybe we are asking too much of everyone, including ourselves, with such romantic, idealistic notions about preaching. Maybe the cost is too high, for us and for them, and we should just say something else . . . maybe.

The second temptation is to turn our "what" questions into "how" questions. We suddenly begin to lose all confidence in ourselves, so that the focus subtly shifts away from the testimony itself to our authority and ability to say it: we become the subject of our own preaching. Maybe, if we could figure out *how* to say it, we could!—we could actually do it! Maybe if we knew how to couch the message, we could get away with saying it. Maybe if we knew how to tell the right stories, strike the right tone, harness the right form, choose the right words, our listeners could hear us without tuning out. Maybe if we knew how to be more politic, we could lower the cost for ourselves. Maybe if we knew how to be more pastoral, we could make it a little easier on them. Maybe if we read another book, took another class, learned how to be more effective, more interesting, more likeable, more forceful, more entertaining, more inviting, *more successful preachers*—we could say what we really saw in this text and really believe to be true. If we knew how to say it . . . we would. Maybe.

The testifying move has a clear moment of reckoning, and it can be a dreadful one. We are nearing the end of the road to the sermon, we can practically see the finish, when those two temptations plant themselves sphinx-like across our path and absolutely refuse to move. They tell us that if we would pass, we must answer their riddles; if we do not answer correctly, we will be devoured on the spot. Choose your path, they say, but beware. If you decide to go forward, there is no stopping the sphinx, and you must give the right answer or perish. If you decide to turn back, you may do so without penalty, but you must give up the road to testimony.

What is so monstrous about these temptations is how they frame the cost: *Answer correctly or die. Submit to these terms, or give up your testimony. There is no other way.* And that is a lie.

The moment of reckoning is the System's last frantic attempt to foist its panic onto the preacher, because what it signals is that the Word is near; it is coming! If we press our ears to the ground, we can hear them, faint voices from the wilderness, crying, "Prepare, prepare the way of the Lord! Make straight in the desert a highway for our God! Repent and believe the gospel! Y'all get ready, because this is it!" The moment of reckoning is only the logic of *leiros* unfolding in its topsy-turvy way. What makes it a potentially dangerous moment, however, is the possibility—if the System's temptations have in fact seized an opportune time—that preachers may be tricked into forgetting how the logic of *leiros* works. Yes, there are shouts of "Nonsense!" about our idle tales, but the logic of *leiros* does not stop there. It does not end in petrified silence as we run away from the tomb or turn back from the sphinx. The logic of *leiros* moves from testimony to testimony and from strength to strength. It pours forth in new kinds of speaking and living while we wait, in faith, for the resurrection of our bodies. It is a logic of fools, and no sphinx ever set the terms.

No one can defeat the moment of reckoning for good. It is as prolific as a weed and just as hardy: we yank it from one sermon and it springs up in the next. It reseeds itself, no matter what we do, and we have to keep up with it, lest it take over the whole field. And maybe that is not a bad thing, actually. The moment of reckoning, that dangerous moment, gives a clarity we find nowhere else. It reminds us of the seriousness of what we are about, and the real cost, and the real goal, which is not to preach ourselves, triumphant. It is to preach Christ, triumphant. Jesus, on his way.

The Most Obvious Question

One of the most consistent ways to keep focused during the testifying move is to think back to our listeners. There are questions we can ask ourselves that will help us over the dangerous-moment hump by reminding us of the relationships at the core of our preaching. Whenever I am stuck, or my students are stuck, we ask one another, "You love these people, right? Well, what is it you love about them? What do you want to give them, in this sermon, and why is it important for you to give it?"

The "love" question may sound like a Pollyannaish diversion, but there is a reason for asking it. We can't preach to people we don't love. We have to love them; otherwise, we are only correcting them. Note carefully, however: *loving* someone is not the same as *liking* them. We may not always *like* our listeners, some of them (ever); they may disappoint us and infuriate us and get on our last nerve; the thought of their company over dinner may be about as appealing as slugs on toast; but we have to *love* them, which I take to mean the practice of extending unconditional grace to another. And if we don't love them yet, it is up to us to figure out a way to do it; that is our responsibility as preachers. It is up to us to watch them closely, to discover what is beautiful about them and in them, to practice attending and describing so that we see those things and name them. None of this happens automatically, and it doesn't happen accidentally, the way infatuations do; it happens slowly, deliberately, over time. We have to work at it, like any relationship. We have to persevere through the dry spells and forgive and be forgiven.

Homiletics has done an excellent job in the last few decades of reminding us that our sermons *do* things as well as *say* things. Thomas G. Long's *The Witness of Preaching*, for example, was one of the first to get very specific about the sermon as word-act. Long's "focus" and "function" statements—clear sentences describing exactly what the preacher plans to say in the sermon, and what the sermon aims to do—are classroom standbys.[7] But I have found it helpful to nuance these by asking direct questions about the *relationship* between preacher and listeners, so that the preacher is constantly reminded that everything she says is with and for these people, not apart from them or against them. Preacher and listeners share the same interpretive space. They practice and receive the same love. They hope for the same freedom of liberation. They listen for the same Word. They may not always agree on what that Word looks or sounds like, as it moves across the pages of the text and flickers through our days, but they at least agree that it is there; it is real; we are all attending, describing, testifying—waiting.

Remind me again: What do you want to give them, in this sermon, and why? What do you want to give to these people whom you love? Sometimes the things that matter most are the things we take for granted most. Sometimes the things we use most frequently are the things we lose most easily, which must be why so many of us have trouble keeping track of our keys . . . and our verbs. A sermon is something we *give*. We do not simply "deliver" it as if we were uninvolved messengers bringing a FedEx from God; we do not "report" it as if it we were consultants hired to fix problems and increase productivity.[8] We give it, as a gift and a blessing that we ourselves have received. The gift is a good word and good news that we have seen and believed; we give it because it is good, and God is good. God for us, not against us. The gift of the gospel. Stop and think: What is it you really want to give?

Theologians-in-Residence: The Word *Lives* Somewhere

In a backwards kind of way, which so often is the gospel way, the most dangerous question and the most obvious question remind us that preachers are not theologians of trivia. We are not charged with speaking a lot of words about God that matter little to anyone but our own egos. We are charged with being *theologians-in-residence*, speakers of God who live in small towns and big cities and suburban neighborhoods and bombed-out streets, and are blessed with the task of speaking to human beings in that particular context. Even better, we are blessed with the gift of living in that context, which means that we will share the people's joys and concerns, and our words will come from someplace real. No one can address a community like its theologian-in-residence because no one knows and loves it like its theologian-in-residence. And as is the case in most covenantal relationships, the love is not blind; it sees the truth and still loves.

"Theologian" is not a title associated with preachers very much any-more, perhaps because we often use it to describe a professional aca-demic. We also caricature it, as a way of expressing the rift between church and academy: theologians (so the caricatures go) are sequestered thinkers who prefer living with books rather than human beings; preachers are pastors who live among the people and care for them, and never read at all. (Some of us would never call a pastor a "theologian" unless that person was intellectually remote, unfeeling, or out of touch—in other words, not pastoral!) But the literal definition of a the-ologian is simply "someone who speaks words about God." The word describes an activity that could apply to any of us—and if we testify, it does. If we preach, it does. It is high time preachers reclaimed the title of theologian, because certainly we *speak* of God—as opposed to read-ing or writing or conjecturing or theorizing—more than most.

"Theologian-in-residence" is a title that draws attention to the con-textual situation of the theologian: where he lives, either permanently or temporarily, in his capacity as one who practices theology. But preachers who are deeply rooted in their communities are already theologians-in-residence, and they know that preaching requires it. We reside among the people so that the people and the Word may reside in us. And when the Word is "in residence" in us, in ways we can see and hear, we have something to say; we have a Word to speak. Preachers are like the bibli-cal Ruth in this respect: we are resident aliens, making a new home. We bind ourselves to a community and vow to put down roots so that there may be life, new life, and justice in the land. *Where you go, I will go, and where you lodge I will lodge; your people will be my people and your God, my God* (Ruth 1:16b). Preaching in the testimony tradition, as a theologian-in-residence, takes a homeless preacher and turns her into a preacher who lives somewhere and therefore has a lot to say about God. She has gleaned between the rows. She will bear new life.

Re-imaging preachers as theologians-in-residence does some strange things to our interpretive space. It suggests that every preacher we meet is a person in whom the Word resides. Every sermon we hear is one preacher's testimony of what he sees and believes in scripture: *every* ser-mon. Not just the ones we like. Not just the ones that meet our needs, or fit our politics, or hold our attention for twenty minutes: every ser-mon. And this is difficult, immeasurably difficult, because of course we are talking about the possibility that the Word may reside in a preacher or sermon that is foolish, ignorant, or downright hostile. We are talk-ing about the possibility that the Word may reside in a sermon that denounces us or in a preacher who has broken our trust. We are talking about leaving room for wisdom and truth that go so far beyond the wisdom and truth we know that to tolerate such a sermon or preacher feels tantamount to apostasy.

Be very careful here, however: leaving room is not the equivalent of affirming. It does not require us to agree with the preacher or the sermon, or to give up what we believe. It does not ask us to be a doormat for Jesus. Leaving room is rather like Jewish hospitality traditions: we welcome the stranger in our midst for the simple reason that we live in expectation that the Messiah is coming, perhaps in the guise of this very stranger. Leaving room challenges us to set aside first impressions so as to look deeper: to change the subject. It asks us to put our own emotions on hold, temporarily, so that we can try to understand how this particular preacher or sermon interpreted this particular biblical text, for these people, on this day; and why. It asks of us a deeper love and respect for God's people than most of us have ever been shown ourselves. Why is it that grace, amazing grace, always manages to speak more powerfully than retribution?

Poet, playwright, and novelist Ntozake Shange writes, "You got to leave room for the fool in everybody."[9] Preachers know all about being fools; it is part of our call. Perhaps we could leave room for the theologian in everybody as well.

The Secret Lives of Sermons
(or "But What Should the Sermon Look Like?")

Here is a secret I never learned in school or books but that I have learned from listening to sermons. The hardest thing for preachers to do is to testify to the Word they see and believe in the text; everything else is secondary. Being honest is harder than being creative; engaging the text is harder than choosing a form. But there is a peace that comes from making it all the way to testimony, and you can see it in a preacher when she sits down after the sermon. You can read it in her eyes: she knows she is on the other side of something that she had to cross over. You can see it in her body: she has spent it all, whatever she had to give. You can even hear it in the blurry way she talks about the sermon—that she isn't quite sure how this particular point developed, or where that image came from, or why this form seemed right, or how any of it came together in the end. The truth is, she doesn't know *how* she did it; she just knows that she *did,* and on nothing but sheer grace. Dissecting the sermon at this stage almost seems beside the point; she's not even sure it's really *hers.* And yes, it could certainly be buffed and polished and improved in places; she can see the rough spots where she stumbled or fumbled a bit. It wasn't a perfect sermon. But it was true; today, it was true. She was true to the Word in the text. She hopes she will be next time. But what the next one will look like—who can say? Sermons keep their own secrets.

Back to the Future

Some Conclusions to Part 3

This book began with a set of questions that every preacher asks, sooner or later, as she faces the biblical text head on.

Can I really say that . . . if the authorities say something different?

Can I really say that . . . if no one will support me, let alone believe me?

Can I really say that . . . if it sounds crazy, even to me?

Can I really say that . . . if it puts my word and life at risk?

Can I really say that . . . if I am only one person, with no special power?

Can I really say that . . . even though I have no proof beyond what I have seen and believed?

Sometimes, a preacher takes a good, hard look at the authority structures around her, including what will happen to her if she speaks and steps out of bounds, and decides that the answer is *No.* She cannot tell what she has seen and heard in the biblical text and confess what she believes about it without some absolute proof to protect her. She cannot say it without bringing down the wrath of those in power. She *would* say it, if she could figure out *how* to say it without risk, but she cannot figure out how; the risk is simply *there;* it will not go away, and she is too afraid of it. Slowly, over time, she may come to realize that she might be preaching but the subject of her preaching is not God. It is she, herself; *she* has become the subject. She is preaching survival, not gospel; fear, not freedom. She has become the very thing gospel seeks to liberate.

We all know this preacher; she lives inside each of us. She is Anne Hutchinson before a courtroom of magistrates, wondering if she can stand fast in her theological convictions when she might be excommunicated or banished for doing so. She is Sarah Osborn before the town of Newport, wondering if she can teach slaves to read God's Word when such an act might get her arrested or ostracized. She is Jarena Lee before her pastor and astonished congregation, wondering if she can answer her call to preach when her church might not allow her to do it. We all know this preacher. She is you. She is me. One person, of no special courage.

How can I say that? How can I proclaim God's liberating Word when no proof will protect me? On the other hand, how can I *not*?

How can I *not* say it, when I really saw it—God, moving in text and life?

How can I not say it, when I really believe it—that God is great and good and more powerful than any system?

How can I not say it, when these people I love are captive to false powers?

How can I not say it, when my words point to God's Word of freedom?

How can I not say it, when I have sealed my life to that Word?

How can I not say it, when this is the pattern of Scripture, the logic of preaching, the mother tongue of my church, and the best-kept secret around?

Now that I am awake, how can I not say it?

How can I not speak—of God?

You can.

You, a woman, a man, of no special courage: glory is your work.

Thanks be to God.

Notes

Introduction

1. John S. McClure, *Other-Wise Preaching* (St. Louis: Chalice, 2001), 1.

2. Ibid., 3.

3. Consider, for example, the richness of Ella Pearson Mitchell's *Those Preaching Women* volumes (Valley Forge, PA: Judson Press, 1985–2004), Marcia Y. Riggs's *Can I Get a Witness? Prophetic Religious Voices of African American Women: An Anthology* (Maryknoll, NY: Orbis, 1997), and Bettye Collier-Thomas's *Daughters of Thunder: Black Women Preachers and Their Sermons, 1850–1979* (San Francisco: Jossey-Bass, 1998).

4. Rosemary Radford Ruether and Elisabeth Schüssler Fiorenza are two of the pioneering women who have recognized the critical need for women to know and claim a theological, historical, and biblical tradition of their own. Historians, too, have made inestimable contributions to our knowledge of women in the church: Jane Dempsey Douglass, Nancy Hardesty, Rosemary Skinner Keller, and Barbara Brown Zikmund, among others, have led the way.

5. One noteworthy collection is *Blessed Is She: Sermons by Women*, ed. David Albert Farmer and Edwina Hunter (Valley Forge, PA: Judson Press, 1990).

6. Ronald E. Osborn, *Folly of God: The Rise of Christian Preaching*, vol. 1, *A History of Christian Preaching* (St. Louis: Chalice, 1999), 413, 424.

7. Joseph T. Shipley, *The Origins of English Words: A Discursive Dictionary of Indo-European Roots* (Baltimore: John Hopkins, 1984), 416; Gerhard Kittel, ed., *Theological Dictionary of the New Testament*, vol. 4, trans. and ed. Geoffrey W. Bromiley (Grand Rapids: Wm. B. Eerdmans Publishing Co., 1967), 475–76. Thanks to Edwin Searcy who brought the Latin derivation of "testimony" to my attention. He writes, "In the Latin world of patriarchy the word that means 'testicle' has a double meaning. It also means one who is able to give testimony. To give testi(s)mony is to risk being neut(e)ralized. If the speech is found to be false, if the testament that has been sworn is broken, then the line of life will, literally, be cut off." Edwin Searcy, "Marginal Reflections on Testi(s)mony and Authority: Discrimen/ating Martyrs Living by Passion/ate Wit(s)ness," D. Min. paper, Columbia Theological Seminary, 20 January 2000.

8. One exception is Lucy Atkinson Rose, who briefly mentions testimony as a characteristic of conversational preaching in *Sharing the Word: Preaching in the Roundtable Church* (Louisville, KY: Westminster John Knox Press, 1997), 124–27.

9. Paul Ricoeur, "The Hermeneutics of Testimony," in *Essays on Biblical Interpretation*, ed. Lewis Mudge (Philadelphia: Fortress Press, 1980).

10. Walter Brueggemann, *Theology of the Old Testament: Testimony, Dispute, Advocacy* (Minneapolis: Fortress Press, 1997).

11. Walter Brueggemann, *Cadences of Home: Preaching Among Exiles* (Louisville, KY: Westminster John Knox Press, 1997).

12. Elaine Showalter's *Hystories: Hysterical Epidemics and Modern Culture* (New York: Columbia University Press, 1997) notes the therapeutic importance of testimony for women, observing that rituals of narrative have become rituals of testimony. Carolyn Forché's *Against Forgetting: Poetry of Witness* (New York: W. W. Norton & Co., 1993), an anthology of twentieth-century poetry written in times of war and global conflict, sees testimony as truth-telling, the most effective means of survival and resistance to power.

13. Mary McClintock Fulkerson, *Changing the Subject: Women's Discourses and Feminist Theory* (Minneapolis: Fortress Press, 1994); Rebecca S. Chopp, *The Power to Speak: Feminism, Language, God* (New York: Crossroad, 1989).

14. Some of these include Mary Donovan Turner and Mary Lin Hudson's *Saved from Silence: Finding Women's Voice in Preaching* (St. Louis: Chalice Press, 1999), Beverly Zink Sawyer's *From Preachers to Suffragists: Women's Rights and Religious Conviction in the Life of Three Nineteenth-Century American Clergywomen* (Louisville, KY: Westminster John Knox Press, 2003), and EunJoo Mary Kim's *Women Preaching: Theology and Practice Through the Ages* (Cleveland: Pilgrim Press, 2004). I have also noticed that one exception to mainline denominational ignorance appears to be Methodist women, many of whom were raised on stories of Susanna Wesley, Phoebe Palmer, Frances Willard, and others.

15. Leif Enger, *Peace Like a River* (New York: Grove/Atlantic, 2001), 311. I thank David Lose for recognizing beauty when he sees it.

Part 1: Waking Up the Details

1. Lucille Clifton, "why some people be mad at me sometimes," in *Blessing the Boats: New and Selected Poems 1998–2000* (Rochester, NY: BOA Editions, 2000), 38. Reprinted with permission.

2. Solveig Hisdal, *Poetry in Stitches: Clothes You Can Knit*, trans. Michele Lock, Else E. Myhr, and Maureen Engeseth (Oslo, Norway: N.W. Damm & Son, 2000), 8. The citation is from the foreword by Agot Gammersvik, Director of the Hardanger Folk Museum.

3. R. Laurence Moore, "Insiders and Outsiders in American Historical Narrative and American History," in *Religion in American History: A Reader*, ed. Jon Butler and Harry S. Stout (New York: Oxford, 1998). Moore hopes that historians will continue to pay attention to the rhetoric of difference (important, he says, as long as certain groups continue to assert it) without succumbing to the temptation to "mainstream" people who were once considered outsiders. A better tac-

tic, he says, is to allow the ambiguities in historical narrative to emerge: "After all, outsiders were as American as cherry pie not because it makes sense to award the ones we admire posthumous admission into a mainstream but because their contests with insiders were the means by which many Americans invented themselves" (218).

Chapter 1: Anne Marbury Hutchinson

1. John Winthrop, *A Short Story of the Rise, reign and ruine of the Antinomians, Familists & Libertines*, 2d ed. (1644), *The Antinomian Controversy, 1636–1638: A Documentary History*, 2d ed., ed. David D. Hall (Durham, NC: Duke University Press, 1990), 201.

2. Winthrop, *Short Story*, 262, 202.

3. See Linda Woodbridge, *Women and the English Renaissance: Literature and the Nature of Womankind, 1540–1620* (Urbana: University of Illinois Press, 1984) for a study of the "querelle des femmes" debate—which, Woodbridge argues, was simply a literary game rather than a serious attempt to change the status of women in society (129).

4. After bouncing in and out of jail for years, Marbury stood trial in 1578 and lost. The proceedings were apparently so ludicrous that in 1590 Marbury published a dramatic and wildly funny account of them, in which he appears as the irreverent yet earnest hero, nimbly defending himself against the forces of obtuse bureaucracy. To say that there is a striking similarity between this account and that of Marbury's daughter sixty years later is an understatement: in both trials we see the Marbury wit and intelligence make short work of their accusers. Marbury wrote at home; it is likely that his daughter absorbed every line.

5. After the English Reformation and the plundering of monasteries, parish life in England was permanently altered. Laypeople appropriated about 40 percent of clerical benefices, or "livings," thus establishing a dangerous form of economic exploitation: by the system of impropriation, local gentry paid the incumbent rectors their stipends, ensuring that thereafter the clergy would be dependent and even accountable to both political benefactors and ecclesial authority. See Alan D. Gilbert, *Religion and Society in Industrial England: Church, Chapel and Social Change, 1740–1914* (New York: Longman, 1976), 3–7.

6. For more on this widely held Puritan belief that emigrants were participating in a grand Protestant commissioning on behalf of the world, see Perry Miller's classic essay "Errand Into the Wilderness," in *Religion in American History* (New York: Oxford University Press, 1998), eds. Jon Butler and Harry S. Stout, 27–41.

7. Winthrop, *Short Story*, 272–73; "The Examination of Mrs. Anne Hutchinson," *The Antinomian Controversy, 1636–1638: A Documentary History*, 2d ed., ed. David D. Hall (Durham, NC: Duke University Press, 1990), 336–37.

8. Anne Bradstreet, *Works* (London, 1650), 196–98.

9. See Joyce L. Irwin, *Womanhood in Radical Protestantism 1525–1575* (New York: Edwin Mellen, 1979).

10. Ibid., 214. This writer takes a humorous, ironic tone; others, such as Puritan clergyman Thomas Edwards in his 1646 *Gangraena*, furiously catalog all manner of heresies and "pernicious practices" associated with women preachers.

11. Selma Williams, *Divine Rebel: The Life of Anne Marbury Hutchinson* (New York: Holt, Rinehart, and Winston, 1981), 67.

12. Winthrop, *Short Story*, 272.

13. Hutchinson never published a definitive statement of what she believed, but we know from her trial that she deviated from Puritan doctrine on at least these points: she rejected a connection between free grace and human righteousness; she rejected what she called a "Covenant of Works" (seeking spiritual comfort and assurance in the performance of moralistic duties as a sign of sanctification) in favor of a "Covenant of Grace" (resting spiritual assurance on the promises of Christ alone); and she advocated "better establishment in Christ" (as opposed to moral behavior) as an antidote to spiritual deadness. On these three points, she and Cotton were in agreement. Hutchinson diverged from Cotton in her rejection of the ministry as an ordained means of grace between God and human beings, her charge that other ministers were preaching a covenant of works, her advocacy of a personal sense of communion with the Holy Spirit, and her claim that those who received immediate awareness of the Spirit need never worry again about their justification (while those who continually looked for "signs" of grace proved that they had never received it in the first place).

14. "The Examination of Mrs. Anne Hutchinson," 338.

15. Ibid. Two of Hutchinson's fellow shipmates, William Bartholomew and the Reverend Zechariah Symmes, testified that she had prophesied and preached corrupt opinions aboard the ship, which Hutchinson denied.

16. Winthrop, *Short Story*, 263.

17. Weld's Preface to Winthrop, *Short Story*, 208.

18. Winthrop, *Short Story*, 263.

19. John Winthrop, *The History of New England from 1630 to 1649*, ed. James Kendall Hosmer (New York: Barnes & Noble, 1959), 234.

20. There is some question as to whether Hutchinson was actually a midwife proper—she clearly had the knowledge and skill to merit the title—or whether she simply helped out when called upon. The distinction is important. Midwives were highly suspect in seventeenth-century England and New England. Presiding over the processes of birth and fertility yielded a kind of power that was upsetting to the male political and religious hierarchy, particularly since so many infants died and questions of baptism often had to be decided immediately. The Massachusetts Bay authorities eventually forbade midwives to baptize children. Scholars have further noted that midwives were among the first to be excommunicated or persecuted as witches, as was the case with Jane Hawkins in Boston, Massachusetts; Hawkins, the local midwife and a friend of Anne Hutchinson, was excommunicated soon after Hutchinson's 1638 trial. See Carol F. Karlsen, *The Devil in the Shape of a Woman: Witchcraft in Colonial New England* (New York: Norton, 1987).

21. Winthrop, *History of New England*, 234.

22. This tragic event became one of the key pieces of evidence in the case against Hutchinson. Mary Dyer, a resident of Boston and friend and follower of Anne Hutchinson, delivered a deformed stillborn daughter on October 17, 1637, and was attended by Hutchinson and midwife Jane Hawkins. When Winthrop later heard of it, he had the body exhumed five days after the Hutchinsons left Massachusetts so that he could examine it for himself. In his *Short Story*, he describes it in detail: "It had a face, but no head, and the ears stood upon the shoulders and were like an ape's; it had no forehead, but over the eyes four horns, hard and sharp" (267). The "monster" delivered of Mary Dyer and the "monstrous errors" of Hutchinson were a critical connection in his account of the controversy. Mary Dyer, it may also be noted, followed the Hutchinsons to Rhode Island, became a Quaker, and was the first female Quaker to be executed in Boston in 1660. The first woman of European ancestry executed in the New World was killed . . . for preaching.

23. David D. Hall, in *Worlds of Wonder, Days of Judgment: Popular Religious Belief in Early New England* (New York: Knopf, 1989), argues that learning to read and becoming "religious" were, in seventeenth-century New England, one and the same (21–70).

24. Winthrop, *Short Story*, 264.

25. Ibid., 263.

26. Weld's preface to Winthrop, *Short Story*, 207.

27. Edward Johnson, *Wonder-Working Providence, 1628–1651*, ed. J. Franklin Jameson (1653–55, repr., New York: Barnes & Noble, 1959), 127, cited in Williams, *Divine Rebel*, 115.

28. Cited in Williams, *Divine Rebel*, 116.

29. Weld's preface to Winthrop, *Short Story*, 211.

30. "A Report of the Trial of Mrs. Anne Hutchinson before the Church in Boston," in Hall, *Antinomian Controversy*, 382–83.

31. Ibid., 371–72.

32. Anne Kibbey, in *The Interpretation of Material Shapes in Puritanism* (New York: Cambridge, 1986), draws a connection between the Antinomian Controversy and the Pequot War of the summer of 1637. One of Winthrop's first actions as reinstated governor was to join forces with Connecticut in the first genocidal war against Native Americans. Vowing to end the Indian threat once and for all, New England troops marched to Mystic and there slaughtered more than two hundred Pequot men, women, and children. Kibbey's point is that one kind of prejudice and violence fostered another; its roots, she argues, are in Puritan iconoclasm.

33. "Examination of Mrs. Anne Hutchinson," 326.

Chapter 2: Sarah Osborn

1. Harriet Beecher Stowe, *The Minister's Wooing* (1859), in Joseph A. Conforti, *Samuel Hopkins and the New Divinity Movement* (Washington, DC: Christian College Consortium, 1981), 193.

2. With Hopkins's help, Quamine and Yamma eventually did raise the money to purchase their freedom and, in 1774 or 1775, left for Princeton to continue their theological studies. Neither man, however, lived to fulfill his dream of returning to Guinea as a missionary. See Conforti, *Samuel Hopkins*, 142–58.

3. "The Great Awakening" (c. 1740) and "the Second Great Awakening" (c. 1790–1830) generally refer to two distinct periods of revivalism in the American colonies and new republic. The terms are problematic, however, since revivals occurred both before and after these dates. Osborn, for example, was instrumental in helping to start a revival in Newport in the 1760s, long after the wave of excitement associated with the Great Awakening had passed.

4. During the Great Awakening, the old Puritan practice of giving one's public testimony to the church as a prerequisite to membership was reinstated. For women, this was the first time they had been allowed to speak publicly in church since the time of Anne Hutchinson. See Harry S. Stout, *The New England Soul: Preaching and Religious Culture in Colonial New England* (New York: Oxford, 1986), 185–211.

5. In these respects, Osborn is an important contrast to more charismatic eighteenth-century figures such as Jemima Wilkinson (who dressed like a man) and Mother Ann Lee, both of whom preached publicly and founded religious sects of which they were the head. See Catherine A. Brekus, *Strangers and Pilgrims: Female Preaching in America 1740–1845* (Chapel Hill: University of North Carolina Press, 1998), 68–113.

6. See Brekus, *Strangers and Pilgrims*, and Susan Juster, *Disorderly Women: Sexual Politics and Evangelicalism in Revolutionary New England* (Ithaca, NY: Cornell University Press, 1994), for two studies of eighteenth-century women who suffered for stepping out of their place. The term "disorderly" is identified by Juster as a common one in church disciplinary records; most often, it referred to women who had challenged authority by speaking out.

7. Joanna Bowen Gillespie, "The Clear Leadings of Providence: Pious Memoirs and the Problems of Self-Realization for Women in the Early Nineteenth Century," *Journal of the Early Republic* 5 (Summer 1985): 210.

8. Two sets of documents furnish the background for this study: (1) Samuel Hopkins, ed., *Memoirs of the Life of Mrs. Sarah Osborn* (Worcester, Mass.: 1799), which includes Hopkins's selection from nearly fifty volumes of Osborn's writings, including journals, a spiritual autobiography, poetry, and commentaries on Genesis and the Synoptic Gospels; and (2) Mary Beth Norton, ed., "'My Resting Reaping Times': Sarah Osborn's Defense of her 'Unfeminine' Activities, 1767," *Signs: Journal of Women in Culture and Society* 2 (1976), which consists of a 1767 exchange of letters between Osborn and her friend the Reverend Joseph Fish, in which the two discuss the propriety of the religious meetings taking place in Osborn's home during the Newport revival of 1766–67.

9. Hopkins, ed., *Memoirs*, 57.

10. Ibid., 9, 36.

11. See Charles E. Hambrick-Stowe, "The Spiritual Pilgrimage of Sarah Osborn (1714–1796)," in *Religion in American History: A Reader* (New York: Uni-

versity of Oxford Press, 1998), ed. Jon Butler and Harry S. Stout, 136, and Norton, ed., "'My Resting Reaping Times,'" 519.

12. Norton is the first to argue that Newport's 1766 revival was precipitated by the black slaves who had been meeting at Sarah Osborn's and whose example inspired "little white lads and neighbors daughters also [to] press in" ("'My Resting Reaping Times,'" 519). The order of groups forming is notable: black slaves, white teenagers, white men. White women had already been coming since 1741.

13. Ibid., 521. The citation is from Osborn's letter to Fish (ca. July 1766).

14. Hopkins, ed., *Memoirs*, 81.

15. Ibid., 83.

16. Ibid., 254–55.

17. Ibid., 325. Note the shift from first to third person; Osborn continues to alternate throughout the rest of the commentary.

18. Ibid., 74–75.

Chapter 3: Jarena Lee

1. See Daniel A. Payne, *A History of the African Methodist Episcopal Church* (New York: Arno Press and *The New York Times*, 1969), 189–96.

2. Ibid., 191.

3. William E. Montgomery, in *Under Their Own Vine and Fig Tree: The African-American Church in the South, 1865–1900* (Baton Rouge: Louisiana State University Press, 1993), describes the growing class divide between educated and uneducated blacks in the generations after the Civil War, a division that deeply affected religious leadership. Elite, upwardly mobile Baptists and Methodists, for example, were highly critical of the emotionalism and occasional moral lapses of the churches' older preachers; they demanded a new generation of highly educated, morally impeccable *male* leadership that could address contemporary social problems. There is strong evidence of this growing division in Payne's *A History*; the older system of lay preachers—which included women—was increasingly under fire as demands for an educated clerical guild grew.

4. Payne, *A History*, 190.

5. Jarena Lee, *Religious Experience and Journal of Mrs. Jarena Lee* (Philadelphia: privately printed, 1849).

6. See Payne, *A History*, 237, 273. For a discussion of how the 1852 ruling never successfully prohibited women from taking leadership roles in the church, see Jualynne Dodson, "Nineteenth-Century A.M.E. Preaching Women: Cutting Edge of Women's Inclusion in Church Polity," in *Women in New Worlds: Historical Perspectives on the Wesleyan Tradition*, ed. Hilah F. Thomas and Rosemary Skinner Keller (Nashville: Abingdon Press, 1981), 276–89.

7. Catherine A. Brekus, in *Strangers and Pilgrims: Female Preaching in America 1740–1845* (Chapel Hill: University of North Carolina Press, 1998), provides the most thorough and incisive discussion of women preachers in the Great Awakenings.

8. For a good example of how the rhetoric for women's ordination grew increasingly political over the course of the century, see Lucy Lind Hogan, "The Overthrow of the Monopoly of the Pulpit: A Longitudinal Case Study of the Cultural Conversation Advocating the Preaching and Ordination of Women in American Methodism 1859–1924 (Phoebe Palmer, Frances Willard, M. Madeline Southard, Georgia Harkness)," Ph.D. diss., University of Maryland College Park, 1995.

9. Jarena Lee, *The Life and Religious Experience of Jarena Lee* (Philadelphia: privately printed, 1836), in *Sisters of the Spirit: Three Black Women's Autobiographies of the Nineteenth Century*, ed. William L. Andrews (Bloomington: Indiana University Press, 1986), 30.

10. Ibid., 29.

11. Ibid.

12. Ibid., 35.

13. Ibid., 36.

14. Ibid., 44.

15. Ibid., 45.

16. See Carol V. R. George, *Segregated Sabbaths: Richard Allen and the Emergence of Independent Black Churches 1760–1840* (New York: Oxford University Press, 1973).

17. Lee, *Religious Experience and Journal*, 22, 24, 28, 30.

18. Lee, *Life and Religious Experience*, 46.

19. Lee, *Religious Experience and Journal*, 87, 23.

20. Ibid., 23. In 1858, Sojourner Truth, after speaking to large crowds at an abolition meeting, was challenged by angry pro-slavery men who declared that they did not believe her to be a woman: her deep voice, stature, height, and (we may intuit) power and authority in speaking did not ring true to their conceptions of "femininity." Over the protests of women in the audience, the men demanded that Truth prove her gender by showing her breasts to a doctor. Instead, Truth bared her breast in public, saying it was to their shame—not hers—that she did so. See Dorothy Sterling, ed., *We Are Your Sisters: Black Women in the Nineteenth Century* (New York: W. W. Norton & Co., 1984), 151–53.

21. Ibid.

22. Ibid., 97.

23. Frances Smith Foster, *Written By Herself: Literary Production by African American Women, 1746–1892* (Bloomington: Indiana University Press, 1993), 2.

24. Ibid., 59–69; 75.

25. For a discussion of independent black churches in America, see Will B. Gravely, "The Rise of African Churches in America (1786–1822): Reexamining the Contexts," in *African American Religious Studies: An Interdisciplinary Anthology*, ed. Gayraud S. Wilmore (Durham, NC: Duke University Press, 1989), 301–17. For more on Richard Allen and the African Methodist Episcopal Church in particular, see George, *Segregated Sabbaths*.

26. See Nathan Hatch, *The Democratization of American Christianity* (New Haven, CT: Yale University Press, 1989), 3–16. This section is a summary of his work.

27. Ibid., 9.

28. Ibid., 20.

29. Lee, *Life and Religious Experience*, 36–37.

30. Ibid., 48.

31. Ibid., 37.

32. Ibid.

33. See Richard Allen, *The Life Experiences and Gospel Labors of the Rt. Rev. Richard Allen* (New York: Abingdon Press, 1960), 55.

34. Marcia Y. Riggs, ed., *Can I Get a Witness? Prophetic Religious Voices of African American Women: An Anthology* (Maryknoll, NY: Orbis Books, 1997), xi.

35. Bettye Collier-Thomas, *Daughters of Thunder: Black Women Preachers and Their Sermons, 1850–1979* (San Francisco: Jossey-Bass, 1998), 25.

36. Jacquelyn Grant, *White Women's Christ and Black Women's Jesus: Feminist Christology and Womanist Response* (Atlanta: Scholars, 1989), 204–5. Expanding on the term first coined by Alice Walker, Grant defines "womanist" as "*being* and *acting* out who you are" (205).

37. Lee, *Religious Experience and Journal*, 46, 44.

38. Ibid.

39. Ibid.

40. Andrews, *Sisters of the Spirit*, 14.

41. Ibid., 15.

42. Lee, *Life and Religious Experience*, 36.

43. Ibid.

44. Ibid.

Part 1: Standing in the Details

1. See Melanie May, *A Body Knows: A Theopoetics of Death and Resurrection* (New York: Continuum, 1995).

Part 2: Waking Up the Secrets

1. Czeslaw Milosz, "Preface to *Treatise on Poetry*," in *Czeslaw Milosz: The Collected Poems 1931–1987* (Hopewell, NJ: Ecco, 1988), 111.

Chapter 4: True Speech in the Mother Tongue

1. Paul Ricoeur, "The Hermeneutics of Testimony," in *Essays on Biblical Interpretation*, ed. Lewis Mudge (Philadelphia: Fortress Press, 1980), 128.

2. Ibid., 129.

3. Ibid., 130.

4. Ibid., 136.

5. Walter Brueggemann, *Theology of the Old Testament: Testimony, Dispute, Advocacy* (Minneapolis: Fortress Press, 1997), 120, 121. Brueggemann cites Ricoeur's work as generative of his courtroom imagery.

6. Ibid., 311. Italics are in the text.

7. Ibid., 273.

8. Ibid., 268. Italics are in the text.

9. Ibid., 373–99.

10. Ibid., 331–32.

11. Ibid., 401.

12. Brueggemann identifies five "form of life" practices for a community of interpretation: "(1) Dwell in the tradition of *Torah*, accepting the narratives and the commands of purity and of debt cancellation as the principal sources of funding for obedient imagination. (2) Engage, after the manner of *royal agency*, in the practice of power for well-being, a practice of power that is always a temptation and always under criticism. (3) Host the disruptive *prophetic voices*, which concern the costs and pains of the historical process, and the possibilities that well up amid the costs and pains. (4) Practice, after the manner of *the Priestly tradition*, the presence of Yahweh, which embraces the sacramental freightedness of all life. (5) In an embrace of the *traditions of wisdom*, know the dailiness of life in all its contested, buoyant density." Ibid., 745.

13. Ibid., 744.

14. Ibid., 746–47.

15. Ibid., 744.

16. As Brueggemann writes, "The reality of Yahweh depends on the compelling case made regularly by the witnesses. And the witnesses make their case in utterance and gestures of mediation" (575).

Chapter 5: Making Trouble and Making Good News

1. With thanks to Margaret Aymer Oget, who shared with me this story about herself and her teaching.

2. "Graf(ph)t" combines the horticultural term with the root of "stylus." See Mary McClintock Fulkerson, *Changing the Subject: Women's Discourses and Feminist Theory* (Minneapolis: Fortress Press, 1994), 10.

3. Ibid., 377.

4. Ibid.

5. Ibid., 384.

6. Ibid., 395. My emphasis.

7. Rebecca S. Chopp, *The Power to Speak: Feminism, Language, God* (New York: Crossroad, 1989), 5.

8. Ibid., 16.

9. Ibid., 32.

10. Elisabeth Schüssler Fiorenza, *Bread Not Stone*, xvi–xvii, quoted in Chopp, *Power to Speak*, 42.

11. Again, the image is Schüssler Fiorenza's.

12. Chopp, *Power to Speak*, 43, 41.

13. Ibid., 62.

14. Ibid., 65. My emphasis.

15. Ibid., 66.

16. The image of "womenchurch"—frequently used in feminist theological literature—is from Schüssler Fiorenza.

17. See Marilynne Robinson, *Gilead* (New York: Farrar, Straus & Giroux, 2004), 161.

18. Robert Frost, "Mending Wall," in *The Treasury of American Poetry*, selected and with an introduction by Nancy Sullivan (Garden City, NY: Doubleday, 1978), 342.

19. Marlo Thomas, *Free to Be You and Me* (McGraw-Hill, 1974).

Part 3: Waking Up the Preacher

1. Mary Oliver, "Work," in *The Leaf and the Cloud* (Cambridge, MA: Da Capo, 2000), 9, 10.

Chapter 6: The Wide-awake Preacher

1. *The Vicar of Dibley*, Series 1 ("Arrival"), British Broadcasting Corporation, 1994.

2. J. K. Rowling, *Harry Potter and the Half-Blood Prince* (New York: Arthur A. Levine, 2005), 385–86.

3. Whenever I ask church groups to brainstorm about why the disciples might not have believed the women's story, they never have any trouble coming up with ideas. Maybe (for example) they were angry that the good news had been told to *women* instead of inner-circle disciples like them. Maybe they were mad at themselves for staying home. Maybe they were paralyzed with fright. Maybe they were thick with fatigue. Maybe they were ready to sober up and move back home. Maybe they were grouchy at having been woken up too early. Maybe they were worried about where all this would lead, if it were really true. Maybe they were terrified to preach a gospel of such pure inversion, without a shred of proof—and so on.

4. With thanks to Chris Henry, an engaging expert himself.

Chapter 7: The Wide-awake Sermon

1. See Anna Carter Florence, "Put Away Your Sword! Taking the Torture Out of the Sermon," in *What's the Matter with Preaching Today?* ed. Mike Graves (Louisville, KY: Westminster John Knox Press, 2004), 93–108.

2. With thanks to Julie Johnson, whose lecture on the spirituality of the preacher in our introductory classes got us all thinking about the spiritual practice of "tending."

3. Mary Oliver, "The Summer Day," in *New and Selected Poems* (Boston: Beacon Press, 1992), 94.

4. See Twyla Tharp, *The Creative Habit: Learn It and Use It for Life* (New York: Simon & Schuster, 2003).

5. With thanks to Dick Baxter, who rewrote the Beatitudes while preparing a sermon for a 2006 class and reminded us of the power of this exercise.

6. With thanks to Marissa Myers, who started the "Text Jam" gatherings at Columbia.

7. Thomas G. Long, *The Witness of Preaching* (Louisville, KY: Westminster/John Knox Press, 1989), chap. 4.

8. With thanks to Dana Steffee Hughes, who waits for her weekly FedEx from God and then preaches it luminously.

9. Ntozake Shange, *Sassafrass, Cypress & Indigo* (New York: St. Martin's, 1982), 99.

Index

CPSIA information can be obtained
at www.ICGtesting.com
Printed in the USA
FSOW01n2324160217
30941FS